B   SHO

About Before Golda: Manya Shochat

"This is a deeply moving...story of a life...Mrs. Ben-Zvi, wife of Israel's second president, describes not only Manya's growth...and her incredible creativity in starting the kibbutz movement, but her love affair with Yisrael Shochat, a charmer with a roving eye, whose infidelities drove her to attempt suicide....

Manya Shochat lived her extraordinary life with strength and idealism, with a pure vision of a world in which all people, especially Jews and Arabs...would one day live together in peace and brotherhood."

> **Ruth Gruber,**
> *author of 13 books; among them,*
> Raquela: A Woman of Israel;
> Rescue: Exodus of the Ethiopian Jews.

"I first heard of Manya Shochat in 1952 on my first trip to Israel as a young journalist from Chicago; but was unable to meet her then or on my return in the 60's. On reading her biography, I see her as a woman for the future, challenging her time and ours for over 80 years of her remarkable life. At long last we may be ready for her and a time of change; for her vision of a homeland at peace."

> **Lillian Elkin,** *reviewer;*
> *literary editor of* Jewish Frontier;
> *past national VP American Jewish Congress;*
> *Board member, Na'Amat USA*

"...an important and fascinating book...an extraordinary woman...possessing enormous inner strength. Both idealistic and pragmatic, she had a vision of Israel as a just society that respects all individuals, a vision that should serve as inspiration today."

> **Judith A. Sokoloff**
> *Editor,* Na'Amat Woman

"...a quite exciting 'read'...Yitzhak Ben-Zvi, 3rd President of Israel, was a much loved man, and Rachel, whom I met in 1962, was as famous and as heroic. Her book of another heroine, is a tale of an Israel we shall never see again. As all scramble to decipher where Israel is headed now, they may want to examine where it once was through the life of the revolutionary and pioneering Manya Shochat. Her idealism and love of country are sorely missed today."

> **Jack Nusan Porter, Ph.D.,** *author,*
> The Sociology of American Jewry,
> *and* Confronting History and Holocaust;
> *founder of the Journal of the History of*
> *Sociology; former research associate*
> *at Harvard*

"Courageous and naive, tough and sentimental, Manya Shochat is the stuff of Zionist legend."

Lesley Hazleton, *author*
Israeli Women *and* Jerusalem, Jerusalem

—and PRAISE from Israel's reviewers
when the Hebrew edition appeared in 1976:

"This is a book which...I recommend to Israeli feminists and to anyone who has been affected by the women's liberation movement in America..."

from **Maariv**

"The history of Eretz Israel during the second aliyah does not lack riveting personalities, but it would be no exaggeration to say that Manya Shochat was outstanding even among these."

Yediot Achronot

"The author does not hide the truth as to Manya's marriage...on the contrary, her brief comments on this subject add an enticingly human dimension to Manya's heroic persona."

Al Hamishmar

"Yanait's book is a true and well-documented testimony which broadens our knowledge through supporting documents...and through various legends which give us a new dimension...

"It is fascinating to becoming reacquainted with those early settlers who were equally adept with pistols as with plows, with fountain pens as with balalaikas
...Yanait's book is a true...testimony which...gives us a new dimension."

from **Haaretz**

LIBRARY OF CONGRESS CATALOGING-IN-PUBLICATION DATA

Ben-Zvi, Raḥel Yanait, 1886–1979.
    [Manyah Shoḥaṭ. English]
    Before Golda : Manya Shochat (Manya Wilbushevitz Shochat) : a
biography / by Rachel Yanait Ben-Zvi ; translated from the Hebrew by
Sandra Shurin ; introduction by Marie Syrkin
      p. cm.
    Translation of: Shoḥaṭ.
    Includes index.
    ISBN 0-930395-07-7 (pbk.) :
    1. Shochat, Mania Wilbushewitch, 1880–1961. 2. Zionists—
Palestine—Biography. 3. Shomer (Organization : Palestine)
4. Haganah (Organization) I. Title.
DS125.3.S522B4613 1988
956.94'001'0924—dc19
[B]
                    88-14522
                    CIP

Cover drawings by Yala Korwin; design by SGW Associates, NY
Book design by Murray Belsky
Manufactured in the United States of America

BEFORE GOLDA: MANYA SHOCHAT

A Biography

By Rachel Yanait Ben-Zvi

Translated from the Hebrew by Sandra Shurin

Introduction by Marie Syrkin

BIBLIO PRESS

New York

Contents

ACKNOWLEDGMENTS

We owe special thanks to Aviva Cantor for having suggested the need for this biography in the introduction to her *The Jewish Woman Bibliography* first edition. We thank both Judith Pearl and Yale Reisner for their help in the preparation of the text, and for the resources of the Zionist Archives and Library and the Slavonic Division of the New York Public Library in New York City; also Pioneer Women-Na'Amat, the Women's Labor Zionist Organization of America.

In addition to her diligence in translating the text from Hebrew, Sandra Shurin supplied careful English versions of complex material in the documents section, including new items. Editing was by Doris B. Gold and indexing by Marylu Koster. Photo and research sources in Israel who kindly cooperated are noted in the photo credits and in the documents supplement.

INTRODUCTION

Manya Shochat's life resembles the substance of myth or the product of a Hollywood producer's untrammelled imagination rather than sober reality, yet the facts are there—authoritatively given in this excellent biography by her friend and colleague, Rachel Yanait. Not that Manya was previously unknown. Fifty years ago she was already a legendary figure notable for adventures in the Russian revolutionary movement and in the building of pioneer Palestine. At last we are fortunate in having a full-length account of one of the most striking women of her generation.

The era to which Manya belonged produced a number of extraordinary women, idealists and activists as varied as Henrietta Szold or the later Golda Meir, as well as women of lesser renown whose involvement in the causes of national and social redemption was total; among these the author of the present biography must be included. It was my good fortune to know many of these women personally. Yet among so impressive a roster I can think of none who resembled Manya in the surrealist quality of her adventures or the extravagance with which she pursued her goals, however implausible they seemed.

Who's Who would have trouble finding the correct pigeon-hole in which to place this woman, who as a teenager was notorious in Czarist Russia as a dangerous revolutionary; who organized the self-defense of Russian Jews during pogroms, and who formulated and helped carry out plans for the first collective settlement in Palestine before the kibbutz became part of an organized movement. And to add to the difficulties of defining her, she was a proud feminist, one of the few women in Hashomer who in picturesque Arab dress, guarded the early Jewish settlements against marauding bands, at the same time obsessed with finding a just solution for the Arab problem; and who as an imaginative humanitarian fearlessly and without self-consciousness never hesitated to approach the world's notables with ethical demands on behalf of victims of oppression. In essentials she never changed. She was as imperious, reckless and unpredictable in old age as in youth, checked only by failing strength.

To be understood she must be seen in the context of her time. In the second half of the nineteenth century the growing revolutionary ferment among Russian intellectuals inevitably attracted Jewish youth who sought the redemption of all mankind and believed that the revolution would liberate all the oppressed in the Czar's domain. These young people rebelled against the rigid orthodoxy of the *shtetl* as well as against the complacency of a small Jewish minority that had succeeded in assimilating and so escaping the most brutal, overt forms of discrimination. Conflicting currents in Jewish life stressed solutions most of which dismissed the dream of a return to Zion as parochial or fantastic. Under the influence of *Haskalah*, the "enlightenment", some stressed cultural secularization. If Jews shed their *shtetl* garb and customs and became culturally, though not religiously, assimilated, they would, with the eventual liberalization of the Czarist regime win acceptance as citizens. The socialist Bund on the contrary recognized Jews as a national entity and sought equal minority rights in Russia, but was furiously anti-Zionist. It propagated its doctrine among the Jewish proletariat in Yiddish, excoriating Hebrew as reactionary.

Not that the ancient dream of the Return had been wholly abandoned. A tiny Jewish community had existed in Palestine since the exile, always reinforced by a trickle of pious Jews throughout the centuries. Zionism as a political movement can mark its beginnings with the *Bilu*, who in response to the pogroms of 1881 went to Palestine to establish agricultural settlements that failed for lack of support. However, continuing pogroms were a clarifying experience for all Russian Jewry, not only because of the bloodshed but because leading members of the revolutionary movement discovered virtues in virulent anti-semitism. Though the revolutionary ideologues admitted the reactionary character of anti-semitism some viewed it as a useful stage in the revolutionary struggle: peasant violence would serve as "cultural manure" for socialism. The extremist *Narodnya Volya* (the People's Will), perceiving pogroms as helpful pedagogic practice, went so far as to issue an appeal urging, "Arise workers, avenge yourselves on the landlords, plunder the Jews and slay the official." Major theoreticians of Jewish nationalism, Leo Pinsker in Russia, Moses Hess in Germany, bitterly disillusioned by the reactions of some of their socialist comrades, concluded that Jews would have to fulfill their aspirations through a national as well as a social movement.

A later generation, among them Ben-Gurion, would go through this by now familiar ideological evolution. One exception would be Golda Meir, who as a five-year old child in Kiev cowered in terror while her father boarded the windows and doors of his house against a rumored pogrom. Half a century later she would explain how the enduring memory of that child waiting for an attack by a violent mob had determined the course of her life, and why she had left the security and good life of America for the wastes of Palestine. The American democracy she treasured and in which she had been reared had given her the will to seek "justice and freedom for all" in a Jewish homeland.

A generation before Golda, Manya was predictably caught up in the vortex of the incipient revolutionary movement in Russia, including a terrorist plot. However, terrorism as practiced at that time by Russian revolutionaries should be sharply distinguished from the monstrous violence that afflicts the world today. Except for a repudiated lunatic fringe, Russian revolutionaries chose a specific oppressor and even delayed an action if innocent victims such as an accompanying family member of the target might be injured. An example, well-known in its time, illustrates the difference.

In 1877 Vera Zasulich, a young Russian revolutionary, shot General Trepov, Governor General of St. Petersburg and Chief of Police, point-blank. After wounding him, the girl made no attempt to escape but remained awaiting arrest. At her trial the jury, despite the evidence, returned a verdict of "not guilty". Though the Czar immediately ordered that she be re-arrested, she managed to escape to Switzerland to the delight of much of Russia and Europe. Even ideological opponents of terrorism applauded her deed and her courage. She entered the pantheon of revolutionary heroines.

The explanation for this almost universal acclaim instead of outrage is understandable. Trepov was a detested official whose brutality was notorious. Neither anonymous nor a symbol, he was the actual perpetrator of vicious cruelties. Because the attempted assassination (Trepov did not die) had been neither random nor cowardly, it was described as a classic example of terrorism that could be viewed as "revolutionary" without degrading the word. But it should be noted that the mainstream of Russian revolutionaries rejected terrorism as self-defeating.

Originally wholly opposed to violence, Manya's single involvement in terrorism came later in her career. Yanait's account of the Russian phase of Manya's life, as related to her in old age by Manya in Palestine, makes some of the most baffling aspects of Manya's complex personality and activities in Russia and Palestine intelligible. How account for so aberrant a woman who managed to achieve so much?

There is no ignoring heredity and family environment. Manya's father was the only member of a wealthy, thoroughly assimilated family who chose loyalty to Jewish tradition in preference to "Russification". He insisted that his children receive a Jewish as well as a secular Russian education. Of his ten children, the sons, with one exception, went to Palestine; the one who departed for Texas also broke the conventional pattern by devoting himself to Blacks. One sister, a reputed beauty who married early, fell in love with a Christian. Not to violate her convictions and remain true to her husband, she committed suicide.

This extremism and impulse for immediate action was a family trait that reached startling proportions in Manya. Religious until the age of twelve, she attempted suicide when she heard a peasant boy she had befriended abusing the "Yids". What kind of God allowed such injustice! At fifteen she ran away to become a worker. Her will proved too strong for her alarmed parents. They finally allowed her to leave the comforts of a middle class home to demonstrate the equality of women and to prove true to her social ideals.

In her new environment Manya got to know the Jewish working class: she learned Yiddish and became involved in her fellow workers' aspirations for social change. At this point the teenage girl advocated reform, not revolution. Nevertheless she was arrested by a police suspicious of her influence. The drama of her imprisonment is related in fascinating detail by her biographer. The arrests, culminating in her sensational relationship with Zubatov, head of the secret police, is one of those grossly misunderstood episodes whose puzzle is decoded by Yanait, basing herself on Manya's account and supported by biographical data.

Consider the script: A twenty-year old girl is arrested, though her activities had consisted of educating and organizing workers; even such mild reformist efforts branded her as a dangerous revolutionary. Constantly interrogated and tormented to reveal her confederates, threatened with reprisals against her mother, she is almost tempted to yield when one interrogator in civilian dress signals that she should remain firm. Suddenly interrogations cease;

she is allowed full use of the prison library and she spends several months in prolonged, candid discussions with her protector.

When alerted by the prison underground she learns that the man is the head of the secret police. She faces him furiously but is convinced by him of his sincerity. Like her, he agrees on the need to form an independent workers' movement. When in evidence of his good faith she demands that he free her and other prisoners to enable her to help form such a movement, he lets her go after a year's imprisonment of which eight months had been spent in ideological debate. Certainly a mysterious business whose repercussions would crop up periodically through her life.

As agreed with Zubatov, in 1901 Manya, together with like-minded comrades, succeeded in organizing a labor movement whose three principal demands were the freedom to join labor unions, free speech and the right to strike. Hardly an extreme program. The modest success of this effort met with small favor among radical activists who dismissed gradualism and moderation as a betrayal of eventual liberation: higher wages and a shorter work week were reformist government tricks to stifle revolutionary discontent.

In 1902 when the notorious anti-semitic, reactionary V.K. Plehve became Minister of the Interior, the iron hand of Czarist autocracy was immediately felt. Zubatov fell into disfavor and was shorn of authority. However, he managed to persuade Plehve to grant an interview to Manya—another puzzler that testifies to the girl's reputation. Undaunted, Manya, after stating her agenda for improving the lot of Russian workers, boldly asked for better treatment of the Jews in the Pale of Settlement. The enraged Plehve turned on the impudent Jewess who dared preach to him about the status of Russian workers. Again wholly in character, Manya grabbed an object from a nearby desk and hurled it at the Minister. She was promptly, though briefly, re-arrested. The reformist idyll was over.

In retrospect, the sincerity of Zubatov may have been tactical rather than ideological. A supporter of a liberalized constitutional monarchy could reasonably have favored measures to deflect discontented masses from revolutionary violence and so spare Russia a coming cataclysm. Since at that time Manya, too, believed that peaceful reform rather than revolution was the right road toward social change, she welcomed the chance. Whatever Zubatov's motives it is obvious that he perceived the intellectual and moral strength of the slight girl who was his prisoner.

In this connection it should be noted that Zubatov and the proletarian priest, Father Gapon, with whom Manya was briefly enchanted, were branded by the revolutionaries as "socialist police agents" to differentiate them from ordinary police agents who infiltrated the radical movement without playing the role of fellow socialists. Gapon was executed by the revolutionaries as a traitor. Despite these suspicions the explanation may be more complex.

Manya herself, stung by accusations from the Left on a visit to the United States in 1922, responded circumstantially to charges of collaboration with police agents in articles in the Yiddish daily *Die Tzeit*. These provide a more circumstantial account than the one she subsequently gave to her biographer. In *Die Tzeit* (April 20–23– 1922) she makes a stunning revelation: Zubatov had indeed been a police agent.

In three articles recounting details of her imprisonment already familiar to the reader she gives a more intimate view of the mysterious Zubatov. When on receiving the damaging information from the prison underground she charged him with being a police agent, he gave her a frank account of his ideological development. As a youth in Moscow he had caught the revolutionary fever. At the age of 18 his closest friends were revolutionaries. He owned a library from which he disseminated illicit literature. In consequence his unwitting, beloved sister was arrested. To save her the boy went to the police to confess his guilt and assume the blame. The official in charge was a devoted monarchist who had a grandiose vision of a future magnanimous Russian emperor who would grant land to the peasants and offer freedom with appropriate controls, not a republic that would lead to the moral degradation of the masses. A modern constitutional government on the European model would destroy Russian nationalism more effectively than a previous attempt by Mongolian enemies. Therefore, it was essential to crush the incipient revolution. Then Russia would emerge as a shining example for the decadent West.

This standard Slavophile doctrine persuaded the impressionable young Zubatov. He renounced what he had formerly believed and in evidence of his good faith betrayed five of his friends; his sister was released, and he was recruited into the secret police. Manya explained this transformation by his "mystic Slavic soul".

But that was not the end of the story. The more Zubatov came to know the actual workings of the regime, its corrupt bureaucracy and ruthless administrators, he suffered another change of heart. Still a devout monarchist, he dreamt of saving Russia from degenerating into a "guillotine" by finding a way to deflect revolutionary rage into acceptable, necessary reform. Manya's proposal provided an answer. This explanation seemed plausible to the girl.

Nevertheless, unwilling to assume sole responsibility for her actions, she took the precaution of informing her friend, Gershuni, a zealous revolutionary, of her cooperation with Zubatov. Gershuni remained unconvinced of Zubatov's regeneration and tried to dissuade Manya: Zubatov was merely using her. But Manya trusted her personal knowledge of the man and her intuition. Once Gershuni knew, she could not be accused of conducting secret dealings with an acknowledged police agent whatever his present motives. Her initial success in helping to organize a trade union movement persuaded her of the soundness of her instincts. The finale came with the accession of Plehve and Zubatov's fall from grace. But attacks on this phase of Manya's early activities would periodically plague her even in biographical references after her death.

The Kishinev pogrom of 1903, instigated by Plehve, proved to be the catalyst in Manya's life. From this point on she lost her qualms about the virtue of direct punitive action against an oppressor. Involved in a failed plot to assassinate Plehve that resulted in the betrayal of her comrades, she fled to Germany to raise funds for another attempt. More significantly she determined to abandon her agitation among the Russian proletariat. A solution for the martyrdom of Russian Jewry became her primary concern. After Kishinev, masses of Russian Jews fled to the haven of the United States and to Western Europe. Only a dedicated handful chose barren Palestine. These men and women would go down in history as the legendary Second Aliyah who had reached the conviction that rebuilding the ancient homeland was the true revolutionary path.

Manya left for Palestine in 1904 at the request of a sick brother, but still uncertain of her role there. In *The Plough Woman*, a collection of memoirs by women pioneers originally published in Hebrew in 1928, in English in 1932, and subsequently reprinted by the Herzl Press in 1975, Manya wrote that she had come determined to find out "what the country meant to me as an individual." This statement, written twenty-four years after her arrival is probably more reliable than the later recollections of Manya given to Rachel Yanait. For a better understanding of the country's possibilities, she went at the problem with her usual energy.

The Jewish colonies of that period were plantations owned by rich Jewish farmers who used cheap, unorganized Arab labor in preference to more demanding Jewish workers. According to her account, Manya spent her first year in touring the colonies and seeing at first-hand the wretched living conditions of Jewish workers forced to accept any terms offered by Jewish plantation owners in order to fulfill their Zionist dream of reviving the land. Ben-Gurion, among others, has circumstantially described the abysmal situation prevailing. In the rich colony of Petach Tikvah, for instance, pioneers slaved for 25 piastres a day (25 cents) and lived crowded eight to a small room. Manya concluded: "My comrades, the workers, were completely mad. The way they were working there was absolutely no hope of creating a Jewish, agricultural proletariat in Palestine." The previous failure of *Bilu* bore out her view.

To demonstrate the feasibility of collective settlements, she studied the records of colonization attempts in Tunis and Algeria and visited the celebrated settlements established by the Jewish Colonization Association (ICA) funded by the philanthropist, Baron Maurice de Hirsch. And she fought with experts who derided the notion of cooperative settlements. In South America she became convinced that agricultural colonies could succeed. Genuine cooperatives would do still better because of their ideological impetus: "What we needed was a substitute for the religious enthusiasm that had made these settlements possible, and for this substitute I looked to socialism." *(The Plough Woman).* Starving Jewish workers housed in stables were beginning to lose faith "in the burning ideal of the conquest of labor—the upbuilding of the country by the physical labor of the working class." Forbidden by their socialist principles "to become individualist farmers and exploiters of others," yet no longer able to endure their intolerable living conditions, many were leaving Palestine. Eventually Manya's forceful appeals to the Jewish National Fund that regularly purchased land from Arab effendis at grossly inflated prices, and to ICA, resulted in the establishment of the first cooperative at Sejera, a process circumstantially described by Rachel Yanait. The success in Sejera, according to Manya, proved "once for all, that a collective settlement economy was possible."

But she had nursed a bolder dream. With her usual verve Manya had set out to explore the country for unsettled land. She and three like-minded comrades rode through the region that included Jordan, then still two-thirds of Palestine, and also Syria, since no border between Palestine and Syria existed. She sought land already bought by the Jewish National Fund or that could be purchased at the usual exorbitant prices. One large tract of land already paid for by Baron Rothschild was the Hauran, a largely unpopulated region, unexpectedly fertile, in the southern part of Syria, east of Upper Galilee. Though a settlement owned by Jewish farmers had been established, they employed only Arabs. There was no place for Jewish pioneers. To Manya this large stretch of land seemed the logical answer to Jewish need. Foiled by ICA representatives to whom she presented her plan, she independently set out for Paris to enlist Baron Rothchild's support. Though he listened politely he was not converted. Max Nordau, whom she did not hesitate to approach, suggested that she consult a psychiatrist. In 1905 Manya's conviction that cooperative settlements were the key to the redemption of Palestine seemed as fanciful as Herzl's vision of a Jewish state had been a decade earlier.

While in Paris her plans had to give way to a more pressing need. An outbreak of pogroms in Russia required immediate succor. Manya was asked to get funds for weapons, smuggle them into Russia and to organize Jewish self-defense. This time Baron Rothschild proved more forthcoming. With his financial assistance she was able to smuggle arms into Russia in the simple conspiratorial fashion that used to hoodwink the Czarist police; the methods of deception were comically primitive if considered from the point of view of the KGB's later expertise. The revolutionaries who had outwitted the Russian police had learned their lesson. They would develop sterner techniques of scrutiny and repression.

During her Russian stint Manya performed the most questionable act of her daring life. In her account in the *Plough Woman* she mentions her role in the Group of Vengeance whose purpose was to avenge slaughtered Jews. She fails to describe her most startling deed. Only in the account given by her decades later to Rachel Yanait does she describe what she had been compelled to do. She had been guarding a secret cache of arms in a house under the surveillance of the Czarist police who suspected her presence and the hoard of arms, but as yet had no hard evidence. By present standards the police were amazingly circumspect. Not over-energetic, they would go home at night. Under the shelter of darkness a young Jew, claiming to need a refuge, managed to enter the house. Quixotically believing his story she agreed to hide him for the night, pretending to be a maid. Alerted by one of his probing questions, she decided that he was an informer. Were he to leave the house, not only she but the arms would be lost. Unhesitatingly, she shot him with a silencer, concealed his body and waited for comrades to dispose of it as in the most lurid mystery story. This episode dramatically related by her biographer illustrates the contradictions in Manya's character. She would risk her life to save one unknown human being, but she would not hesitate to kill to save her cause. Fortunately, in the rest of her long life no similar act was required; but because of its occurrence, on subsequent occasions in Palestine when a spy would be identified and anonymously executed, false suspicion would fall on Manya.

In his circumstantial biography of Ben-Gurion, (Ben-Gurion, The Burning Ground, 1886–1948) which appeared in English in 1987, Shabtai Teveth, who does not share Rachel Yanait's enthusiasm for Manya, interprets the Zubatov involvement differently. Though calling Manya extraordinary, a born rebel, "ardent for a cause and utterly fearless," he writes:

> "Vilbushevitz fell in love with the infamous agent provocateur Zubatov,* an outstandingly successful officer of the Okhrana (secret police), who after their release created and led a new revolutionary group for the purpose of capturing her confederates. Trusting her beloved Zubatov, Vilbushevitz led many of her friends into his trap. Out of her mind with grief and guilt, and on the run herself, she took revenge on a door-to-door salesman who called at her hide-out in Odessa, thinking he was an Okhrana agent who had tracked her down. Inviting him in, she shot him, dismembered his body, packed the pieces in four suitcases, and dispatched them to four remote parts of the empire."

This lurid account for which no evidence is given, contradicts the known dates and seems far less plausible than Manya's explanation.

On her return to Palestine she met the fascinating Israel Shochat whose dedication to his mission of organizing a group whose function would be to "work and watch," was as intense as Manya's to the idea of collective settlement. In temperament and ideology they seemed perfectly matched. Manya persuaded the manager of a model training farm for agricultural workers at Sejera to establish an autonomous collective settlement in part of the settlement for one year. In it the twin dreams of Manya and Shochat were to be fulfilled. Manya served as bookkeeper. At the end of the year Manya summarized the success of the experiment. "We overcame

---

*In a letter to Zubatov, Manya herself takes note of this rumor in her circles and asks him to do what he can to dispose of it.

the doubts about living collectively on the land and the way was paved for the kibbutz movement." The collective also established the Watch as "a quasi-legal organization to defend what it had created and to feel the pride of nationhood." She added one note of regret. "However we were unable to bring the Hauran plan to fruition."

An added light on Manya's future clashes with Ben-Gurion is provided by Teveth. Ben-Gurion had gone to work as a day laborer in one of the tenant farms at Sejera where he endured the hardships described. The then unknown David Gruen was immediately attracted by the collective in one part of the settlement, but though he was drawn to this glamorous elite and was allowed to participate in some of their activities he was not taken into the inner circle. In the meantime Manya and Shochat had married and obviously directed all major events. Though Ben-Gurion was allowed to stand guard, when Hashomer was formally inaugurated and the newly arrived Rachel Yanait, as well as her fiancé, Ben-Zvi, were admitted, the "veteran" David was rejected, though both Rachel and Ben-Zvi pleaded for him. How deeply this rankled is indicated by the biographer who relates that even when internationally famous, Ben-Gurion, on meeting Shochat or his associates, would hiss, "You didn't want me."

Apart from his injured pride, Ben-Gurion, once in authority, would not countenance rival political factions of the Left or Right. After Hashomer disbanded in 1920 to become part of Haganah, it nevertheless continued as an underground force with its center in Kfar Giladi, the Shomer kibbutz. Shochat formed a Labor Legion with its own activist program. In 1924 an ultra-orthodox anti-Zionist suspected of spying for the Arabs was shot by order of the Haganah, a fact known to few. Because of her past, Manya was arrested as a suspect. Manya, aware of her innocence and Ben-Gurion's knowledge of the truth, sent him an outraged letter on her release. "Ben-Gurion. . . I hadn't thought you were capable of such means to hurt the Legion. I respected you too much as a person. The path you chose will destroy us and you. There's no forgiveness in my heart, and I'm breaking off all personal relations with you!"

Teveth claims that because of the Odessa murder Ben-Gurion had "real cause to fear for his life." The affair was eventually patched up with the cooperation of Ben-Zvi. By 1933 Ben-Gurion placed Manya and Shochat in command of squadrons to defend organized workers against attacks of Jabotinsky's Rightist Revisionists.

While this episode shows how readily Manya's political opponents would accuse her of acts of which she was guiltless, she would in any case never accept the unswerving discipline on which Ben-Gurion and other elected representatives of the Yishuv insisted. The invaluable documents that supplement Yanait's biography indicate not only Manya's continuing challenges of the labor movement's policies, but the respect she inspired throughout her life in those with whom she disagreed, including Ben-Gurion.

Manya met her biographer in connection with the activities of Hashomer. Rachel Yanait had arrived in 1908 at the age of twenty. Then Manya was twenty-nine and already a notable figure, a woman who dressed like a man and rode in Bedouin garb to defend the settlements. That Rachel was a kindred spirit can be seen from the memoir she wrote of her early years in Palestine. Conditions that would have discouraged others filled her with a curious exaltation. "The slight of all the barren ground filled me with a kind of joy—joy that fate had kept the soil of Judea uninhabited . . . In my mind's eye I saw it brought to life by Jews returning from far away." The swamps delighted her: "No village, no farmer in sight. Why are we waiting?" Why did Jews fail to take "the great chance". The "chance" included both immigration and the purchase of uninhabited land for agricultural settlement. The latter was then being done in limited measure by I.C.A. and later by the Jewish National Fund.

At the first formal assembly of Hashomer, Rachel was inducted into the select group of thirty, including four women. Manya on horseback arrayed in an Arab abeya was a welcome sight to the young pioneer feminists resentful of the relegation of women to the kibbutz kitchen and children's house. For a while the romantics in Hashomer dreamt of emulating Bedouin lifestyle and living in tents—a notion that was abandoned. Manya herself stressed the importance of women in the Watch. In the Plough Woman several women comment on the liberating effect of seeing the physical valor of the women members of Hashomer. Rachel describes the indignation of girls like herself who resented exclusion from backbreaking work like digging roads and clearing rocks. When shortly before the close of World War I hundreds of young women sought to enlist in the newly formed Jewish Legion, they were rejected. Rachel Yanait writes, "That rebuff left us flat and wearied. We were not to participate in the Great Moment." (In this connection, it should be noted that women now serve in the Israeli Army but not in combat.) Manya repeatedly raised the issue of discrimination against women, particularly on behalf of Shomer wives who were not admitted to Shomer meetings or discussions. However, part of the reason lay in the initial nomadic existence of the Watch. When they established a permanent collective in Kfar Giladi, women worked as equals and took shifts in guarding the settlements.

The puzzling Turkish interlude described by Rachel Yanait, must be seen in the context of the period. At the time, Palestine was part of the Ottoman Empire. The notion of another country supplanting Turkey seemed so unlikely that even after the outbreak of war, an astute observer like Ben-Gurion and others were convinced of a Turkish victory. To function effectively in Palestine, Ben-Gurion, Ben-Zvi and Israel Shochat thought it advisable to study Turkish law. Manya, by then with a small son, accompanied her husband. When World War I broke out, the extent of the miscalculation resulting in Manya's imprisonment and exile to Anatolia where her daughter Anna was born, is fully described by Rachel Yanait who did not accompany her husband. Turkey did not view Russian Jews as loyal subjects but as enemy aliens. The family did not get back to Kfar Giladi until 1919, except for one interlude.

What of Manya's personal life? Again the contradictions appear. Readers are often surprised to discover that in their intimate lives, apparently granite feminists and revolutionaries suffered from thwarted love like frailer members of their sex. In a recent biography of the anarchist Emma Goldman*, the disclosures of letters exposing her pathetic, wheedling subservience to men she loved shocked some of Goldman's admirers. The difference, however, lay in the fact that though personally unhappy, these women never wavered in the pursuit of their cause. The rational Simone de Beauvoir and the fiery Rosa Luxemburg are other examples, as is the life of Golda Meir.

Israel Shochat, an extremely handsome man according to most accounts, was an inveterate womanizer. Manya's personal misery, driving her at one point to an attempt at suicide, as well as the generosity she displayed to her errant mate, are revealed in the poignant descriptions by Rachel Yanait. As a mother, however, Manya's ideological commitments took chilling preference. Both her children felt cast away. The searing account given by her daughter to a reporter in an interview that appeared in the Israeli *Haaretz* in 1986 when Anna was seventy years old, reveals in devastating detail the daughter's and son's sense of abandonment and the

Love, Anarchy and Emma Goldman by Candace Falk. Holt, Reinhart, 1984.

depth of a resentment that lasted into old age. Once on a visit to Kfar Giladi, Ben-Gurion turned to the girl and asked about her parents. She answered, "I am an orphan." Expecting a panegyric, Ben-Gurion indignantly reminded her that the settlement existed thanks to her parents. But the old woman writes bitterly that neither she nor her brother Geda had a mother or father; instead of a "home" they had a "homeland." "I felt alone but I knew it was for the homeland . . . My parents carried the burden of the homeland relentlessly on their backs." The child's unhappiness was mixed with a sense of guilt. She knew she should accept the poverty, stern discipline and danger of the Hashomer children without cavilling. But the mature woman judged her parents more harshly. This extraordinary document is one of the most intriguing of the documentary supplement to this biography.

It should be noted that the Shochats were a extreme instance in this as in other aspects of their lives. The kibbutz was geared to meeting family and work needs through a children's house that allowed for the children's and mothers' normal desires for contact. At the end of the work day, the children went to their parents' room, a time daily cherished by the family. But Manya was too busy with various activities to rate a room. In this respect she was atypical as in others. In *The Plough Woman*, the young Golda wrote a prescient account of a woman torn by the balancing claims of her family and career. But at no point did she neglect her children. They loved her and honored her greatness in sharp contrast to the reactions of Manya's son and daughter.

Though in 1920, Hashomer had joined Haganah, the underground defense force of the Yishuv in which all groups of the labor movement participated, this change in no way inhibited Manya's gift for individual unorthodox action. Illegal immigration into Palestine in the twenties in response to anti-semitic legislation in Poland and Russia supplemented the quota allowed by Great Britain, while Arabs from the adjoining countries poured unimpeded into Palestine to take advantage of new opportunities created by Zionist development. Jewish Agency officials, fearing that even the small legal quota would be jeopardized by illegal immigrants, tried to discourage independent efforts by the kibbutzim to assist immigrants trying to cross the border from Lebanon. "Hotel Kfar Giladi," (as it was named in the immigrant grapevine) situated in the north, proved geographically and ideologically a temporary refuge from detection by the Arab police and British authorities. Manya's ingenuity in devising stratagems for escape did not endear her to Jewish officials. The daring of Hashomer in smuggling illegals and arms for defense elicited ambivalent responses, even in the Haganah, whose disciplined members criticized the riskiness of some of the ventures.

As in the past, Manya was still possessed by her vision of wasteland that could be purchased and fructified by Jewish labor without dispossessing a single Arab. The Negev, the bare southern desert, entranced her in 1921 as compellingly as it later did Ben-Gurion, who ended his days in Sdeh Boker. Receiving no encouragement or funds from Zionist authorities, she turned directly to the committee for agricultural settlement, demanding that a special committee for the project be appointed, despite the opposition of Zionist officials who objected to the deflection of scarce funds to romantic enterprises. In a letter written in 1925, she specified those who should constitute the committee: "These four must be: Ben-Zvi, Yisrael Shochat, Rachel Yanait and myself, because we have already been working on this project for four years; it is in our blood and we have decided to dedicate ourselves completely to its fruition."

The first Negev outposts that exported flowers and fruit even to Italy did not come into being till the late thirties and forties. They became blooming kibbutzim, so fully justifying their founders' hopes, but Ben-Gurion's call to "go South" was answered only by the hardiest and most idealistic.

Another cause on Manya's docket was friendship and coexistence with the Arabs. In Hashomer, she and her comrades had always stressed the need for friendship and understanding with Arab neighbors, particularly with the Bedouin whose bearing they admired and whose dress they imitated. After the shock of the Arab riots in 1929, Manya established contact with the circle of Jewish academics whose guiding spirit was Judah L. Magnes, president of the Hebrew University and founder of Brit Shalom and later of Ihud; organizations that advocated a binational state organized on the principle of parity.

But at no point were there any Arab takers of this proposal. When urged by Magnes to negotiate with Arab leaders, Ben-Gurion, with the authority of head of the World Zionist Executive, began negotiations that extended from 1933 to 1938.* The finale came when Musa Husseini of the powerful Husseini clan bluntly informed Ben-Gurion that peace could be attained only if Palestine

*See *My Talks With Arab Leaders* by David Ben Gurion, Keter Books, 1972.

became an Arab state whose Jewish population would never exceed one-third of the whole; immigration would be restricted accordingly. This proposal was made in 1938 when the desperate need of European Jewry was all too apparent. There was nothing left to negotiate. To accept minority status meant abandoning the hope of eventual national independence and closing the doors of the only haven left to Nazi victims.

Manya, no more than Ben-Gurion, would have been likely to concur in such an outcome. That she remained on good terms with the more discreet intellectuals of the Magnes circle despite her temperamental inability to limit her activities, indicates the respect and affection she inspired even among individuals not inclined to subscribe to her unilateral attempts.

In 1931, on one of her missions to the USA for the Histadrut, she formulated a list of the guiding principles for a League for Arab-Jewish coexistence. Like many in the labor movement, she was convinced that once the Arab masses perceived their identity of interest with Jewish workers, they would resist the instigations of the Mufti and join hands in a cooperative effort with Jews. In the program quoted by Rachel Yanait, Manya offers a realistic appraisal of the value of joint labor unions and the participation of Arabs in social institutions. Despite this realism, she quaintly begins with "cultural action." Arab youth should be given the opportunity to read great literature in Arabic translation instead of the "fascist-chauvinist poison" they were being fed by the Mufti's cohorts.

She sought funds for this purpose as energetically as for arms. In 1940, on a later visit to the U.S., she addressed a meeting of *Avukah*, the leftist organization of Zionist college students. One of the women present at that meeting gave me an account of that occasion. The last thing the young students expected from the fabled Manya was an exposition of the urgency of translating Tolstoy and other European classics into Arabic, and an exhortation to collect funds for this purpose. Such was Manya's eloquence that she completely persuaded the usually disputatious students: salvation lay in a great books course. In retrospect my friend laughed at the simplicity of these sophisticated, and usually belligerent students. But Manya's magic prevailed. They started to collect money for translations as a priority.

With the outbreak of World War II, when knowledge of the Holocaust reached Palestine, Aliyah Beth illegal immigration became her consuming passion, as it was that of the entire Yishuv. As usual she did not hesitate to castigate and complain. On 5-12-42 she fired off a letter to Ben-Gurion accusing him of "political expediency" and delay. He answered temperately, "Although I don't agree with all you say, I have no doubt as to your sincerity and pure intentions". And he signed his response, "With fondness and blessings." She too had signed "with respect and fondness". But she wholly misjudged the small Yishuv's ability to influence the policies of the allies in wartime. Anyone familiar with the difficulties of Haganah in bringing in illegal boats despite the British blockade, understands how illusory was Manya's demand for mass immigration at that time.

At the end of the war, after the establishment of the state, she worked indefatigably in the transit camps for new immigrants, living with them until forbidden on medical orders. As a result in 1950 she had advice for Golda, then Minister of Labor. After spending several months in the camps she concluded that idleness was destroying even the best individuals: "Some want to go into business and only a small part choose to be farmers." Her solution: they should be sent at once to agricultural settlements to be trained and then be sent to work on undeveloped land.

Considering the still festering resentment of those newcomers who initially had been dispersed in developing communities rather than sent to urban centers, one can imagine the practical result of this proposal that represented what the those in charge actually wanted. Years earlier Manya had urged Henrietta Szold, who loved and respected her, to persuade Hadassah to fund a desirable project. Hadassah, as Henrietta dejectedly explained, was running a deficit and could undertake no further commitments. But Manya had no talent for pragmatic compromise.

In 1959, two years before her death and seven years before Israel had to wrestle with the problem of occupied territories, she complained to Ben-Gurion about discrimination against Israeli Arabs; "There are in the defense department enough smart and capable people who could find the means to fight against a fifth column among the Arabs without resorting to martial law." Ben-Gurion, then Prime Minister, answered affectionately; "I am a full partner with you in the aspiration for equality and justice. The difference is in our perception of realities. But I was happy to hear from you, happy that you turned to me."

My only meeting with Manya was at the end of 1940 when she was in the United States on her several missions, public and secret. She came to my apartment and we talked of various matters, particularly the Arabs. Instead of summarizing those few hours, since my recollections of nearly half a century ago are hazy, I quote from the interview that appeared in *Jewish Frontier*, January, 1941. It gives a clearer glimpse of her many-faceted personality than would a general impression.

There was nothing formidable or picturesque about the small woman, dressed in a curious zipper coat and wearing a little fur hat that looked like a relic of student days in Russia. She was carrying a bulging brief case full of plans and projects that she proceeded to show me. I quote verbatim a part of our conversation:

"As soon as I get the money," Manya said, "I must go home. It's time. Only it takes over two months through India—"

Manya made a grimace of displeasure and shook her grey, clipped head. It would have been silly to ask if she were afraid of bombs, of torpedoes, of the perilous journey in wartime—so I waited.

"It's the sea-sickness," she went on. "I always get sea-sick. That's the only thing I mind."

One doesn't often have a chance to drink tea with a heroine—Manya Schochat's revolutionary activity in Czarist Russia, her years in Palestine are already legendary—or to chat casually with a member of that strange, fearless race, who are as much apart from the rest of us as the unicorn or the phoenix. It was rather comforting to think that Manya could be sea-sick.

"Do you mind fasting?" I asked, because recently I had fasted for a day and had felt quite virtuous.

Manya's dark eyes, bright and undimmed by her sixty years, gleamed behind her spectacles.

"Who minds fasting? But the most I ever managed was twelve days."

"Twelve days!" I gasped. "When did you fast twelve days."

"Oh, that was in prison in Russia. We had such a style then—hunger strikes," Manya smiled. "I don't remember now what we were striking about that time, but it was twelve days. However, we drank water. Without water it's hard. The most I ever managed without water was five days. With water, twelve days are easy. You feel light and your mind is so clear. As long as you keep walking up and down in your cell, you feel fine."

I knew how much opportunity for developing the technique of the hunger strike Manya had managed to acquire in Russia. Those were the days when she had joined the terrorist conspiracy against the Czar's minister Von Plehve, when as a slight, young girl she had led Jewish self-defense groups during pogroms. I remembered how she had smuggled arms, how she had been hounded from lodging to lodging by the Czar's police in St. Petersburg. And then, after 1904, the great pioneer years in Palestine—Sejera, Kfar Giladi. The same revolutionary valor and passion harnessed to her people's cause. What daring she had shown in thought as in action—the first to fight for the idea of the agricultural collective as well as among the first to guard the young communes.

And now she sat in my chair in New York, a little, unpretentious woman with a brief-case instead of a banner, with spectacles instead of an aureole, and discussed revolutionary fasts as other women might discuss the merits of the Hollywood diet.

"When was your last long fast?" I asked.

"Ten years ago in Palestine, but that was not political. It was a scientific experiment on metabolism. They needed volunteers so a young chap and I offered ourselves. We drank five glasses of tea with lemon a day but we ate nothing."

"No sugar?"

"No, no sugar; it was easy after the first two days but the young fellow got tired of it after twelve days. Besides it was interfering with my work. I had to come to Haifa every day to have my blood-pressure taken, be examined and all that kind of thing. There was too much to do at Kfar Gileadi."

I made a mental calculation. Ten years ago Manya was about fifty, and she was still demonstrating how strong the spirit could be, when it is strong.

We started to talk about the Arabs. Manya has her own views as to how the Arab problem is to be solved—win the Arab masses rather than negotiate with the Arab leaders. Manya's theories have been labelled as Utopian but she battles as ever.

"I know the Arabs. I've lived with them for thirty-six years. Take Aziz for instance."

"Who was Aziz?"

"Aziz was my friend." Manya stopped for a moment remembering Aziz. "You know how I met Aziz? The automobile I was riding in on the way to Haifa overturned, and we were pinned down on the road. Then Aziz came along with another Arab and began to rescue us. He was only eighteen years old then, and it was a complicated job, extricating us from under that car but he did it with great skill. I kept marvelling at the technical ability of this Arab."

"For God's sake, Manya," I interrupted. "You were lying pinned under a car and you were meditating on the technical talents of Arabs."

Manya looked annoyed. "I wasn't dead, was I? And besides such technical abilities are unusual in Arabs. They haven't had the training. But Aziz was different. We became friends."

She told me about Aziz. He had run away from Palestine as a child. He had lived by his wits in Syria, being bootblack, newspaper vendor—the real life of a street gamin—but he had become literate. He wanted to learn. Then he returned to Palestine, picking up odd jobs. After their accidental meeting, Manya had helped him. She got him apprenticed to a Jewish locksmith and Aziz became a skilled craftsman.

The locksmith was an anarchist but, under Manya's guidance, Aziz was not led astray. Though he served his master faithfully, he swallowed no false sociological doctrine.

"I made him a socialist." Manya said proudly.

And then Aziz fell in love with Leahle, a Jewish girl. But he wouldn't give up Islam. He prayed each Friday in the Mosque despite his enlightenment. When Leahle's parents got wind of the romance, they packed her off to Tel Aviv. But Leahle couldn't forget and threw herself into the sea one cold night. After she was pulled out, she contracted pneumonia and died. Aziz was never the same after that.

"He used to be such a gay boy but then he became gloomy," Manya related.

When the terror broke out in the thirties, Aziz would go out among the Arabs and argue against the Mufti. In due course, the terrorists attacked him. The first time he was badly wounded. When Manya visited him in the hospital, he asked her to make sure that Leahle's photograph be put in his grave when he died. He knew that the Mufti bands would get him sometime.

"What good will her picture do you?" Manya had asked rationally, and Aziz had explained that it was easier to recognize the beloved dead if one had a photograph along.

"Imagine," Manya turned to me in genuine bewilderment, "I made him a socialist and this is the nonsense he believed. That's an Arab for you."

"What happened to Aziz?"

"The terrorists shot him later, just before I left for America, and I wasn't able to put Leahle's picture in his coffin."

Manya showed no visible emotion when speaking of Aziz but we were silent a moment, thinking of the young Arab who had loved a Jewess, who had technical skill, who had been shot by terrorists, whose socialism had been so paradoxical according to Manya's lights. And I had a feeling that even Manya was perhaps sorry that Aziz lay mouldering without Leahle's photograph to guide him through the heavens.

"Aziz was only one," I ventured.

"No," Manya said with conviction, "There are many more. They have to be found."

When she was leaving I asked her, "So all will be well." She turned to me, bright, confident, "Of course."

After the state was declared and Israel lost Old Jerusalem to the Arab Legion, Manya resolutely ignored the barbed wire fence and the Mandelbaum Gate that divided the city. Determined to maintain contact with her many Arab friends, she would repeatedly disregard the barriers and stray into forbidden territory. The Arabs, who knew her, would just as regularly send her back instead of imprisoning her.

For what would Manya agitate today had she lived to see the impasse that emerged despite her optimism. On the one hand she would be looking for another Aziz or his modern Arab equivalent. At the same time, she would probably be as merciless as in the past with planters of bombs in Jerusalem markets or killers of children in a peaceful kibbutz in Galilee. Readers now have an opportunity to evaluate this extraordinary woman and make their own prophecies and judgments. Biblio Press merits high praise for its enterprise and perception in making this biography available in English.

MARIE SYRKIN

Readers' Note

Words and terms starred with an asterisk(*) in the text and documents section
are defined on pages 152–157.

Prologue

The personality of Manya Shochat is one of the most striking in the history of the labor movement in Israel. Her multi-faceted image serves to symbolize the period of the second wave of immigration, when the foundations of a working Israel and its values were laid. Many special people blossomed in this period, and Manya, who was both an imaginative thinker and energetic activist, epitomizes this era.

After all, it was Manya who created, from her deep introspection and soul searching, the first collective in Sejera, thus laying the groundwork for the kibbutz movement in Israel. Together with Yisrael Shochat, she was among the first members of Hashomer and its living spirit, a pioneer of the Haganah and Aliyah Bet. During her lifetime, Manya was already a legend.

I see a personal duty to perpetuate her memory and to tell about her childhood and youth, about her revolutionary activity in Russia, but mostly about her action-packed life in Eretz Israel.**

About her early years, I relate the events as I heard them from Manya herself, some of which were publicized in *Devar Hapoelet* beginning in 1961. As far as her goals and methods in Eretz Israel, I have as sources friends and community leaders who knew her well, her brave heart, her pure soul and her belief in humanity.

Rachel Yanait Ben-Zvi

**Eretz Israel is used throughout this book to indicate the land of Israel before the state in 1948.

Introduction

In 1959, when Manya was getting on in years and her health was slowly deteriorating, I invited her to stay with me for several months in the President's house in Jerusalem, hoping to assist in her recovery.

In the evenings, we would sit and chat, and I would try to encourage her to talk about her complex and colorful past.

The testament of Manya's life was long and involved, studded with lofty dreams and daring acts. It was difficult to grasp the endless complexities of her personality. For more than half a century, she had been ceaselessly, inexhaustibly immersed in a multitude of activities, investing in all a unique kind of fervor.

Manya's nature was a blend of earthy femininity, compassion, logic and pragmatism. When she was taken with an idea she committed herself totally to its fruition, devoting herself completely and involving others, as though she were fulfilling a divine mission. Whether a particular idea originated with her or with a friend, she would seize the initiative and within a short time, thoughts would be transformed into actions.

From the first time that I met Manya I wondered about the origin of that zeal; from what source had she derived her enormous inner strength? I was always amazed by her diverse activities and her tendency to ignore her own bodily needs, often making do with a small piece of carob as her source of nutrition. She seemed to require of herself a degree of asceticism consistent with her need to conquer the passions that seethed inside her. Powerful longings competed within, as she instinctively tried to free herself from them, to acquire the self-discipline needed to fulfill the idea or the dream; to give all for others to the point of self-sacrifice. In her fierce desire to help every individual for the sake of humanity as a whole, she inspired in others feelings of tremendous faith in her;

feelings of respect and honor—even among those who opposed her.

In order to reach her heart of hearts, I would sit with her and attempt to make her recall the past.

"No, not the past," she would reply, placing on my shoulder her good hand, her warm hand, warm as the gaze in her eyes. She did not like speaking about the past. Her body was growing weak, but her soul was young and fresh as ever, and her spirit was whole. She would continue living each current experience as it came, as if starting her struggles anew.

Even when she finally gave in to my repeated requests and began to speak about events of the past, she relived them in the telling, and in her speech past became present. The present and the future—these were her concerns until the end of her days.

Reminiscing about her childhood and youth, she temporarily overcame her frailty, raising her head, as if shedding the weight of years. Opening her wonderful eyes wide, she would set sail to the distant past, becoming transported to a far-off world, reliving her youth. Often, she seemed so totally immersed in her recollections that she completely forgot my presence.

Remembering her father, a spark of love and respect shone in her eyes. Recalling her trip in the hot air balloon, she became angry at herself, and desolation filled her countenance when she recalled Gershuni. With renewed energy, she told about the activities of the Bund in Russia, and it seemed then that she still had not resolved her debate with them. With deep sadness, she told how Chayka Kagan, her childhood friend from Minsk, had left the Poalei Zion. "Chayka, Chayka," she whispered, "how can it be that you went over to the territorialist socialists? Was this your way of looking for a final resolution to the suffering of the Jewish nation?" And when she spoke about the end of Gapon, she was in deep sadness. To that day, she could not believe that he had been a traitor to his worker comrades. Though he had been found guilty of treason and executed, she was convinced that a mistake had been made. After all, she knew him so well! A noble man....

Once more she became filled with rage when she remembered how, for many months, she had had conversations with the head of the Czar's secret police, Zubatov, without being aware of his identity. When she told me of her visit to Zubatov in order to accuse him of treason, armed with a pistol in her pocket, her hands trembled and her heart pounded. She felt the old depression in retelling how her friends had been imprisoned after their thwarted effort to assassinate Plehve. In the springtime of her life, when she was not yet twenty years old, Manya had acted together with the movers and shakers of government and revolution in Russia, putting heart and soul into the workers' movement. Alas, alas, what efforts she had wasted in the diaspora when she could have come to Eretz Israel sooner—this was her regret.

In talking about her aliyah*, a new note was sounded in her words, a note of peace, of contentment; also a feeling of excitement, as though she were once again landing at the pier in Jaffa. Speaking slowly, with great detail, she seemed to feel once again her first contact with her homeland, to live again the transformation of that moment which had extricated her from her past in the diaspora, to feel again the joy of rebirth.

Yes, how good it was to delve with Manya into the past.

1. Childhood

Manya Wilbushevitz was born in 1879 in the village of Lososna near the city of Grodno. Her father's parents were wealthy, assimilated Jews who lived the life of Russian landowners, "regular squires," in the words of Manya.

Her grandfather was a supplier for the Russian army, and was thus able to secure privileges that few Jews received, such as a permit to enter Petersburg and Moscow. He lived like a Gentile, with an abundance of women and wine. His house was open to army officers. The walls groaned with the weight of valuable pictures, particularly of czars and generals. Even the holidays were Christian. To Manya, the whole scene was repulsive.

In the grandfather's absence, all business was conducted by his wife, who also acted like a Gentile, seeking to emulate the women of the Russian aristocracy. Manya could never understand how a woman who came from such a splendid Jewish family could so estrange herself from her people. Her mother's brother was the author, Samuel Joseph Fuenn, editor of *Hacarmel;* and the Ramm family, owners of the well-known publishing house in Vilna, were close relatives.

The Jews of Grodno had reason to hate these turncoats; Manya loathed them too. She never forgot her one opportunity to demonstrate the extent of her hatred. She was seven years old. One Shabbat, the little girl was brought to her grandmother's house. When Manya walked in, the old woman was reclining on the sofa, supported by several colorful pillows. One of her many aristocratic affectations was her habit of smoking a pipe and even on the Shabbat the pipe hung from her lips. Looking imperiously down at the child, she extended her hand to her to be kissed, in the manner of the noble Russian matriarchs. Without knowing what came over her, Manya bent down, took the dowager's hand and sunk her teeth into it. Thus, she poured out her anger toward her grand-

1

mother, perhaps because of the suffering that woman had caused her father.

Manya loved her father more than anyone, and even at that tender age, she could almost literally feel the terrible trials that he had undergone in his youth at his mother's house. Manya's father was the only one of his entire family who remained loyal to Judaism. His brothers were the first to attend the Russian *gymnasia** that had been then erected in Grodno and they soon abandoned Jewish tradition. Eventually they married non-Jews and were lost to the Jewish people.

When he was a young boy, Manya's father would run away to the Jewish quarter in Grodno, where he felt a real kinship for the pious teacher, Reb Nachum. The teacher had no children of his own, and he poured out his enormous love to the poor children of the city, spending all his time with them. The boy became very dear to Reb Nachum and the Rebbe was like a father to him. When his mother found out that her son was close to Reb Nachum, she did all she could to separate him from his mentor and to convince him to study in the Russian *gymnasia* like his brothers. But the boy continued to go to Reb Nachum and persevered in the study of Torah. His mother beat him and scolded him and berated him until he finally decided to starve himself and end his miserable life. He hid in the stable in the courtyard and covered himself with straw. The family looked for him at home but could not find him. They sent messengers to Reb Nachum to demand that he return the boy, but he too had not seen his student for two days. Searches were organized in the courtyards, in the roads, in the attics and finally even along the banks of the river, looking for his body to wash ashore. On the third day, one of the servants happened to be in the stable and saw boards over the stall. He removed the planks and found the boy unconscious. Barely alive, he was brought to his mother who summoned physicians to bring him back to life. After he was revived, the boy threatened that he would try to kill himself again if they would not let him live as a Jew. From then on, he spent all day under the roof of Reb Nachum, and studied and ate there. He went home only to sleep. There he spoke to no one and took no meals, so as not to eat unkosher food.

When he turned eighteen, his mother hurriedly married him off, convinced that this would make him a "man". He was married to the great-granddaughter of the Vilna Gaon*; but at the end of one year she died in childbirth. After a while, his mother married him off again, but this time it was only under the express condition that he would live in a village at a distance from his mother, so that she could no longer interfere in his life. His resourceful mother bought him an estate, not far from Grodno; Lososna. Despite his unwanted proximity to her, from then on he lived his life according to his beliefs as a proud Jew, who obeyed all the commandments and was engrossed in the study of Torah. He was a man of noble spirit, with a deep religious feeling, and these lofty attributes he passed down to Manya and her talented brothers and sisters. It was he who instilled in them the values of Judaism and implanted in their hearts the love for Eretz Israel.

In particular, he loved the village, the forest, the river bank. On the shores of the river, he constructed a flour mill, and there he worked on his various inventions. One was a machine that used water power—the turbine engine—totally unaware that it had already been invented*. His inventions were not developed for personal gain; rather he took a special joy in the act of creation. Manya's mother managed the farm and handled the money while her husband spent it on his inventions.

Manya's mother was a wise and intellectual woman, who was educated in the spirit of the "Haskalah"* movement, as was the custom in those days. She could converse equally well in Polish, Russian or German. It is not surprising, therefore, that she strove to transmit a university-style enlightenment to her children, opposite to the wishes of her husband, who preferred to educate them in the spirit of the Jewish tradition, hoping his sons would become rabbis. After unending arguments about the education of their children, the parents reached a kind of compromise. The children were sent to Bialystok, to the home of Dr. Joseph Chasanowich, who would later become one of the founders of the Jewish National and University Library. The Wilbushevitz children studied in the Russian *gymnasia*, but there, under the influence of Chasanowich, became imbued with the spirit of Judaism and Zionism.

There were ten children in the family; Manya was the eighth. The oldest sister, who was very beautiful, married Chasanowich at the age of twenty-one. Later, during her studies in Petersburg, she fell in love with a Christian. In order to be true to herself, and not cheat on her husband or on her love, she committed suicide. This occurred even before Manya was born.

Her second sister, Anna, was especially loved by Manya. She was also very beautiful, but her end was also tragic. When Manya was about eight years old, Anna returned from the big city, enveloped in smothering depression. Manya could read Russian, and

Anna asked her to read from the writings of Dostoyevsky, Tolstoy and the literature of the Russian revolutionaries. Although Manya understood practically nothing in these books, she read aloud to her sister for hour upon hour which seemed to soothe her.

Her oldest brother, Isaac, emigrated to Eretz Israel when Manya was a baby, but the impression he made on her was a deep one. Isaac had a great influence on the entire family, ingraining in them a strong feeling of Zionism. They all admired his confident and proud attitude while attending the Russian agricultural academy, although this behavior caused his expulsion. In one of the lectures, the instructor casually remarked that the "Zhids"* were sucking the blood of the Ukrainian farmers. When Isaac heard this, he leaped out of his seat and slapped the lecturer's cheek right in front of the class. It was no surprise that he was expelled immediately. But this led him to achieve his lifelong dream. In 1882, he emigrated to Eretz Israel with the Biluim*. His letters home were always an exciting event for the family; his dynamic words subliminally binding Manya to Eretz Israel.

Her brother Gedaliah was also a Zionist from his youth, and in 1892 he emigrated to Eretz Israel to develop industry there. After a time, he travelled to Berlin, with the purpose of inducing investors to support the industrial development of Eretz Israel.

Of all her brothers, Manya was closest to Nachum. Only one year separated them, and they grew up together. When she was about fifteen, Manya gave Nachum her picture, and on it she wrote in Russian: "There will always be a strong tie between us and we will always help each other in times of trouble." These words eventually came true.

The only brother who was not destined for Eretz Israel was Binyamin. Like the other children, this brother was also very gifted but full of strange notions. He studied pharmacy, but because of his socialist leanings, he was persecuted by the government. Somehow, he ended up in Texas, where he ran a drug store. He became very devoted to caring for the Blacks in the community and was viewed by them as a saint. Although he did not accept payment from the poor, he nevertheless became very wealthy. He had a large following, and admirers frequently came to his home and left donations for his good works. In 1902, he died of a debilitating illness, and bequeathed all his belongings to his siblings. Eventually, it was that inheritance which paved the way for Manya's trip to Eretz Israel and her travels there with Nachum.

On hot summer days, Lososna bustled with students, both male and female, and on the Wilbushevitz estate, heated debates were conducted on socialism and revolution. Manya would listen to these words, and lofty thoughts and aspirations were thus awakened in her heart.

On one of those summer days, the conversation turned to the story of William Tell, and all were inspired by him. Manya's brother, Moshe, who was then seventeen years old and influenced by the books of Dostoyevsky and Tolstoy, suddenly interjected into the students' discussion the idea that there was nothing remarkable about shooting at targets. And to prove what a sharpshooter he was, he called Manya and asked her to stand near a tree. Before she could grasp the meaning of those words, something sped past her head. It seemed to her she had been wounded—her head felt warm. Everyone seized Moshe to punish him. But Manya would not let anyone touch him, even though she then understood that he had used her for target practice. Years later she asked Moshe if he would still aim above her head. His answer was that only in one's youth can a person do such things without weighing the consequences beforehand.

Moshe was ten years older than Manya and she was fervently bound to him. In her eyes he was a miracle man—agitated, ranting, full of mighty ambitions, so like her father. Although he excelled at his studies, he decided to become an ordinary worker among workers, and not, God forbid, the son of a landowner. He therefore left home and went to far-away Odessa to work in a mill. After some time, his parents were able to convince him to return home and become a worker there. He returned, wearing the clothes of the peasants, toiling with them, eating their simple coarse food, living in the dank atmosphere of one of their huts. Only on Shabbat eve would he return home, when Manya would adoringly bring him clean clothing for the Sabbath. On Friday evening he would dine with the family and delight them all, but on the following night, as soon as the Shabbat was over, he hurried back to his workers. After all, how could he live in the home of the rich during the week? The life of poverty and the simple villagers attracted him. Manya adored Moshe and aspired to a lifestyle like his.

From her father, Manya absorbed the feelings of love of God, nature, forests, earth, and humanity. At a very young age she gave much thought to the paradoxes of life. Until the age of twelve, she was very religious and felt a closeness to God. She always addressed Him aloud, as though she was talking to a close friend; never using a prayer book but simply pouring out her heart. This turning to God as to a friend was typical of Manya, who always spoke plainly and expressed her feelings in simple words which moved others.

2. Youth

As Manya developed and began to hear the adults discuss faith and religion, doubts crept into her heart. That period became one of the most difficult in her life. She continued to read avidly, but found no replacement for her pure faith in the Almighty.

In those days of religious growing pains, the twelve-year-old Manya befriended a 14-year-old Russian boy, the son of workers on the estate. The boy told her tales about the misfortunes of the farmers and how they were being exploited by the landowners. These words resonated strongly in Manya's heart, since she had not yet been able to reconcile the differences between the rich and the poor. Manya believed every word he told her, and through him she became friendly with other village youth. In the boy's company, she often visited the farmers' huts, and in her idealistic fervor, the rich home of her grandmother became even more distasteful to her.

One day Manya approached the boy's home unnoticed while he was absorbed in a conversation about the rich and the poor with a group of youngsters. Suddenly, he started talking about the "Zhids"*, who were—according to him—the culprits who caused all the suffering of the poor villagers. Manya was dumbfounded. He was not talking about landowners, he was talking about the few Jews in the area, who were to be a scapegoat for all. "The Zhids,"*—that meant Manya and her family. . . She shuddered and fled the scene, paying no attention to the feeble excuses of the boy running after her.

When she arrived home, she ran up to her room and cried out to God, this time not because of "injustice" but because of injustice to her people. Why did God spread out the Jews among the nations; why did everyone hate them, whether they were poor or rich?

Although Manya tried to pour her angry heart out to God, her faith was already somewhat shaken. She felt heavy with despair and confused; climbed up to the attic, where she wandered until her eye happened upon the medicine chest. Suddenly something seized her. As if in a trance, she opened its lock, and removed a vial of poison. She drank it and fell to the floor. That night, her mother felt ill and asked for medicine to be brought to her. Her father went up to the attic where he discovered Manya lying unconscious. A doctor, who by chance was visiting that evening, was summoned and was able to revive her. Manya later became furious because without faith in God, she could see no reason to live.

Actually there was a great deal of purpose to her life, and a heavenly spirit seemed to guide all her actions. From the atmosphere of contrasts in her home—the anti-religious fervor of her assimilationist grandmother and the pious attachment of her father to Judaism; the affluent home in which she was raised and the hovels of the nearby villagers; a total disregard for God or man and a belief in morality and ethics—from this home of paradoxes and from the spiritual growing pains that this atmosphere fostered, Manya was able to retrieve one precious set of values which remained at her core: her simple faith in people and their humanity, her striving for justice and the burning desire to fight for a worthwhile life for every person. Even after she went to the other extreme and saw herself as a completely free thinker, there remained with her a kind of religious attitude in her approach to people. Her love of people, individually and collectively, was expressed in all she did and so she ultimately became a living legend.

During this period of despair, Manya's mother tried to raise Manya's spirits. Under her influence Manya began to consider the study of medicine as a means of helping her fellow human beings. A private tutor hired by her mother began preparing Manya for the exams, but her father objected and the whole plan collapsed. This did not come as a great blow to Manya, because in truth she was not drawn to the idea of becoming a doctor. After all, through medicine, she might cure sick people, but would not be able to help all the other suffering masses.

At that point in time, her parents decided to relinquish their control and allow Manya to do what she herself wished. Teachers were brought to the house (her father would not permit her to attend the *gymnasia*), and thus she learned the Bible and read the New Testament and the Koran in its Russian translation, searching everywhere for her lost faith. But her belief was already undermined, and her soul filled with yearning for justice and a burning desire to correct all the wrongs of human society.

Thus, through an identification with the working class in all its suffering, she decided to become a "male" worker and to live among workers as an equal, regardless of her religion or her gender. Of course she knew that her parents would never allow her to leave home (she was only fifteen years old) in order to be a "worker," so she decided to run away. Decision translated into instant action. She travelled to Lodz without identity papers. She found board at the home of a Jewish family and started to search for a job. In a Jewish bag factory, she was at first rejected, but after endless pleading they accepted her as a porter at her own suggestion despite the fact that they had the impression she was not entirely in her right mind. Manya earned a living, and before long she proved her worth as a porter; stronger than many men who worked there.

Meanwhile, her parents searched for her. Before long, the police located her and forced her to return home. And once more she sank deeply into her studies and her examinations.

3. Social Activism

But Manya could no longer remain at home. Finally, she turned to her brother Gedaliah, who was then a partner in a large carpentry shop in Minsk, and he agreed to accept her for design work. But design did not attract Manya; what did appeal to her was the actual labor of carpentry. And so she apprenticed in the shop, and with her own hands built crates. In Minsk and in Grodno, stories were beginning to circulate about the girl porter, about the girl carpenter—legends of Manya. But she was still at the beginning of her journey.

For about a year, she lived with Gedaliah. Once she was earning more than a subsistence wage at the shop, she decided to rent her own room. Before long, it was transformed into a meeting place for her friends, who filed in and out day and night. On any number of occasions, Manya would give her room to the homeless while she stayed in her brother's house. Even the basic necessities that her mother sent her she distributed to her friends.

Her mother continued to urge her to study medicine, but Manya's response was that in her view this was not the way to help others.

In Lososna, Manya had gotten to know the lives of the peasants, but until she lived in Minsk she knew practically nothing about the lives of her fellow Jews. Now she got to know the Jews, she learned Yiddish, and her connection with her people became stronger. On her frequent visits to the factories she came into contact with Jewish laborers and their families, whose lives were very difficult in those days. In most places, the work day was fifteen hours long. Gedaliah's workshop was unique: the workers put in only an eleven-hour day, possibly because of Manya's urging. Incidentally, Gedaliah's factory was also unusual in that it employed about forty Jewish workers, compared with the majority of the factories that hired mostly Poles.

In Minsk, Manya met the famous Bundist*, Grisha Shechovitz. It soon became clear to Manya that Grisha, who was very perceptive, did not totally agree with the philosophy of the Bund movement. Later she became interested in the Poalei Zion party in Minsk, the nucleus of what was to become the Labor Zionist movement.

During her contacts with the workers, Manya was first and foremost devoted to the idea of establishing educational groups, in her belief that only knowledge could transform them into activists. In this matter, she differed sharply from the Bundists who argued that knowledge only raised doubts. But Manya stood firm and put all her efforts into her groups.

In 1898, the year of the great famine in central Russia, there arose among the Russian youth a movement to help the hungry. In Minsk, a delegation of about twenty-five people was formed to help the starving in the Tatar villages of central Russia, and Manya eagerly joined the committee. The committee headquarters, which included a doctor and a secretary, was in Kazan, while the other members dispersed among the more remote villages.

As soon as she reached her village, Manya hurried to set up a kitchen. She received the basic necessities from Kazan. Her so-called assistant was the village head, but it became entirely clear to her on the very first day that she was dealing with a *kulak** who was sucking his people dry. Although Manya was ostensibly in charge of the operation, on a practical level, when it came to distributing the rations, the village head took control. Her situation became unbearable. The hungry looked to her to extend some help, but she was powerless; their leader controlled the distribution. Manya wandered among the helpless Tatar mothers feeling equally hopeless. One day, they pleaded with her to find a shroud for a young woman who had just died. Where would she find a shroud? She had already given away most of her nightgowns and underwear. Finally, she took the few linens she had left and went to the dead woman's home. There she discovered a bundle of bones. The woman was twenty-five years old when she died of hunger, but her appearance was like an ancient scarecrow, her skin nearly transparent.

The starving were covered with sores. Many suffered from syphilis. Manya asked the attending physician how to treat the sores, but when she started to work among the sick, she developed a dread of contracting the disease herself. She had found out that one member of the delegation, Sonia, had contracted the disease and had committed suicide. Manya no longer feared the illness; she now felt that she knew at least one "cure" for it.

In later years, Manya could never free herself of the memories of those miserable days. Later, during the Holocaust, when she heard rumors of the death camp victims, the "Musselmen"*, before her eyes were the images of those dreadful times in the starving Tatar village.

For four solid months, Manya worked in the Tatar village. She felt as though many years had passed. At times she thought she would never emerge, locked in that desperate world forever. However, as fall approached, help finally arrived from the government. Food was delivered to the hungry, and horses and seed were sent for plowing and planting. The delegation's mission was completed.

Before the delegates scattered, an assessment was conducted as to the merits of their work. A stormy debate ensued; with the majority arguing that it was better to bring about a fundamental change for the masses by concerted efforts to change the regime than to spread their efforts thin by scattered attempts at aiding individual sufferers.These debates would rage on for days.

When Manya returned to Kazan, she went with the members of the delegation to watch an experimental launch of a balloon by the army. The launch directors announced that anyone who wished could travel in the balloon. The delegation's doctor began coaxing Manya to join him for a short flight. Suddenly, Manya had the uncontrollable desire to soar above the earth. Spontaneously, she accepted the suggestion. She hurried to the office and changed into men's clothing so that none of the soldiers would know that she was female. The doctor, sixteen other men and Manya (in disguise) climbed into the basket. As the balloon began to rise, warning shouts were heard from the group below that a storm was approaching. Manya knew that the storms occurred frequently in Kazan but she did not know their severity; after all, when she had entered the basket the sun was shining. In a short while, the sky was covered with black clouds, and the balloon began to tremble. All the travellers were wearing light clothing, and they grew cold. Day ended and night came. The shivering passengers underwent many terrifying hours. Only after twelve hours did the storm abate and the captain realized that they were flying over the Ural Mountains. Little by little, he released gas, and after a while the balloon basket landed in a stream that ran near the godforsaken village near the town of Ufa. It was daybreak when the farmers going out to work noticed the balloon falling into the stream. In their innocence they believed that demons had appeared from the heavens, and when the passengers rowed toward shore with their last ounce of strength, the farmers attacked them with sticks to get rid of the "demons". Quickly, the captain showed them the cross hanging around his neck, and made the sign of the cross. The others follwed suit and soon as the farmers became convinced that these were not demons, they were immediately given aid. Some passengers collapsed when they reached the shore. Manya did not faint, but became quite weak. The farmers escorted the victims to their homes, fed them warm milk, and after a night's rest brought them to the train, even helping them buy tickets to Kazan. The whole incident was well publicized in the newspaper, and featured Manya, the girl who dressed like a man.

This event aroused pangs of remorse in Manya. Later,she could not reconcile herself to this event, although it had not been even a fraction as demanding as the immense effort she had invested in the Tatar village. Although on one level she understood that she had merely wished to free herself from the terrifying visions of her experience, she could never forgive herself for acting on the spur of the moment simply for the sake of her own personal pleasure. She often regretted leaping so readily from the intensity and self-sacrifice of her work in the Tatar village into the selfish, self-serving adventure of a balloon flight. In the eyes of most people, it had been an adventure, but to Manya it became a guilty burden.

In the fall of 1898, Manya returned to Minsk. She again worked in the factory, and was again absorbed by her political circles, but this time she had a stronger sense of purpose and dedication. Every evening was devoted to educating the apprentices and the workers. Now too, differences of opinion flared up between Manya and the Bund members, because according to her the Bundists focused on the "masses" without really seeing the individual. In their eagerness to change the government, they persuaded crowds to attend demonstrations, endangering their lives without ever explaining the rationale to them. Her soul was in anguish over the Bund's cavalier attitude toward the Jewish worker, the individual. While the Bund wanted blind obedience, Manya protested strongly against using ignorant workers as cannon fodder.

At first she led two groups, but as time passed, they expanded. Until very late every evening, she taught Jewish youth, lecturing them on both culture and economics. The preparation of the lectures was very time-consuming. The groups would meet in the home of a poor woman who earned her living from selling cakes to the group members and who volunteered to guard the door to warn them of the approach of the police or government agents. This good Jewish woman was as devoted as a mother, and she kept the secret of the group gatherings from her neighbors.

That winter, Manya moved closer to the Poalei Zion faction,

known as "Poalei Zion of Minsk." Among others, she met Abba Rubenchik and Lapidus. The Poalei Zion members attracted her far more than the Bundists. She was drawn by their efforts to organize the Jewish workers toward immigration to Eretz Israel, and she also identified with their desire to improve their living conditions without getting involved in attempts to destroy the Czar's regime. Still, she continued to meet with Bundists, becoming good friends with Grisha Shechovitz and Meir and Chayka Kagan, who were also opposed to the Bundist method of encouraging mass demonstrations without explaining their purpose.

For about a year, she was immersed in this work in Minsk. Occasionally, she would return to Lososna for a short test and she would revisit Minsk keyed up with excitement for her work. At this point, the police started to notice her, suspecting that she was inciting the workers to demonstrate. The searches followed soon after: the room where the groups gathered, Gedaliah's apartment, and also Manya's room. And soon enough they found certain letters in her room; she had not yet mastered cloak and dagger methods.

At that time, Manya was in Lososna because her mother had fallen ill. At two A.M., the police stormed in and began to tear the house apart. Her mother was lying in bed with a high fever. When they tried to search her bed, Manya pleaded with them not to disturb her mother. Suspecting that she was hiding something illegal under her mother's mattress, they ignored her pleas. Manya leaped up and tried to stop them. They arrested her and imprisoned her in Grodno.

The prison in Grodno was overflowing with detainees, including some of Manya's acquaintances. The prisoners were soon moved to Minsk, and from there to the Moscow prison. In Moscow, Manya was placed in solitary confinement, and soon she was called for interrogation. Actually she had nothing to hide, since her only involvement with the workers had been to educate them. But her interrogators suspected that she was a revolutionary, and they demanded of her names of her co-revolutionaries. Manya laughed at this suggestion, and her questioners started to restrain her. First they put mice into her cell, but Manya responded to them as if they were birds, sharing her food with them and even playing with them. Once, a guard arrived to bring her to interrogation. He did not know about the mice; so when he opened the door and the mice burst out, he became frightened, screamed and bolted.

When the interrogators realized that this method of torture was ineffective, they threw her into a different cell and took another approach: they began by giving her very bad news. First she was told that her mother was dying, and if she would reveal her associates, they would allow her to visit. Manya was silent, in spite of her fears. Then they would drag her out at midnight and tell her about close friends who were imprisoned and suffering on her account. One night, they informed her that all the workers in her brother Gedaliah's factory had been arrested. Manya kept silent, in spite of severe pangs of conscience. Was her mother really so ill? Were her brother's workers really arrested because of her? While the matter of the workers' arrests was still gnawing at her, the interrogators started on a new tack. They asked her to help them with a small matter—what did she know about Gregory Gershuni and his work? When did she first meet him? She answered that she did not know any Gershuni, but she knew they would not leave her alone, because in fact she had had close ties with Gershuni and had been at his house on a number of occasions.

Gershuni was Manya's first love. It was love at first sight. She knew his family—full of Torah scholars and intellectuals. The son looked like a young rabbi: his demeanor was aristocratic and his face was clothed in an air of spirituality. As he became steeped in the superior ethics of Judaism, he transformed them to more generalized radical beliefs. His entire spiritual inheritance was redirected to the Russian revolution. Manya found it difficult to grasp how he, with his delicate and pure expression, had become an active social revolutionary.

How she believed in this man! How she loved him.... Manya became aware that a Russian woman and mother named Radionova had fallen in love with Gershuni and was devoted to him with total abandon. She worked with him in the Social Revolutionary Party, and when they arrested him, she too was taken. When the interrogator began to question Manya about Gershuni, she kept silent, full of fear for his fate; but then he showed her letters which she saw were in Gershuni's handwriting. He began to read from them—love letters to a girl. Then he selected yet another letter written to another girl, and then a third and a fourth. The interrogator stated that when he had read these letters to Radionova, she had become so disturbed about Gershuni's philanderings that she almost lost her mind and told all she knew about him. Manya knew that they were trying to break her as well. She declared that this tactic would not work with her. These Gershuni letters held no interest for her and she could not tell them anything.

Although her words were strong, in her heart she was devastated. She could not believe that Gregory Gershuni, the dedicated revolutionary idealist, so sincere that he had given up a family life, could be romantically involved with several women. She played deaf to the interrogator's questions, but finally deeply agitated, she burst out screaming that she be left alone. She underscored this by flinging a bottle of ink at him. A great commotion ensued, and additional guards appeared who threatened her with dire punishment. But the thought of retribution did not upset her peace of mind as much as her grief about Gershuni's behavior.

Sometime later, Gershuni was arrested, imprisoned in Petersburg, where he languished for three years. Finally, he was sentenced to death, which was commuted to hard labor in Siberia. In the public eye, his travail added to his brilliant image, but Manya's vision of him was forever clouded by the memory of that packet of letters. Eventually Manya realized that when one is young, more is expected from others than from oneself, and that one must learn to differentiate between private and public lives. Despite this rationalization, Manya could never reconcile herself to this dichotomy in Gershuni's character.

While she was in prison, Manya suffered greatly, both physically and spiritually. She was continually pressed for information about her revolutionary comrades.

One day she was told that they were about to rearrest Babushka, and that it was in Manya's power to save her. The interrogator declared that, in her brother Moshe's house, there was a secret gathering in which Babushka called for opposition to the government. Since politics was firmly prohibited to Babushka after her return from Siberia, the suggestion of further imprisonment was enough to drive Manya insane. Would they actually rearrest Babushka after twenty-five years in Siberia?

Katerina Brashko-Brashkovskaya was the daughter of a wealthy landowner, a member of the Russian nobility. In her youth, she was influenced by the Decembrists* and, since she was one of the revolutionary leaders and one of the founders of the Narodnya Volya*, she earned the name "Babushka," literally "grandmother" of the Revolution. Babushka was one of the first people sentenced to hard labor in Siberia. Originally, she was given fifteen years, but when she attempted to escape and was caught, an additional ten years were added. Her name was held in esteem by the revolutionaries, and when she returned from Siberia, enthusiastic homecoming celebrations were held at every train station, despite the fact that the police forbade these demonstrations and arrested many of the participants. Now Babushka had settled on the land of friends of hers from near Minsk, a place of refuge for a number of comrades of the revolutionary party. Once she guaranteed that she would not participate in revolutionary activities, Babushka was allowed to live there in peace. (Incidentally, Babushka was separated from her husband, and her only son, who was educated by his father, was brought up to have an entirely opposite point of view from his mother.)

Manya had often visited Babushka and felt very close to her. In particular, Manya was amazed that all the years of imprisonment had not broken Babushka's spirit. Most people who came out of prison after long incarceration were bitter and defeated. Yet, after twenty-five years in prison, Babushka's spirit was not damaged. How she loved life; how she loved to meet with young people whom she inspired with her revolutionary spirit! At her advanced age, how she loved to dance. During her stay in Minsk, she secretly met with the high school students, most of whom were Jewish. Often, Manya tried to discuss the Jewish question with her, the lack of hope in their condition, but Babushka was totally uninterested in the Jews. She would say that she was a cosmopolitan, that all the nations of the world were close to her heart. In point of fact, Babushka was totally devoted, heart and soul to her own nation— Russia.

Manya loved Babushka and respected her. She was good-hearted, elevated in spirit and devoted to others. She believed wholly that only the Social Revolutionary Party could save Russia. Secretly, she had kept her alliance with this group and encouraged terrorist actions against the government with her philosophy, "he who comes to kill you, kill him first!" Her thesis was that in Russia there was no justice, and in order to save the Motherland, it was necessary to wipe out the government by means of terrorism. More than she was influenced by Babushka's philosophy, Manya was drawn to her strong personality and charm. Babushka, like other social revolutionaries, was mostly devoted to the villager, the peasant, and not to the factory worker in the city, and on this issue, the women differed sharply.

While Manya was still wavering about her response, she saw a man in civilian clothes standing behind the interrogator, staring at her as though he were trying to convey something. His handsome face drew her trust. She wondered who he was.

All that night, she paced back and forth in her dark cell, pacing and wondering. What should she do? In order to save Gershuni, in order to reach her mother's sickbed, in order to free the factory workers,in order to prevent the imprisonment of Babushka— should she reveal the names? She finally decided to reveal a few names and then end her life. At least she had found a solution. She banged on the cell door, asserting her readiness to speak. When the officer came, she told him to bring paper and she would list the names she knew.

Immediately after the officer left the room, the man in civilian clothing appeared. Speaking very quickly, he pleaded with her to be silent, saying she should not believe her interrogators. He spoke and then disappeared. Manya had no idea who he was or what he was doing there. Was it possible that here was a friend of the social revolutionaries? In any case, her heart was filled with gratitude for the man who had saved her from becoming a traitor. When the officer returned with paper, Manya told him that she had changed her mind. He left muttering to himself.

About two weeks passed until they once again called Manya to be questioned. To her amazement, she was brought this time to a lovely room that seemed a kind of private office. For a while she remained alone in the room, her eyes darting back and forth at the spines of the books which lined the walls. What a wealth of books, and in all languages! There were books on utopianism and philosophy and *belles lettres*—all the classics in Russian and in translation— and also books on worldwide labor movements, labor unions, revolution, and other illegal topics.

Soon someone entered, and when she turned around, she saw the "civilian", the man whom she had met earlier. He extended his hand and mumbled his name, but Manya did not catch it and did not really care, since in her mind the character seemed more important than the name. After all, it was he who had saved her from becoming a traitor. When she now thanked him , he replied that he had acted because he felt that she might then be totally lost and broken in spirit. Manya expressed her surprise about the library, and they began to speak about books. The man tried to understand Manya's point of view, and they talked for over an hour. It seemed to Manya that the man was of one mind with her about the need to educate the people and to improve the living conditions of the workers.

From that time forward, Manya was often called to that room for open conversation. It was, in essence, a long debate which lasted for months. The debate focused on one issue: would the economic struggle of the workers inevitably lead to war against the regime or

could the workers fight for better living conditions without resorting to revolution?

Often the man remarked that the Czar's grandfather was the one
who freed the peasants from the oppressive landowners, but this
claim only strengthened Manya's argument that helping the workers was a positive act, and that the government should stand united
with the factory workers during a strike, rather than on the side of
the capitalists.

Each meeting strengthened Manya's impression that the man
agreed with her and related positively to her struggle. Her instincts
told her that he spoke sincerely. The man spoke at length about his
past, how he had joined the social revolutionaries, but later dis-
associated himself from them when he realized that their main goal
was revolution, overthrowing the government and taking power.
He accused the social revolutionaries of speaking loftily about the
suffering of the people, but actually doing nothing to improve their
lives. On this point, Manya agreed. Over and over, she elaborated
on the need for an economic union of workers, on the need to fight
the owners, and that the government should not put obstacles in
the path of the workers. She told him about her goal to raise the
cultural level of the workers and about the differences of opinion
between her and the Bund members on her efforts to educate the
people. Month after month, the discussions continued until opinions and viewpoints crystallized. Manya was able to select any
books she wanted, and had ample time to read and think. At the
end, she spoke of her idea to establish an independent movement
of workers that would be non-political, but would completely devote itself to improving the conditions of the workers. She firmly
believed that if the government would not create obstacles, the
workers would be able to help themselves within a relatively short
period. Every day, she felt more optimistic.

In the meantime, Manya learned to decipher the rappings on the
walls that were the secret language of the prisoners. One day there
was a knock on her cell wall. It was a new prisoner named
Herschele, a brush factory worker and Bund member whom
Manya had known in Minsk. Herschele told her that many of the
young people in Minsk agreed with Manya, that what the workers
needed, most of all, was education. The next day, he again knocked
on the wall and told her that he had been called by Zubatov for
interrogation. Manya was puzzled and asked him which Zubatov
was meant. Surely he didn't mean the head of the secret police
himself? In this prison? Herschele described in detail the room in

which he was questioned and also the appearance of the interrogator, and to her astonishment, Manya realized that he was
describing the room that she went to regularly and the person to
whom she had been talking. This knowledge was a heavy blow.
She could not believe that she had been having dialogues with the
head of the secret police! Her conscience gnawed at her—how
could she have talked so openly with this man without even asking
who he was? Although she finally came to the conclusion that she
had not revealed any names to him, that their conversations had
been purely intellectual, she still smarted over not having dis-
cerned what manner of man he was.**

The next morning, Manya was again summoned to the room.
This time she entered angrily, and asked the man if it was true that
he was Zubatov, the head of the secret police. He tried to calm her
down, saying that he had introduced himself at their first meeting.
Manya replied that she had not caught his name and that she
certainly did not know his position—what had interested her were
his books and his appearance, not his name. It never occurred to
her that he was *the* Zubatov. Had she known, she fumed, she
would not have spoken to him. Then she rose and stormed out of
the room.

A deep melancholy fell upon her. All that day, she did not open a
book or respond to the tappings on her wall. She was deep into her
own black thoughts, blaming herself for speaking to Zubatov without knowing his identity. On the other hand, she told herself,
perhaps it had been for the best. After all, Zubatov had agreed with
her point of view in the end, even expressing willingness to help
the workers in their economic struggle.

The next day, Manya was again called to Zubatov. This time she
spoke more quietly but with sadness. Again she claimed she had
spoken with him openly only because she had not known his
identity. Then she asked whether his words had been sincere,
whether he would, in fact, be willing to help the workers. He
replied that he was ready and willing to help a workers' movement,
that his main purpose in his conversations with Manya and the

**For a fuller description of Manya's activities with Zubatov, see Dimitry Pospielovsky, *Russian
Police Trade Unionism*, Wiedenfeld & Nicolson, 1971, pp. 89–93 and Jeremiah Schneiderman,
Sergei Zubatove and Revolutionary Marxism, Chapter 9, Cornell University Press, Ithaca/London,
1976.

In April, 1922, in *Die Tzeit*, a Yiddish daily newspaper, Manya's own explanation of her
activities with Zubatov appeared in 5 columns (Yiddish). She was then visiting the USA to raise
funds.

other detainees was to separate the labor movement from the revolutionaries.

This time Zubatov also spoke about himself, about his trials, about the many who opposed him in his own department in their belief that the workers would not oppose the capitalists without an anti-government revolt.

In her conversations with Zubatov, Manya remained true to herself. Her devotion to the workers was total, believing in her goal to educate them and improve their lives. Manya thus influenced Zubatov rather than the reverse. In their conversations, she felt that he respected her opinions. During that time, their views fused, and both agreed it would be beneficial to establish a non-aligned labor movement whose purpose it would be to shorten work hours and raise wages. Zubatov even stated that he would support the right to strike. Manya had no basis for doubting Zubatov's honest aspirations to help the workers. After all, she reasoned, was not that why he himself had broken with the revolutionaries?

During her stay in prison, Manya received kindly treatment from the guards, perhaps because of her attitude toward them. She saw them as not only government representatives, but also as human beings. Some were simple folk who fulfilled their tasks without cruelty. Once, she saw a guard outside her cell who appeared ill. Manya told him that he looked feverish. The man then went to his supervisor and received permission to leave. When he returned to his post several days later, he greeted Manya through the small window on her cell door and thanked her for her concern. Another time, she asked a guard why he looked so worried. He told her that he had many children and that his situation was very bleak; he too was grateful for her interest in his condition. Manya understood that these people fulfilled their tasks mechanically and that they were no more than blind pawns of the government. Even among their superiors, there were those who treated her politely.

When she would go to Zubatov, the guard would lock the door after her, and upon her return, she would knock on the door, when the man would again lock her in and take the key with him. On one occasion, she returned from the library and found the guard in a good mood, perhaps a bit tipsy, inspired by the first snow of the season that had just fallen. Manya requested and was given permission to go outdoors for a moment. For several minutes, Manya stood in the doorway and beheld the lovely vision: all the ugliness covered by a pure, sparkling carpet, the snow continuing to fall, and the sun peering through the clouds. With enormous difficulty, Manya wrenched herself from the spot and returned to the guard so that he would open her cell. And there was the man sprawled on the couch in a deep sleep; on the chair his coat and hat. Without a moment's hesitation, she put them on and retraced her steps. She lifted up the collar of the coat and, slipping by the sentry, made an exit. Suddenly, she was filled with a wonderful sense of freedom—the pure snow and the brisk air intoxicated her. Years later, Saadia Paz, a member of Hashomer, recalled the legends that circulated in Minsk about Manya walking around the city in the snow, dressed like a prison guard. In truth, all she had done was stand briefly outside the prison gate enjoying the snow. When she returned to the gendarme, covered with snow, she saw to her surprise, that the man was still asleep. As she entered, she moved the chair, waking him. He stared at her, amazed. He saw the snow on her and understood what must have happened, but said nothing, merely rubbing his eyes and opening her cell. Manya was silent too, but then she became agitated: had she once again exposed herself to danger simply for momentary pleasure? She silenced the voice within her that said she was entitled to a few moments of fresh air after all these months of confinement. With so many suffering here, how could she think she deserved her moment of pleasure?

Manya was confined to prison for a year, eight months of which consisted of continuous dialogues with Zubatov.** During this year, she read a great deal, and crystallized her ideas. Finally, she insisted to Zubatov that, if he really agreed with her, he had no choice but to release her and provide her the opportunity to work freely for the unaligned movement. She suggested that he organize the prisoners, offering them the opportunity to work for this effort. It was clear to Manya that if those people would no longer fear reprisals, they would be eager to participate in the new unaligned workers' organization. Zubatov did as Manya suggested, gathering a group of about sixty Jews and Russians, exhorting them that workers could only benefit from an end to the struggle between them and the government. Some were convinced, but the rest, mostly Bund members, seemed perplexed by the turn of events.

When Manya was finally released, she immediately rushed to her sick mother's bedside. But the next day, she traveled to Minsk,

---

**Sergei Vasil'evich Zubatov, 1864–1917; a high Okhrana (Moscow secret police) official, who created "Zubatovshchina"—police-sponsored trade unionism which tried to direct workers toward economic and social self-improvement rather than political revolution. In 1903 he was dismissed in disgrace and committed suicide in 1917 when he learned of the Czar's abdication.

and began organizing a labor union based on the principle that the workers could organize within the law to improve their lives. Manya became deeply enthusiastic and engrossed in this effort. The Social Revolutionaries, the Social Democrats, and the Bundists were opposed to her movement, but many workers from all sectors, Jews and non-Jews alike, willingly and gladly used the opportunity to join openly with the non-aligned movement. It became known that there was an agreement between the government and the movement which allowed them to organize freely and to declare strikes.

Manya came to regret her contact with Zubatov. The revolutionaries were opposed to the idea that the workers could have a purely economic struggle, and claimed that Zubatov was merely a hypocrite; that he could not be trusted—since he had left the ranks of the workers and joined the secret police. To them he was a traitor, and they charged Manya, or anyone who accepted Zubatov's assistance, of treason. But Manya believed in Zubatov's good intentions, knowing that he had been disappointed by the social revolutionaries. She honestly believed that he wholeheartedly wished to help the peasants and the workers in their struggle against the rich. She saw in him a man of vision who continued in his post as head of the secret police within the prison walls, because of his desire to prevent the persecution of the non-aligned movement. With her own eyes, she had seen how hard he tried to differentiate the workers' movement from that of the revolutionaries.

During that period, Manya's bond with the Poalei Zion members in Minsk grew stronger. They too refrained from struggling against the Czar's government. Although Eretz Israel was far from her, her relationship to it stemmed from the childhood influence of her brother Isaac who had immigrated there with the Biluim* in the early 1880's and who wrote ardent letters home. Since then, she had inherited a deep affection for Eretz Israel, but it was only an abstract love. In Minsk, by contrast, she was immersed in the bleak realities of the Jewish quarter, and was swallowed up in the non-aligned movement, believing that it would be possible thus to save the Jewish workers from poverty and suffering. And, in truth, the movement grew and spread to the cities and villages, until it included hundreds of thousands of Jews and non-Jews.

In late 1901, the founding committee for a non-aligned labor movement was formed with governmental permission. Manya was elected to serve on the central committee. It was then that she renewed her connection with Grisha Shechovitz, who had left the Bund and was committed to organizing labor unions in Odessa. Other workers included her dear friends, Chayka Kagan and Sasha Chemerinsky, who gave heart and soul to organizing Jewish workers. By an ironic twist of fate, Sasha later became the head of a group of self-hating Jews—the Yevsektsia*—a group of Jewish Bolsheviks who destroyed all semblance of Jewish culture.

One day, Zubatov arranged for a meeting with Manya in his home. Manya agreed, curious to see the home that he had already described to her so often—his conservative wife and his small son, who did not love his father, and his wife's revolutionary sister.

As soon as Manya entered Zubatov's home, a cloud of gloom surrounded her. Zubatov's wife, a sad, depressed woman, looked at her husband with hate-filled eyes, and it seemed to Manya that the feeling was directed at her as well. And Manya observed that even the son did not lift his eyes to look directly at his father. Zubatov, appearing troubled, quickly ushered Manya into his study. No sooner had Manya sat down, when in the doorway Zubatov's sister-in-law appeared. She said something to him, but gave the impression that she had actually come to observe Manya. Manya felt uncomfortable and asked Zubatov to postpone the conversation to the following day in his office at the prison.

The next day, she went to Zubatov's office. This time the conversation was brief and spirited. Manya reported how the movement was growing rapidly, encompassing many groups of workers, and informed him that she was returning to Minsk to dedicate herself totally to the work of the movement. Zubatov seemed distracted, as though making a great effort to concentrate. Finally, he stated that he relied upon the Minister of the Interior, Sipiagin. This man was an Anglophile, interested in labor unions, and in his opinion the Russian labor struggle could be purely economic, thus preventing the spread of revolution.

When she returned to Minsk, Manya found great ferment. From everywhere, workers streamed to the non-aligned movement, and in many neighboring villages, new unions were formed. Open gatherings were arranged, a fact that infuriated the revolutionary underground. Manya often visited the factories and workers' quarters and derived great pleasure from direct contact with the workers and their families.

Chayka Kagan and her brother, Meir, also worked for the movement, even though Chayka was principally devoted to the Poalei Zion who were forming their own labor unions and conducting their own strikes. No one saw a contradiction between Chayka's work in Poalei Zion and her simultaneous participation in the non-aligned movement.

In that period, Manya and her friends established a small commune having about a dozen members. The commune did not last long—perhaps half a year—but the memory of those days remained in Manya's heart, as her first experience in communal living. Manya, Chayka, and two other girls lived in a spacious room, and the young men lived in two small rooms. Between them were the dining room and kitchen. All the members would rise early, and would sing their way through household chores—mopping floors, preparing breakfast, readying the next meal. After the household was put in order, each person went to work. All free hours after work were reserved for the movement.

Commune life was like family life. All money, both wages and savings, was handled cooperatively. There was something uplifting about collective life. Manya loved the shared work, feeling that one transcended oneself in labor for others as contrasted with labor for oneself.

Thus Manya was already envisioning a fully collective existence, a way of life in which one would be freed from the pettiness of everyday matters, from the stifling qualities of jealousy and hatred. Only in Eretz Israel, did she ultimately fulfill this dream of group living and working in the collective of Sejera.

The non-aligned movement continued to blossom. In Brisk (Brest-Litovsk), in Bialystok and their surrounding villages, other unions were formed, and the movement began to establish itself in Odessa. In those days, Vasiliev, one of Zubatov's proteges, who sanctioned meetings and strikes, governed in Minsk.

In early 1902, the workers' legal economic struggles intensified and a round of strikes broke out. The movement organized countless strikes; in Minsk alone there were perhaps a hundred. Although most were begun by skilled Jewish workers whose condition was only slightly better than that of the unskilled workers, several strikes were also organized in the large factories, by Jews and non-Jews alike.

At the height of the movement, Grisha Shechovitz and his friends came to Odessa, where the strikes comprised some fifty thousand people, Jews and non-Jews. Grisha, who kept close ties with Zubatov, succeeded in organizing tens of thousands of workers with his great energy and fervor.

The movement had now succeeded to an extent that none had dared dream of, winning higher wages and shorter work hours.

4. The Turning Point—Aliyah

While the members of the movement were immersed in strikes, word reached them that the Minister of the Interior, Sipiagin, had been assassinated by revolutionary terrorists and was being replaced by Plehve. It took only a few days for it to become common knowledge that Plehve was a cruel autocrat who was persecuting the revolutionaries, oppressing the Jews and extinguishing every spark of independent thought throughout Russia.

On the heels of the movement's success, the government began to be wary of it—what if it could no longer be controlled and would pose a threat? Also, business owners had started to press Plehve, demanding that he control the movement, and sharp differences flared up between Zubatov and Plehve.

It was clear to the new movement's leadership that without authorization to conduct strikes, there would be no possibility of continuing, and that without the fulfillment of the three founding principles—freedom to organize, free speech and the right to strike—there was no reason for its existence. With this in mind, the central committee sent Manya as an emissary to Petersburg, the capital, to obtain the needed authorization from the government leaders.

In Petersburg, Manya met the priest, Grigori Gapon*. Their first encounter was on the street. She had accompanied her sister on some errands, and when her sister entered a store, Manya waited for her outside, watching the passersby. Suddenly she heard the sound of someone crying. Manya turned toward the voice and observed a policeman attempting to arrest an old Jewish man. At that moment, a young priest appeared on the scene who grabbed the policeman's hand and begged him to stop. When the policeman exclaimed indignantly that this was nothing but a Jew, and Jews had no right to be in the capital, the priest grew angry and raged at the policeman that he was an anti-Christ, that God had created the world for all people. Displaying his own identity card, the priest announced that he would take personal responsibility for the old man. Stupefied, the police officer released the Jew, and the priest took the old man by the hand and accompanied him on his way.

Manya watched the priest with amazement and respect, and was only sorry that she had not thought to ask his name. Quite by chance, however, she met him several days later at a small party of students. When Gapon was introduced to her, she reminded him of the incident on the street and they began a conversation. There was something unusual in Gapon's appearance which touched Manya; the man gave the impression of nobility, purity and honesty.

After the student party, the two of them met often and Manya's first impression was reinforced: a concerned man, looking for justice on this earth. With time, the two became close friends, and Gapon told Manya the story of his life—about his youth in a remote village in central Russia and also about his girlfriend sho soon became his wife but who then had died at an early age. She had been the daughter of a priest and a member of the revolutionary party; under her influence, he too was attracted to revolutionary politics. His one point of departure with them was the movement's negative attitude toward religion. After the death of his wife, he had journeyed to the capital, where he met leaders of the socialist parties and joined the social revolutionaries. Often he expressed to Manya his anger about his comrades who were destroying the faith of the masses, by giving them doses of rhetoric instead of practical advice that could truly help them.

Manya and Gapon met often, and through their conversations their views began to converge. Gapon well understood the concept of differentiating between the struggle to improve the lives of the proletariat, and opposing the Czar's regime. In this matter, Manya influenced him greatly. In her unshakable belief that first and foremost, the workers' living standards and consciousness had to be raised, she requested that Gapon help them broaden their knowledge and develop leaders from within their own ranks.

Manya brought Gapon to the forefront on the matter of the non-aligned movement, and together they began to work in Petersburg.

**Georgi Apollonovich Gapon, (1870–1906) a Christian reformer, known as "Father Gapon" who led the Jan. 22, 1905 march of workers and peasants to the Czar's winter palace. The event, known as "Bloody Sunday" was a turning point when 130 were killed and hundreds wounded. See *A History of Russia* by Nicholas V. Riasanovsky, Oxford University Press, 1984, 4th ed.

She enjoyed going with him to workers' meetings in the factories. He was able to penetrate the largest business establishments, such as the famous Potilov factory. "Father Sergei," as the workers called him, would open the meeting with a prayer, and only afterwards would he broaden the talk to the workers' demands from management. He then would end the meetings with a short prayer. At first, this seemed strange to Manya, but slowly, she had to admit how great his influence was on those in attendance, who were, for the most part, religious. The prayer lifted their spirits, and its aftermath left a hushed silence. When she saw the faces of the audience, the realization deepened in her that there was no reason to exorcise religion from the hearts of the workers in order to improve their lives.

In those days, Gapon often met with Zubatov and talked with him at length. With all his heart he believed that it was possible to improve the lot of the laborers, just so long as the government did not deliberately place obstacles in their path. On several occasions, Manya and Gapon discussed Zubatov, trying to determine if he spoke sincerely. For example, they argued about whether it was permissible to accept the money Zubatov offered to organize strikes, for according to him, he had discretionary funds for which he did not have to account. Manya expressed strong opposition to this, fearing that they could be accused of treason if Zubatov's handouts were accepted. After all, despite all his efforts to help the movement, he was still a member of the secret police, and Manya did not want to give an opening to those who would claim that the movement was organizing strikes with the help of the government. Her Jewish friends agreed with her, but Gapon did not hesitate to accept Zubatov's financial assistance. This eventually returned to haunt him when, in 1905, he was accused of treason and was executed by the Social Revolutionaries.

Although Manya resisted taking donations from Zubatov, both she and Gapon still believed in Zubatov, who was then trying to prove to the government the legitimacy of the movement. Gapon's trust continued even after Manya began harboring doubts. But as for Gapon himself, Manya could never have qualms. There was no one who met Gapon face-to-face who could help but believe him. His very appearance was enchanting. There was something in him that drew respect and admiration from all who met him. Purity and sadness were reflected in his black eyes; his appearance was ascetic. In fact, under his clothing, on his emaciated body, he wore a kind of chain; from each of its links, there extended a pin which would pierce his body with every movement. He felt that a man needed to suffer in order to control his evil impulses. His room was like the cell of a monk: the bed—two boards without mattresses; in the middle—a small table and footstool; in the corner—a bookcase laden with holy books and revolutionary literature; and on the wall—icons of saints surrounding one of Jesus. When Chayka Kagan, Manya's friend from Minsk, came to Petersburg and had no permit to stay in the city, Gapon brought mattresses and a blanket for his guest, and he himself stayed with friends.

Chayka, who was the daughter of a wealthy family which had lost its fortune, was especially well-liked by Manya and influenced her a great deal. In her childhood her father died and she was forced to work hard to help support her mother and her two young brothers. But despite all her cares, she gave her full devotion to the Poalei Zion movement and was among the founders of the first cell of the movement in Minsk. Chayka was very beautiful—her eyes were large and soulful and her bearing was aristocratic. But she did not draw people to her with her beauty, but rather with her warm nature and her fiery words. When she was delivering a speech on her visions about the land of her Fathers, where she envisaged the solution to the sufferings of the Jewish people, a silence would descend upon her audience. Everyone would listen enraptured, even those who opposed her. Gapon, who until then knew nothing of Zionism—despite his love for the Jews—listened to her and told Manya that Chayka was delivering words of prophecy. On another occasion he remarked that Chayka was a sister to the disciples of Jesus. Gapon, the man of faith and morality, credited the Jews with the fact that they gave the world the gift of Jesus of Nazareth. His simplicity and purity led him to a conclusion opposite to the prevailing one that the Jews were guilty for the crucifixion of Jesus.

Meanwhile, Zubatov continued to support the movement, and according to him, he was even trying to influence Plehve the way he had influenced Sipiagin before him. But very soon, the relationship between the two soured and Plehve began to carry out his plots, arresting leaders of the movement.

One day, the police came and arrested Grisha Shechovitz. It happened that a messenger had just delivered a letter to him from Zubatov (who would write to the movement leaders by hand and leave no traces of his correspondence in his office). Shechovitz shoved the letter into his pocket without even glancing at it, but the police grabbed it from him. In the letter there was, among other things, a reference to "the donkey"—none other than Plehve. When this letter found its way to Plehve's office, a tempest erupted. At first, he was going to imprison Zubatov, but he settled—for the moment—for house arrest. It became obvious, however, that he was going to eliminate Zubatov and destroy the nonaligned movement.

Manya learned about all of this much later. For several months, she had not had any personal contact with Zubatov, and knew nothing about his disintegrating relationship with Plehve. It was no surprise then that Manya felt great shock upon hearing of Shechovitz's arrest. After all, Zubatov had promised that no member of the movement would be harmed as long as their demands were purely economic. Had he lied to her? Was he a traitor? It was Manya, after all, who had influenced her compatriots to trust him. Feelings of guilt overwhelmed her, and she sank into the deepest depression she had ever known.

Finally, she pulled herself together and went to the capital, a pistol in her pocket. Storming and raging, she entered Zubatov's prison office, and thundered to him that he had betrayed her and therefore had to die.

Zubatov looked at her, and in a stifled voice told her that a bullet in his heart would only be a blessing. Then he poured out his heart, once again revealing the visage of a tragic, broken man. The image she saw before her came from a Dostoyevsky plot; this could not be the person who had arrested her friend. He himself was a suspect in the eyes of the secret police, just as he had previously been ostracized by his former comrades, the revolutionaries. The real villain now was the cruel Plehve, and Zubatov had aroused his wrath. Any day, he might be formally arrested and sent to Siberia. Again Zubatov spoke of his complex relationship with the revolutionaries, about the difficulties he had endured, about his despondency, and about his idealism.

Manya listened to him quietly, and it seemed to her that his voice was rising from the depths of the soul of the Russian nation. Zubatov fell silent. Then he pointed to the secret back door of his office and told her she could shoot him and leave unobserved. It was as though he knew his fate, that he would not have long to live before being exiled to Siberia.

Manya did not feel the gun dropping from her hand, and with an aching heart, she left. She passed a tortured night, weeping until dawn. Everything had gone up into smoke, all her hopes were shattered. Her movement had suffered a mortal blow.

The next morning, still devastated, she went again to Zubatov, intending to tell him that she would recommend the dissolution of the movement. But at this meeting, Zubatov came up with a new plan: to try to talk to Plehve himself. Perhaps Manya could influence him and explain to him that the non-aligned movement could yield nothing but benefit for Russia. Perhaps he would then understand that there was a real difference between the labor unionists and the revolutionaries. And he might just allow the workers to struggle for the improvement of their lot without revolution.

Manya was shocked at the suggestion. Was Zubatov suggesting that she, a Jew, go to this autocrat who was sending the Jews to destruction? Zubatov continued to insist that it was her obligation to try at least. In his heart, he was totally pessimistic about Plehve, but in his desire to find a solution, he grasped at any straw.

When Manya returned home from this encounter, she sat alone and began to weigh the possibilities. Well, why not try? Didn't she believe that any person could be influenced? Maybe Plehve would be convinced that her movement presented no threat to the government and would allow her to continue her work.

After much soul-searching, she decided to present the issue to her comrades at headquarters. At first, they were all as shocked at the suggestion as she had been, but after long deliberation, it was decided that Manya should make an effort to talk to Plehve. In preparation for the meeting, three demands were drafted for Manya to present: the right to form labor unions, the right to strike, and free speech.

Toward the end of 1902, Plehve agreed to invite Manya as a representative of the non-aligned movement. This was the last time that Zubatov influenced Plehve. Manya worked long and hard on a frank and honest presentation to Plehve—in favor of the workers, but not against the government. She was summoned to Plehve's house that evening. As dusk approached, she arrived at his estate which was outside the city limits, surrounded by soldiers and police. They took her through a dozen corridors until she finally reached the spacious salon where Plehve sat. Guards were posted at the entrance. Although Plehve knew without a doubt about her arrival—since he had arranged the appointment—he looked surprised; perhaps because she was so young. He asked to hear about the non-aligned movement and Manya began to describe the pain and suffering of the workers. First Plehve listened patiently, as though he was making an effort to understand. But when Manya touched on the subject of the difficult situation of the Jews in the

Pale of Settlement* and presented the three demands of the movement, he jumped out of his chair and began to scream. How did she, a Jewess, dare to think she could come to him about the Russian workers and about demands for freedom? He would destroy them all, he ranted, non-aligned and revolutionaries alike.

When Manya heard his words, her blood boiled and she hurled biting words at him. If he would try to destroy the movement, she said, he would himself be destroyed. Raging, she lost control, grabbed an object off the table and tried to throw it at her enemy. At that moment, something pincer-like grabbed her shoulder and she almost fainted from the tremendous pain. She was then dragged out and arrested. This time she was not kept in prison for long, but to Manya and her friends, it was now crystal clear that the non-aligned movement did not have even a prayer of survival.

Closing down the operation was arduous and bitter, and even more so because working covertly now put her in the realm of the revolutionaries who had never disguised their disdain for her movement.

Only Gapon continued to work openly. As a man of faith, he pinned his hopes on a religious demonstration as a way of arousing the Czar's pity for the plight of the workers. This plan was put into motion two years later when Manya was already in Eretz Israel, but it resulted in abject failure. With total faith in the Czar, Gapon led tens of thousands of workers and their families to the Czar's winter palace, holding religious banners. But when the demonstrators approached the palace, bullets rained on them, and there were many casualties. It seemed that the police were afraid that the crowds would storm the palace. Following this event, the revolutionaries accused Gapon of provocation and executed him.

On Easter 1903, the pogroms of Kishinev* erupted and the Jews of Russia suffered a devasting blow. Although it was well known that the "Black Hundreds"* had fomented anti-semitism and that the government sought to channel the rage of the masses against the Jews, these blood baths still came as a terrible shock. A sense of hopelessness pervaded Manya and many others among the Jewish youth. It is difficult to describe the tremendous upheaval in their consciousness. They felt as though they had sinned against their own people, and they were tormented by great guilt. The best of the Jewish youth had, after all, devoted themselves heart and soul to the Russian revolution on all its fronts, and had deserted their own people, despite its hardships. Now the blood of their people was being spilled under the wheels of the revolution—and their sense of shock ran deep.

Manya and her comrades hastily met and determined not to concern themselves with the Russians, but to devote themselves completely to the Jews alone. In their hearts there grew the realization that first and foremost, they needed to organize for self-defense. And, thus, every city and every village began to hastily prepare itself for defense against the pillagers. The notion of self-defense cut across all factions. The first to call for action were the Poalei Zion*, but the Bundists* were ready to participate as well. From then on, all their efforts were devoted to one end: to defend themselves, no longer to be fair game for their enemies.

The pogroms led to a fundamental change in Manya. The ideals which had previously consumed her were dissipated. From now on she was rededicated to only one purpose: defending her people. Towards this end, she travelled everywhere, raising money for self-defense. Even this, she felt, was not enough. Some other action was needed to prevent further attacks upon the Jews.

Manya and her friends—three Poalei Zion members and four Russians—met to try to decipher the root cause of the Kishinev massacres. After careful analysis, they came to the conclusion that Krushevan, the maniac who incited the Kishinev pogrom*, was only a tool—that the real responsibility lay with Plehve, who hated Jews and revolutionaries. After much deliberation and soul-searching discussion, it was decided that they had no choice but to eliminate Plehve, and a plan was drawn up for his assassination. Plehve's compound was known to be heavily guarded and seemingly impenetrable. It was therefore decided to tunnel into the compound. This plan was formulated by Sergei, one of Manya's acquaintances from the non-aligned movement who had also been affiliated with the militarist faction of the social revolutionaries. In his plan, Sergei was assisted by Azeff, the well-known provocateur.** It was Azeff who encouraged them to act on this plan, and it was also Azeff who revealed this information to the police after the digging had begun.

The plan was difficult and daring, and large sums of money were required. The comrades delegated to Manya the responsibility of raising the money, and so she travelled to Berlin, a place where

---

**Yevno Fishelevich Azeff was a double agent for the Czarist secret police and a Russian revolutionary.

there was a large Jewish community of Russian emigres who feared for the fate of their fellow Russian Jews. She arrived in Berlin at the end of 1903 and before long met a Jewish banker, a Lithuanian emigre who was devoted heart and soul to his fellow Jews in Russia. He expressed his readiness to use all his power to help them. Manya revealed the tunnel plan to him and he immediately sent a large sum to Russia and made sure it got into the right hands.

In Berlin, Manya stayed with her brother Gedaliah, who lived in temporary quarters, and was one of the pillars of the "Chovevei Zion"* movement there. He had already visited Eretz Israel once. As an engineer, he dreamed of returning there to dig wells and to irrigate the land. After hearing from Manya about the Plehve situation, Gedaliah told her, good-naturedly, that the Jews of Russia would not be saved by Plehve's death, that another tyrant would doubtless rise in his place, and that the Jewish nation could be saved only in its homeland. His wise and measured words struck a chord in Manya's heart, and the notion of building a Jewish homeland in Eretz Israel began to take root within her.

Suddenly, a telegram arrived from Sergei's "fiancee" which said that Sergei was "sick." Manya understood that this meant that some disaster had taken place. In the letter that arrived later, the details were recounted: the police had uncovered the tunnel and arrested the conspirators, including Sergei. It soon was revealed that Azeff had informed on them. This calamity shook Manya to the core. There was no doubt that death awaited them all, particularly Sergei who had been the most active participant in the group.

Manya became deeply depressed, and Gedaliah, who watched over her day and night, quickly sent a telegram to their brother Nachum in Israel, reporting on her serious condition. Upon receiving this, Nachum sent a telegram to Manya, saying he was very ill and begged her to come help him. Manya had to fulfill the promise that she had made to him so many years before, to always be there for him if he needed her—and she immediately departed for Eretz Israel, her heart full of uneasy anticipation.

With her arrival in Eretz Israel, a chapter was sealed for Manya— it was as though she was reborn. She soon regretted only that she had not lived her entire life in her homeland.

5. First Steps in the Homeland

On January 2, 1904, Manya reached the shores of Eretz Israel*. The skies were azure and sparkling, and the sun shone as if it were spring. But Manya paid no attention to the sky or the earth or the people around her. She was still shrouded in depression, and her only happiness was in finding her brother Nachum healthy.

During that period, Nachum was the guiding spirit in the beginning of industry in Eretz Israel and was constantly developing new schemes. That year, he was engrossed in the search for water sources; later he would become the founder of Shemen, a major oil and soap factory in Haifa.

Subdued, Manya followed Nachum, her heart still in torment. Within a short time, however, she began to savor the taste of her homeland, thanks most of all to her contact with Nachum. How could she walk along the beach of Jaffa without being intoxicated by the beautiful scenery, without being moved by the importance of this great moment?

Nachum brought Manya to Yehoshua and Olga Hankin, and they received her warmly. In their company, she began to relax, and the two of them soon became Manya's very close friends. Yehoshua was a wise mentor and he illuminated her path in the land.

From the start, Olga spoke to Manya in Biblical Hebrew, with a soft Ashkenazic inflection which had a pleasant, musical ring. Manya was fluent in Biblical verses since her childhood, and very quickly was able to grasp much of what was said to her. Little by little, the Hebrew words rose from her memory, even though many years had passed since she had learned them. The language had been rooted somewhere deep within her. After a while, she tried to string together simple sentences, and Olga corrected her mistakes, helping her to draw from her subconscious the Hebrew that she once knew.

Manya was aware that Nachum and her new friends already knew, perhaps from Gedaliah, about all that had happened to her—about the terrible calamity that had befallen her group, about the death sentence that was awaiting her friends, and about her own spiritual crisis. With great delicacy and care, they stroked her wounded soul, in order to free her from her sufferings. What would her reward be, Hankin would say, if she continued to torture herself about the disaster in Petersburg? After all, there was nothing she could do to help. And he continually emphasized the fact that revenge and terror were not solutions, that terror would only increase the sufferings of the Jewish people. The only logical path was to uproot the Jews from the diaspora and bring them to Eretz Israel. These words—words that she had heard long ago from Gedaliah in Berlin—came from Hankin's lips with such total conviction, that they left no room for doubt, and Manya understood that this was a different kind of Zionism, a practical Zionism, that would ultimately be truly revolutionary for the Jewish people in their homeland.

Hour after hour, Manya listened to Hankin's plans to liberate the Jezreel Valley from the effendis* and to build new settlements, and in her heart a new faith began to grow. Hankin's words and plans were not theoretical, but rather living ideas that required action.

Together with Hankin's family, Manya travelled to Rishon LeZion, to the Feinberg family. She had heard many stories about Lulik (Yisrael) Feinberg, and in her mind, he personified the Bilu man.* Her expectations were not disappointed. Despite all their sufferings, Lulik and his wife were alert, energetic and possessed a deep love of the land. In that same settlement, Manya also met other original members of the Biluim, but the brilliance of the movement was dimming, and all that remained was a group of people, embittered by their struggles with Baron Rothschild's bureaucracy.

Manya explored by herself the main road of Rishon LeZion, entranced by the whitewashed houses and the rows of palm trees. She would wander in the vineyards. The sight of the foliage was enchanting. The idyllic picture was somewhat marred one day when she met some youngsters who had just arrived in Eretz Israel. It soon became clear from their conversation that they could not find work. This was totally incomprehensible to Manya—after all, hadn't the Biluim started out just like them? How could it be that they were hiring cheap Arab labor and had no concern for their own fellow Jews who had just immigrated, who were yearning to work the land?

In the days that followed, Manya also visited Rehovot, Nes-Ziona and Gedera. Although she was enchanted by the appearance of these settlements, every place she went she met immigrants who could not find work. After each such visit, she would talk about this with Hankin, but his mind was mainly preoccupied with redeeming the land.

Manya visited Petach Tikvah, where she met Eliezer and Yisrael Shochat, with Yechezkel and Chaya Sara Hankin and a number of other friends. She was delighted by this dynamic group, whose members were ready to lay down their lives to repossess their homeland. In Petach Tikvah, the workers' condition was revealed to her in all its seriousness: lack of work, starvation and malaria. Manya saw their suffering, and was amazed by their unrelenting ambition to obtain work, even if it meant having to live in conditions more primitive than those of the Arab workers. She could not reconcile herself to this concept of work at all costs.

Within a month after her arrival, Manya was so completely immersed in her new lifestyle, it seemed she had always lived this way. She gave much thought to the situation, and often discussed it with the Hankins and her other friends. It was clear to her, that under the conditions that she saw, the land could not absorb the masses of the Jewish nation, and she, therefore, came to the simple conclusion that a new way must be found.

Nachum spoke to Manya at length about his dreams and schemes, and suggested that she join a six-week cross-country expedition. It was his plan to visit unsettled territory on both sides of the Jordan River, with the objective of finding sources of water— a task which he had already begun—to search ravines and streams, to study the geological formation of the mountains and to collect all the data necessary to investigate possibilities for industrial development. Manya enthusiastically accepted his invitation. The thought of the expedition fired her imagination and firmly planted in her the realization that she had already started to strike roots in the land.

There were four companions on this trip: Manya; her brother Nachum; Mendel Hankin (Yehoshua's brother); and Sophia Zvenigorodska, the girl who had single-handedly brought many of the orphans of Kishinev to Shefeya. Mendel was fluent in Arabic, and he prepared for the expedition four horses, two pack mules, a tent, sleeping bags and food. For funds they used the inheritance money from Manya's brother Binyamin, who had died in America in 1902.

Many legends about Manya originated on this trip. It was said that she never got tired. Even when her horse was dropping from exhaustion, she would dismount, leave the group and explore the hills herself. Fascinated by the fellahin*, she expended great effort learning Arabic from Mendel Hankin. During the trip, she would stop passersby and engage them in conversation. Upon passing a Bedouin camp, she and Mendel would boldly engage the surprised sheiks in conversation.

At the beginning of February 1904, the four left Jaffa. Nachum's destination was the hills of Judea; Manya quite naturally concluded that he would first show her Jerusalem. Actually, his primary objective was the Jericho Road, and so the group stayed only one night in Jerusalem, and with the dawn they went to cross Nabi Musa.

How amazed Manya was when, hardly out of the city, she seemed to leap into a desolate wilderness, surrounded by bare mountaintops. Along a rocky mountain road, the group travelled south, and after a little while reached Maaleh Adumim, the place where Nachum hoped to find traces of bitumen. When Nachum saw the variegated ridges—yellow, red and green—he dismounted, and with a small pick-axe began scraping the earth off the ridges and filling his sacks. Manya led her horse out to graze, lay down on the ground at the foothills, and lazily took note of the unfolding view: to the east—the Jordan, Jericho and the hills on the far side of the Jordan. The plain of Jericho seemed to stretch endlessly in the dusky horizon. There was poignancy in the fact that the whole expanse was barren and deserted. It had been like this since the last fighters of ancient Israel had been led away captive, she thought, since then the land had been deserted. She raged inwardly at the generations of her people who had not bothered to return. The wasteland of Jericho juxtaposed in her mind with the fate of her people, and she carried a heavy burden of guilt for herself and her whole generation.

They never actually entered Jericho itself, because Nachum and Mendel wanted to go north toward Shechem (Nablus). The entire way, Manya took in the spectacular sights. When the group reached the hills of Ephraim, Manya was filled with awe—ancient olive trees and remnants of old settlements from days gone by were lodged among the neglected Arab villages. Mendel Hankin loved to engage passersby in conversation and in particular to investigate the sources of the village names. It was amazing how the names of the towns had been preserved from Biblical times, and only a few had been changed by the fellahin. Mendel and Nachum told many stories of ancient times, and in Manya's eyes the fellahin were reincarnations of Biblical characters.

According to Nachum, every day, Manya looked more alert, more radiant. Her thoughts became clear and she once again wanted her part in life. Without even being aware of it, she began to love the land and to be nourished by its light, and, slowly—almost unnoticed—thoughts of returning to Russia evaporated.

At night, she would lift open the flap of the tent, and gaze up to the stars, enveloped in a feeling of contentment that she had never known before. Often, she would stay up until sunrise. It was wonderful living with nature, drinking in the mountain air. And when she saw the beautiful skies and scenery, she said to herself that this air, these skies and this land had filled Jewish souls with the spirit of promise and victory, enabling them to withstand the tortures of the diaspora through two thousand years of wandering with the hope of a return to the homeland.

The group wandered in the area of Shechem without entering the city, camped near some ruins and travelled to the villages. Then they headed east, past Damia and Zarka, and crossed the Jordan.

The four spent more than two weeks in Trans-Jordan. Among other places, they visited Amman and Salt and the ruins of Gerasa. Standing before the pagan temples in Gerasa in the amphitheater in Amman, Manya reflected on the tremendous labor that had gone into these structures that now lay in ruins. On the other hand, the Bible had gone into exile with the children of Israel, was alive, and was a source of inspiration for the Jewish fighters, who were now beginning to return to their land.

The four crossed the length and breadth of the country, reaching Syria in the north, then going eastward and finally south. In those days, there was no border between Eretz Israel and Syria and they crossed the Jordan several times. Thus they devoured the miles, riding ten and even twelve hours a day, resting for a while in an isolated village, eating the dried food that they had brought, and continuing on the road again. Manya was not at all tired, accustomed as she was to riding from childhood. Not so Sophia, who delayed the group on more than one occasion. The two girls disguised themselves as boys, both for comfort and safety. Manya had her hair cropped short, but Sophia had long braids, and on the road, she had to be careful that they were always concealed inside her hat.

Once they got lost. Night was approaching and they could not find a living soul. They had no more water, and they began to be concerned, although no one would admit to being afraid. The four hurried their horses until they saw before them a small village. Upon reaching it, they sought out the home of the mukhtar* and Mendel entered while the others dismounted and started to set up camp. None of them paid attention to the fact that Sophia had taken off her hat, and her two braids hung down her back. The Arab boys did notice, however, and they began to laugh. They started to encircle her to see this amazing sight—a girl dressed like a boy! Sophia didn't shrink from them, but smiled back, making them all the more curious. They came closer, taunting and yelling, until they blocked off the whole tent. Mendel and the mukhtar both asked the boys to leave, but to no avail. Realizing that his guests were in imminent danger of assault, the mukhtar invited them into his house, and Mendel again went out to the group and asked them in his best Arabic to be cordial hosts toward his people.

Night fell, and Manya and Sophia entered the women's apartment. But the attitude of the Arab women was not appreciably different from that of the young boys, and it was necessary to call Mendel in to explain to them that it was easier to ride and also safer dressed this way. After a quick dinner, they gathered their belongings, folded up the tent, and in the middle of the night, when everyone in the village was sleeping, the compassionate mukhtar escorted them out of the town by a back road. When they were some distance away, they broke into a gallop, and only stopped at daybreak.

Thus went the month of February. The winter of 1904 was very warm and spring came early.

A useful book for readers interested in more about Eretz Israel, *A History of Israel From the Rise of Zionism to Our Time*, by Howard M. Sachar, Alfred A. Knopf, NY, 1976.

6. Collective Living

While Nachum was exploring every wadi and each ravine, examining the structure of the ridges and mountains for sources of water, Manya was fully absorbed in ruminations about her new reality. The situation was perfectly clear to her even though she had only been in the country for a short time—perhaps even more apparent because everything was new to her. On the one hand, she saw Jewish farmers using cheap Arab labor, and on the other, unemployed Jewish workers were living in inhuman conditions. The workers seemed to be experiencing the delusion that their salvation lay in taking over the workforce and that this alone would somehow pave the way for the absorption of new immigrants. As for the farmers, she was completely convinced that developing Jewish settlements with non-Jewish labor was not the way to rebuild the country.

In her usual straightforward fashion, she decided that since the existing situation was untenable, she would have to change it. She focused all her thoughts on devising a new lifestyle, a way that would entice many immigrants to come and work the land, one that might lead to a class of independent farmers. Since childhood, her soul had ached from the class structures she had observed—a paper-thin layer of rich superimposed upon a multitude of layers of poor, starving masses. Now, as she wandered through the countryside, she envisioned a society which did not consist of the exploiters and the exploited; she dreamed of a truly cooperative work system. During the long journey, she tried to ride at a distance from the others to be alone with her thoughts. Often she would dismount and walk alongside her horse, deep in thought. Little by little, her thoughts crystallized.

Through vast, deserted plains, they finally reached the Bashan and from there they continued north to Hauran*, where they rested for a few days. This place impressed Manya deeply. Nowhere else had she come upon earth so lush, with such an abundance of water. She was drawn to this fertile patch of earth. And it was in Hauran that her plan took shape: this was the place to settle, this was the earth where everything could be started anew—and in a new way.

The agricultural settlement belonging to Baron Rothschild was Hauran, and there Manya met Zalman Cohen from the settlement of Mescha (Kfar Tavor) and several Jews from the Galilee settlements who worked as overseers managing the Arab workers. Again she wondered about the strange phenomenon of Jewish settlements without Jewish labor. How could it be? Zalman Cohen told her about the dismal saga of the land purchases in Hauran. Towards the end of the 1880's, the Baron had ordered his clerk, Ossowetzky, to buy a large parcel of land in Hauran, an area known for its fertile earth and plentiful water, with the objective of settling new immigrants there. Ossowetzky bought 120,000 dunams*, but he neglected to include in the contract a specific stipulation that the workers on the land must be Jewish. This omission caused major problems, for when the Baron's people established the first field school to train Jewish workers, they were forced to hire Arab labor and could only hope for some kind of agreement with those who sold them the land. Although a number of Jews did attempt to farm the land, according to the contract they could be forced out. Only Cohen, who was appointed as foreman of the farm that had been built with the Baron's money, remained for several years. Eventually the landholdings dwindled, and the Baron retained ownership of only 80,000 dunams.

Manya fell wholeheartedly in love with Hauran, and she resolved to do all she could to repeal the miserable contract and to liberate this beautiful acreage for Jewish settlement. She was entirely possessed by the idea of living in Hauran in a communal settlement, imagining vivid scenes of new settlers working the land, full of desire to develop it with their own hands. She had no doubt that this was the beginning of something big.

Manya suggested to Zalman Cohen that they import workers from Petach Tikvah, not as supervisors but as independent settlers, who would hold the land dear and guard their own fields. To keep the peace, they would allow the Arab tenant-farmers to continue working those areas they always had. Zalman Cohen, who was both an intelligent person and an excellent farmer, grasped the spirit of her words and agreed that in this way it would be possible to guarantee a real Jewish presence in Hauran.

Before long the word "Hauran" became a secret slogan in Hashomer*. Manya brought the group this slogan and excited her friends with it. So attractive was the concept that Hashomer members dreamed about going to this land for the purpose of redeeming it. Manya believed that neither negotiation nor bribery stood a chance of countermanding the restriction on Jewish settlement in Hauran. Her conclusion was that only direct action would free the land, that the prohibition could only be lifted by the arrival of Jewish workers who, without permission, would dare to work and guard the land themselves, with the iron-clad determination to stay put.

At the same time that Manya harbored dreams of a communal settlement, she was developing practical plans for implementing them. In her eyes, this was no daydream, but rather a real mission whose realization would be determined by realities—good earth, an abundance of water and top-notch workers. She had no reservations about her ability to acquire all the ingredients needed for success.

Manya's flights of fancy led to the fulfillment of the Hashomer idea of redeeming the land. And who knows whether Hashomer would have later accepted the notion of independent workers liberating their own land if Hauran had not been acquired in this way.

Even if the Jews had not succeeded in the redemption of Hauran, thanks to Manya's aspirations the idea of communal settlements did materialize. This idea, which Manya planted deeply in the hearts of her comrades, was successfully brought to fruition soon after in the first collective—Sejera, the beginning of collective settlement in Eretz Israel. From Sejera, some Hashomer comrades went to Umm-El-Juni in order to redeem that land with cooperative work. Together with members of the collective in Hadera, they also laid the foundation for Degania, the mother of kibbutzim, in the same way that Manya had the historic privilege of being the mother of the idea of collectivism in Eretz Israel.

Nachum was interested in travelling further, and for his sake, the group also visited Damascus and Beirut, but Manya was impatient to implement her ideas. Immediately upon her return, she hurried to her close friend Yehoshua Hankin and presented to him her plans for taking title to the land of Hauran. Hankin listened intently and encouraged her, and though he himself was totally absorbed in farming the Jezreel Valley, he introduced her to the officials of the I.C.A.*. They listened to Manya politely, but did not grasp at all the heart of the matter—to fundamentally change the established methods of settling the land. The shameful condition of the workers in the settlements of Judea did not seem to trouble them in the least, nor were they disturbed by the prospective problems of mass immigration. The truth was that they did not really seem to understand anything about settlements. The proof? In all twenty-three settlements that existed at that time in Eretz Israel, the farmers were greatly frustrated. The officials tried to cool Manya's enthusiasm but, while she gave up on them, their negative responses only strengthened her stubborn determination to establish collective settlements managed by the settlers themselves.

But who would these settlers be? In order to bring her plan into being, Manya wandered through the settlements of Judea and talked at length with the starving workers. Almost all the members of Poalei Zion disagreed with her. To all who countered her with the need to take control of the workforce, she responded that that was a lovely idea but that without a foundation for the existence of work there was no future for the Jewish worker in the land. In truth, the situation of the Jewish workers was deplorable. The Arab workers were relatively better off, because they at least could return home to their villages, where they could have a patch of earth to grow vegetables. For the Jewish workers, there was nothing. On one of her sojourns through the streets, Manya found eight roommates sleeping in a single room. Could they continue to work as hired hands, she asked, under such conditions? Could they support families? Could they pave the way for a massive Jewish immigration? When she told the workers that they should demand apartments, public buildings, a communal kitchen, and so forth, they objected vehemently, saying that this notion smacked of charity and they wanted no part of it. Manya respected their moral position and marvelled at this specimen of humanity that represented the best of Jewish youth. At the same time, she was deeply saddened that this was how it was expending its energies. Despite all this, she did notice a strong spirit of cooperation, and her sharp eye detected little sparks of collectivism that grew unnoticed out of deprivation and suffering in this worker community, both among the Poalei Zion* and the Hapoel Hatzair* members.

Mutual assistance was necessary both at work and for basic living conditions because of the horrible realities—lack of work, shortage of living space, starvation and disease—all coupled with a yearning to live and work on the land. An immigrant arriving in Petach Tikvah with nothing would find other workers who had also just arrived, penniless like himself and be accepted like a brother in sorrow. Naturally, he would join his barefoot compatriots and lie down with them on their straw mats. If someone was lucky enough to get hired for a day, his friend would also share his piece of bread and his orange. People who had never met became bosom friends within two or three days. Thus were formed small communes of a kind.

When Manya observed this new way of life in the midst of the "chalutzim,"* (which they were not yet called), she was more strengthened in her resolve for equality in the workplace without exploitation. Her indefatigable dreaming ultimately led to the kibbutz movement in Eretz Israel.

She found a more positive approach to her "collective" concept among the workers who worked on farms in the Galilee. Many of them aspired to be farmers themselves and were determined to learn all they could about agriculture. The Galilee workers were also in dire straits, many of them sleeping in stables. There were those among them that were unconvinced by the notion of taking control of the workforce and there were others with socialist leanings who did not want to become farmers and did not want to compete with cheap Arab labor. There were, however, quite a few who understood the spirit of Manya's dream. In those days, the Keren Kayemet L'Israel (Jewish National Fund) was beginning to buy parcels of land, and Manya hung many hopes on the possibility of nationalizing the land, envisioning the prospects for collective settlements.

Included among the friends with whom Manya would debate were Eliezer Shochat and his brother, Yisrael. Eliezer was impressed, as were others, by her good nature. Years later, he recalled how one night, as he lay alone in a hut, tired and feverish with malaria, Manya suddenly appeared. She took him to the home of the Gissin family in Petach Tikvah where she was then rooming, and fed him warm milk and slices of white bread with honey. Eliezer listened respectfully to Manya's words about Hauran, but he was completely consumed by his need to seize control of the workforce in the existing settlements. To him, Manya's plans were only dreams.

The only one of the entire group who agreed with Manya at this point was Yisrael Shochat. With him, there was no need for much talk, because he immediately grasped the essence of the idea. He, too, was a visionary with original ideas of his own. His plan was to form a group of Jewish "Watchmen," ("Shomrim" in Hebrew) and he searched for brave comrades who would be willing to endanger themselves by going with him on guard duty in the settlements of the Galilee. On the surface it was a simple and necessary concept. Yet, in those days, it was a bold new concept to go out on guard duty, riding a horse and carrying a rifle. Much effort was expended to find stout-hearted comrades who would transform the idea into reality, and much effort was required to convince Jewish farmers to pass the guard duty onto Jewish hands.

Soon Manya and Yisrael** joined forces in both work and in life. At first, at least according to Yisrael, Manya thought more of his brother, Eliezer. She would say to Yisrael that she preferred to work with Eliezer because he was far more rational, sensible, and logical. Yisrael, she felt, had a stormy temperament, virtually exploding from the force of his own imagination. After a while, she reconsidered and told Yisrael that the land needed spirited people, whose imagination could soar. They understood each other. Her idea of collective settlement and his of Jewish Watchmen complemented each other, and it would be worthwhile to work together to find new ways of accomplishing their goals—two powerful ideas linking two powerful people.

**Born 1886, Lishova, Grodno; d. 1961, Israel.

7. At the Baron's in Paris

In order to discredit the existing modes of settlement, Manya decided to conduct an independent investigation. Yehoshua Hankin, Manya's mentor in matters relating to Eretz Israel, encouraged her by saying that one could learn from the negative as well as the positive.

Thus, Manya began her travels among the twenty-three existing settlements. She observed the miserable condition of the farmers, met with the complaining farmers and with the officials of the I.C.A. and asked them probing questions. What was their work program? What were the goals of their settlements? Why were they not hiring independent farmers who would be responsible to themselves? Why did the agricultural settlements inevitably end up in the red each year, forced to request bureaucratic assistance? How could it be that community funds sunk into the settlements were somehow metamorphosed into private wealth? Why were they unwilling to hire Jewish workers? With all her heart, Manya resisted the self-defeating bureaucratic attitude, the net result of which was dependence on both outside funding and Arab workers.

For many months, Manya immersed herself in this research. Upon her arrival at a farmer's house, she would explain her purpose, trying to convince him that the investigation was being conducted for his benefit. Despite her efforts to win the farmers' trust, she was received with suspicion. Everything about her seemed alien to them. The farmers spoke to her cautiously. Several actually told her they suspected she had been sent by the I.C.A. as some kind of spy.

Manya eventually discovered that some even suspected her of being a man dressed as a woman in order to be more readily accepted into their homes. Tova Portugali, from Kfar Giladi, who lived in Rosh-Pinah, recalled that even the children were intrigued by the arrival of Manya Wilbushevitz at their settlements. She was an inexplicable phenomenon to them. Rumors flew that she came from France, that she had been sent by the Baron, that she was a boy dressed in woman's clothes. To lend credence to the rumors was her unusual appearance: a strong and self-confident manner, exuding health and energy, cropped hair, galloping in on a noble horse. On one occasion, she visited Tova's aunt's house, having heard that she had just given birth that week. Manya congratulated her and kissed her on her forehead. And when Manya left the room, the frightened woman burst out crying, believing that it was a man who had just kissed her.

From the vast amount of data that she gathered, Manya came to two fundamental conclusions: first, the immigrants from the labor movement, the socialists, need not accept a method of settlement based on private property; second, a method of communal settlement must be found which would not only be appropriate for the conditions of the land, but which would also be true to the fundamental principles of Keren Kayemet.

Thus Manya grasped the essence of the problem, finally concluding that there would be no salvation from the officials of the I.C.A. and decided to meet with the Baron himself. Her passion for the workers moved her to attempt unheard of strategies, and she was completely confident that she would be able to influence the famous philanthropist. After all, Manya knew that the Baron was completely dedicated to settling the land, and had heard that he graciously received anyone coming to him from Eretz Israel to talk about settlement issues.

In 1905, Manya left for Paris, where she was received warmly by the Baron in his magnificent office. She was very impressed by his appearance and was amazed at the extent of his knowledge about the particulars of each individual settlement. More than that—he could even remember the names of many of the farmers. However, when she presented to him the conclusions of her investigation, his face darkened, furious that she would dare to criticize his methods of settlement, as though she considered all he had done to be a total waste. Nonetheless, when she described Hauran, he started listening again, and his eyes lit up when he heard her description of its rich earth and abundant water supply. Now Manya dared to elaborate on her plan: to bring to Hauran three hundred brave young men who would work and guard the land themselves. Her confident delivery conveyed the impression that three hundred men were in fact on call, ready to go to Hauran, and that she was their envoy, just waiting for the go-ahead. With unbridled enthusiasm, Manya elaborated upon her vision of the noble individual growing up in his homeland, the image of a young man who would live and work on a collective without exploiting the work of others. As she spoke, she was conjuring up in her own mind images of the workers in Petach Tikvah and Rishon LeZion, images of the Shochat brothers and their friends.

With great anticipation, Manya waited for the Baron's reply. But he stared her down coldly, stating that all this was merely a pipe dream. In all the world, there were landowners and hired hands and that was that. On the other hand, if he thought for one second that her plan would help to eliminate the prohibition against Jewish settlers in Hauran, he would not hesitate to support her. For a short while, he was silent, and then he remarked that in theory, he was not opposed to mass settlement in Hauran; he was prepared to give her the land, but no monetary support—the settlers would have to fend for themselves.

When Manya left the Baron, she was full of hope. Soon, however, doubts began to assail her. Would the settlement workers agree with her? Where would they get the means? What was the best way to achieve settlement of this magnitude? After wrestling with these questions, she concluded, quite characteristically, that the problem must be studied in a fundamental manner. With the help of her nephew, who was working as an agronomist in the settlement bureau of Paris, she visited government offices and examined the statistics on the development of French settlements in North Africa. She soon realized that she could not equate the French colonial settlement methods with those of a nation returning to its homeland. In her search for a new way to establish socialism she went back and re-examined the utopian texts that she had read while in prison in Moscow. Once again she devoured the descriptions of the French Utopians, such as Saint-Simon and Fourier, and the Englishman, Owen. Like them, she rejected the capitalist form of government and loved the masses of workers, but when she finished analyzing the various utopian plans and began to grasp the web of complex concepts, she came to the conclusion that the writings were not substantive and that it was impossible to find in them practical methods for establishing a just, collective society.

At that time, Max Nordau* came to Paris. Manya had heard that he was noted for his mockery of accepted norms, so she turned to him as a possible ally, hoping that he would find in her a kindred spirit and possibly even help her. He received her graciously and, for an hour and a half, listened raptly to her passionate words about the workers in Eretz Israel, about the corrupt administration in the settlements, about her concept for the settlement in Hauran, and about the need for independent, collective work, without exploitation. When she finished, Nordau scrutinized her sadly and quietly advised her to see a psychiatrist in order to free herself from these delusions.

In July 1905, Manya travelled to the Seventh Zionist Congress in Basel. That was where I first met her. I had come to Basel as a representative of my hometown—an eighteen-year-old girl from a small village. Manya fascinated me. She wore a gray dress with a white collar, with pearl buttons up to the neck. Her walk was strong and confident, and above her shoulders was a proud head, from which shone wise eyes that cut a path straight to one's heart. But the main thing—she was from Eretz Israel! How amazed I was at this new image from the Land. One could inhale the atmosphere of the homeland from her. It was an image that symbolized for me the beginning of our renewal in the land of our ancestors. In something of a trance, I followed her, shadow-like, absorbing her every word, yet never daring to actually approach her for all those days.

Manya stayed in Basel only a short time, because she had to rush back to Paris to begin preparing for her return trip to Eretz Israel.

8. Self-Defense for Russian Jewry

In Paris, Chayka Kagan's brother Meir awaited Manya. During the period of 1901-1903, he had worked with Manya for the unaligned workers' movement in Russia, and their friendship had continued. He visited her with another friend as spokesmen for the movement of self-defense for Russian Jews. The two pleaded with Manya to find a source of weapons for them, because the sword of destruction was dangerously close to the Jews.

Manya could not deny her friends, although she was herself then completely committed to matters in Eretz Israel. Shocked by the ferocity of those massacres, she once again turned to the Baron. When she arrived at the Baron's she found him sprawled out on the floor, intent upon a map of Eretz Israel. The sight was inspiring. With a flash of insight, she perceived clearly that this map was the blueprint of his dreams, his vision of settlement. The Baron assumed that she had come to bother him again about the Hauran matter, but Manya quickly explained to him that this time she had come to request his donation on behalf of Russian Jewry which was living under a cloud of terror and desperately needed to organize itself for defense. The Baron rose to his feet and stated that as a French Jew it would be impossible for him to supply arms for his coreligionists in Russia, because it could embroil his government in political complications.

Manya left in a state of agitation—where would she find the means for defense?

That evening, Manya met with a group of French socialists and described for them the organization for self-defense by the Jews of Russia and the urgent need to extend monetary help to them. Among those present was a French official who was very interested in the defense issue and wanted to know if their operation would be kept completely secret. After conversing with him for a

51

while, Manya became aware that this official was a member of the Baron's staff. The two of them decided to appeal to him again.

During the next meeting with the Baron, Manya once again expressed her fears for the Russian Jews because of the imminence of widespread pogroms. The official convinced the Baron that there was no risk of a political incident because the entire matter would remain top secret, at which point Manya gratefully accepted fifty thousand francs from the Baron. The official continued to support Manya, buying arms on her behalf and connecting her with a munitions factory in Liege, Belgium.

She then devoted all her strength and energy to obtaining arms and getting them across the border to Russia, and for a while she postponed all matters relating to Eretz Israel. This was a most dangerous undertaking. It was necessary to obtain false passports and to smuggle the contraband—which included pistols and ammunition—across four borders. Fortunately, the Russian government was still relatively unsophisticated and it was possible to maneuver quite a bit. On one occasion, Manya disguised herself as a French woman transporting suitcases full of expensive dresses; the suitcases had false bottoms containing the arms. Another time, she passed herself off as the wife of a young Rabbi from Frankfurt carrying a forged German passport, bringing with her eight big trunks full of "holy books," the gift of the Jews of Frankfurt to yeshivot in the Ukraine. She had all the required documentation in hand, and the trunks were passed through with hardly an inspection. This was the largest shipment of Browning rifles and ammunition and also the last shipment, because the money had run out.

During the morning, Manya reached Odessa, where she was met by Bat-Zion Mirsky from the Poalei Zion; she too was involved in the self-defense effort. Bat-Zion brought Manya and the trunks to the apartment of a wealthy family which was away on vacation and had opened up its home for this purpose. Manya stayed there in the guise of a servant and waited for friends who were supposed to deliver the weapons to various caches. A few hours later, Bat-Zion appeared and told her that the house was surrounded by secret police for some unknown reason, and that they would have to delay the transfer. In the afternoon, the doorbell rang and Manya opened the door. Before her stood a pale young man who asked if there was a student in the apartment named Akimov. She said that she had never heard of him and began to close the door, as the boy fainted. Manya took pity on him, dragged him in and revived him.

When he came to, he told her a tragic story about his wife running away with his best friend, Akimov, a revolutionary. He said he had been trailing them in order to take revenge, that he was penniless and hadn't eaten for several days. For two hours he poured his heart out to Manya and stirred her compassionate nature. Suddenly, he casually asked the "servant" if she had heard the rumor that someone had brought to this house a trunk full of weapons for the revolutionaries. Apparently someone in the munitions factory had leaked the story to the Russian secret police. From her startled reaction, the boy knew that he had come to the right place. Manya then realized that the whole story had been a smokescreen and a lie, and that if he left the house, all was lost because there were doubtless secret police right outside waiting for his answer. Feeling completely cornered, Manya removed from her pocket a small gun equipped with a silencer—a gift from the munitions factory—aimed straight at him and fired. The boy fell, looked at Manya with sad eyes and died. Manya hid the body in a large closet, cleaned up the blood and waited for Bat-Zion's arrival. Late in the evening, Bat-Zion returned and reported that the police had left the yard and that all was quiet. Manya told her what had happened and suggested that they put the body into one of the trunks and take it to the train station. Bat-Zion left and returned with a husky carpenter, who put the corpse into one of the trunks. The next morning, Manya hired porters, brought the trunk to the train station and sent it to a fictitious address. When the matter was concluded, Manya closeted herself in the apartment and did not utter a sound. During the next three days, Bat-Zion's comrades brought the arms to hiding places. Manya's Odessa mission was over.

Then Manya began to travel in the villages of the Pale*, and for that whole winter and spring of 1906, she worked in the secret defense organization. The idea of self-defense was becoming very appealing to the young and Manya accomplished much in spreading the word. But her heart was still in Eretz Israel.

At the end of summer, Manya returned to Paris. From there, she set sail to America for a two-fold purpose: self-defense for the Jews in Russia and settlement of Jewish workers in Hauran. She had letters of introduction to Dr. Magnes* and Henrietta Szold*, both of whom became her lifelong friends. With the help of Dr. Magnes, she received the means for self-defense in Russia, but as far as the collective settlement, she received no support. Neither Magnes, nor Henrietta Szold, nor any in the Zionist establishment in the United States was interested in the idea.

In her quest for support, Manya also met with the members of a religious commune, the Dukhobors*, whom she remembered from her days in the Tatar village in central Russia. She discovered that they had been persecuted by the Czar and had emigrated to America, and she was interested in seeing their way of life and how they were managing as a cooperative work unit. In her meeting with them, she was struck by the fundamental difference between their outlook and hers. The basis for their communal lives was a strong religious feeling, while Manya's outlook was nationalistic and humanistic. She believed that the survival of the Jewish nation in its historical homeland must be coupled with settlement in the spirit of the prophets of Israel.

In the early part of 1907, Manya returned home. When she was far away from Eretz Israel, she yearned for it, more convinced than ever that Eretz Israel must be resettled and turned into the center for the Jewish nation.

Her first stop was Petach Tikvah where hundreds of workers were gathered, and again she breathed the atmosphere of seizing control of the workforce. One evening, she discussed the situation with Eliezer Shochat, Alexander Zeid and about ten others who crowded together on the straw matting in Shochat's room. Listening to them speak about the employment problem, it became very clear to her that to work in Eretz Israel, they were ready to sacrifice everything. But in spite of her respect for them, she could not make peace with their willingness to work under such degrading conditions. The debate once again raged on with the members of Hapoel Hatzair, who shrank from any form of official help, viewing it as charity, and with the members of the Poalei Zion who still felt that any form of communal life would undermine class loyalty.

Soon after, Manya left Petach Tikvah and turned to Shefeya, to Yisrael Shochat, because his hopes and dreams excited her, and their souls were connected by the same passions. Manya was falling in love with Yisrael.

9. The Sejera Collective

Surrounded by the boulders of Shefeya, Manya was nourished by the ancient spirit of the nation as she and her friends explored the surrounding hills. The group was small in number but overflowed with aspirations for bold, new actions.

At that time, Yisrael Shochat was the secretary of the foundation established by Yisrael Belkind in Shefeya for the orphans of the Kishinev pogroms. Every so often he would go up to Zichron Yaakov in order to greet the new immigrants and recruit from among them special individuals to form the nucleus of his dream.

In Shefeya, Manya also met Yisrael Giladi, whom Shochat had recruited. These two were a study in contrasts: Shochat had a stormy temperament, while Giladi was quiet and deliberate. Giladi had the eyes of a dreamer, and gave the impression of absolute tranquility, but inside he was on fire. The two complemented each other. Giladi did not like to speak in generalities and would convert lofty conversations into practical ideas. After listening to Yisrael Shochat's visionary words, he suddenly removed his shoes, gave them to Shochat and said that from now on he would walk without them, that he had to feel the earth to aspire to it and prepare his body for the difficulties ahead. During one of his barefoot walks in the vineyards of Zichron Yaakov, he met a man plowing. He stood and stared at him until the farmer asked him what he wanted. Giladi asked for permission to plow. The puzzled farmer gave him the plow. Giladi grabbed it and the reins of the horse and plowed one furrow after another, his face gleaming with happiness. A similar event occured the first time he rode a horse. Confidently, he held the bit, started with a slow walk, gradually accelerating into a gallop, wanting to achieve absolute mastery over the horse. To no one's surprise, he quickly became an expert both in plowing and horsemanship.

Among the small group that gathered in Shefeya and Zichron

Yaakov, were also the fiery Moshe Givoni and Zvi Boker who had just come from the Caucasus. Although Zvi had been a tailor in the old country, his demeanor was that of a native of the hills of Samaria. It was difficult to find anyone more enthusiastic than he or his other friend, Yechezkel Nisanov, to work the vineyards and guard the settlement. Nisanov had intriguing eyes and a sharp tongue. Self-education had led him to the same conclusions as his friends, and they were among the first of Shochat's secret group representing Jewish strength. Included among them was also the broad-shouldered, jolly and intellectually gifted Mendele Portugali. But the most impressive candidate was the courageous Alexander Zeid, whose spectacular looks evoked awe in Manya. In Zeid, were fused the heightened spirituality of the Jews of Lithuania, his father's legacy, and the charm and looks of his mother, a Subbotnik* from the wilds of Siberia. Zeid, who was an associate of Michael Helpern and Aaron David Gordon, was very close to both Yisrael Shochat and Manya, and together they dreamed of the Jewish Watch and Jewish work.

This was a remarkable group, and Manya felt that with them it was really possible to create something brand new; with them it would be possible to establish a collective even without money. And since it was not possible to go as far as Hauran, the idea was conceived to first acquire land in the Galilee and to begin their new experiment there.

Meanwhile, several friends hiked to Jerusalem and despite the ever-prevalent malaria, they marched along singing. Zeid, who arrived first at Jerusalem, was one of the first to respond to Professor Boris Shatz's call for stonecutters in Jerusalem. For this project, a group of about forty young men gathered in Jerusalem, including some of the Shefeya group. On Shavuot of 1907, they all participated in the Poalei Zion convention in Jaffa, where the slogan was "To the Galilee!" as conceived in Shefeya.

In the course of this convention, Yisrael Shochat was elected delegate, along with Izhak Ben-Zvi*, to the Eighth Zionist Congress to be held that Passover in The Hague. On their way back to Eretz Israel from the Congress, the two of them often fasted because they were penniless. For a while, they worked as porters at the port of Trieste, but lacking the funds for lodging, they made do, even sleeping on some occasions in a cemetery. Hungry as they were, they continued to plan their strategy, and when they returned to Eretz Israel, Shochat quickly assembled his comrades to a secret meeting in Ben-Zvi's room, which was on the edge of an orchard in Jaffa. At this meeting, which was on Simchat Torah of the year 1908, the foundation was set for the initial settlement of Hashomer, which was at first named "Bar-Giora" in memory of the ancient freedom fighter.*

The Bar-Giora organization had the character of a secret political faction. Its mission* was two-fold: work and watch, but it was obvious that the first could not take place without the second preceding it.

Manya admired her comrades for their idealism, for their absolute faith in their own abilities, for their daring spirits and their readiness to lay their lives on the line without a moment's hesitation. They also had a highly developed sense of self-discipline which became second nature over time.

When Izhak Ben-Zvi and Yisrael Shochat returned from the Zionist Congress, Manya talked with Ben-Zvi on several occasions and heard from his lips the history of the Jews in ancient times. Ben-Zvi was then devoting much study to each and every period in the history of Eretz Israel before the destruction of the Temple and thereafter, and he had assembled a large amount of information about Jewish settlement in Eretz Israel throughout the ages, as well as folklore from the various Jewish ethnic communities. Before writing about these matters, he would often discuss them with Manya and Yisrael.

Manya liked and greatly respected Ben-Zvi, becoming deeply inspired by his research into the unending link between the people of Israel and their land, a link which survived times of trouble as well as times of peace. While she had already absorbed the spirit of the land from her brother Isaac before his emigration with the Biluim, her actual knowledge about the history of the land was sparse, and therefore she eagerly drank in Ben-Zvi's narrations. She was surprised to learn that there had been an unending succession of immigrations to Eretz Israel over the generations despite unbearable conditions. It had not been unusual for Jews to come from Eastern Europe by foot, spending long months on the road, and often dying from the rigors of the journey. Manya would conclude from the spirit of events recounted by Ben-Zvi, that the Jews could not seize the land as had Europeans in Africa; the nation of Israel was returning to its source, to the land of its ancestors. One of Ben-Zvi's primary goals was to raise the standard of living of the new settlers by finding new modes of settlement that would be based on justice and equity.

During Yisrael Shochat's stay in Europe at the Zionist Congress,

Manya redoubled her efforts to realize her dream of the collective, coupled with the idea of the Watch. For this purpose she turned to Yehoshua Hankin, her good friend, who also strove to penetrate the Galilee settlements with Jewish labor and a Jewish Watch. Hankin stood by her side and helped her persuade his brother-in-law, Eliahu Krause the agronomist, to accept the idea of the collective.

Among the mountain ridges between Nazareth and Tiberias was nestled the tiny settlement of Sejera. Spread out in the foothills, were two rows of farmhouses, and up above on the hilltop, opposite the development, loomed the farm of the I.C.A., completely surrounded by a wall, like some ancient fortress. The manager of this farm was Eliahu Krause, and one day Manya and Hankin went to him requesting that he allocate a small group of workers on their own responsibility to bring in the crops and work in the stables, from the time of planting to that of threshing. At first Krause hesitated, thinking of the negative reaction he could expect from the I.C.A. officials. But being a good Zionist at heart, despite the possibility of his own dismissal, he agreed and also offered the group of workers two thousand dunams of land and dozens of mules and teams of oxen. He even consented to advance them a stipend until after the threshing season.

Manya greeted Yisrael with these wonderful tidings upon his return to Eretz Israel. They were very optimistic, as was the whole Bar-Giora group. There were eighteen members already, including six girls. Right after the holiday of Sukkot of 1907, the group travelled to Sejera**. Thus was quietly born the first collective in Eretz Israel.

They put all their energies into farming, assisted by Krause who valued their labors greatly. Krause was also notable as the first person to train the girls not only in the traditionally female housework and gardening; he also gave them teams of oxen and taught them to plow the fields, a most unusual attitude for those times.

Manya was a bookkeeper at the farm. She was also the living spirit of the collective and she had a hand in every pot. It was she who formalized communal life—both the collective purse and the collective kitchen.

David Yisraeli, one of the original members, recalled a characteristic episode:

One of the Sturman sisters was the first to receive a team of

**Above is Arabic; the Hebrew name is Ilaniyyah.

young oxen for plowing. During the plowing, the oxen suddenly became wild and began running to the other side of the farm. The girl did not release the plow; with all her might, she surged after the oxen trying to control them. One of the male workers, apparently not devoted to the notion of equal rights, enjoyed the spectacle tremendously and burst out in a gale of laughter as he watched the girl chasing after the oxen. Manya found his behavior unforgivable. In fact, she harshly criticized the work supervisor for having given this girl young and hot-tempered oxen for his own amusement. Manya insisted that he be given a taste of his own medicine—that he try plowing with the same team of oxen. From that time, the girls received well-disciplined oxen and had no further trouble.

This type of intervention was intrinsic to Manya's character, to her lifelong battle against the status quo.

In the middle of that year, the members started refocusing their energies to taking over the Watch. Even among the farmers of Sejera were several hired hands, and the watch was done by Circassians*. The farmers could not believe that Jewish workers could withstand Arab terrorists and bandits and properly guard their properties and lives. The Circassians were born fighters, they claimed—even the surrounding Arabs were afraid of them.

Even in Sejera, a Circassian from the nearby village guarded the farm. The Sejera pioneers were determined to take over this watch themselves. They observed that every night the Circassian would return to his village for a few hours. On one of those nights, they quietly removed Krause's horse from the farm and hid it in one of the yards in the settlement. Then they woke Krause and informed him that his horse was stolen and the guard was missing. Krause walked around the yard fuming until the Circassian returned to his post. He fired him on the spot, and despite his fears of a Circassian retaliation, he decided to accept a Jewish Watch. Zvi Boker was the first Jewish guard in the Galilee. The comrades returned Krause's horse, and every night Zvi went out to guard the grounds as well as the area behind the walls and the fields. The comrades went to sleep fully clothed, ready to come to his assistance if needed. To no one's surprise, he was ambushed several times by the Circassians and was saved by his ready comrades. Manya participated as well and was once beaten by one of the Circassians. After a while, however, the Circassians came to terms with the Jewish Watch and left them alone.

Thus, the first watchman passed the test; little by little, Jewish guards could be seen patrolling the fields of Sejera. After a while, the Watch was also active in Mescha (Kfar Tavor), Yama (Yavneel) and Bet Gan. The comrades in Sejera started to dream of plowing all the fields in the Galilee and encompassing the north, beyond to Hauran, and eventually going south and taking over the work and the watch in all the settlements of Judea and Samaria.

Manya summarized the first year in Sejera in these words:

"This has been the happiest year of my life. For all of us, these were beautiful days. We sanctified each working day, all of us feeling ennobled by the work. We felt that our experiment would serve in the future as a cornerstone for many workers who would take over the land of the Keren Kayemet on their own responsibility; we believed that we were laying the groundwork for collective work for all time, for us and for our children to come.

"The human material in the collective was quite remarkable—its dedication to work was exemplary and as Krause watched over us from the 'sidelines,' without our feeling it, in order to protect us from mistakes and also giving us intensive lessons in agriculture, we completed the year successfully and with a substantial profit—for the first time in the history of Jewish farming in the land! When Yisrael Shochat recommended that I join Bar-Giora, and explained its purpose, it was completely natural for me to do so....

"The positive results in the Sejera experiment led to several important outcomes: (1)We overcame the doubts about the possibility of living, creating and working collectively in the land and the path was paved for the kibbutz movement; (2) The collective life of the comrades in Sejera during this year and the collective goals tied us together strongly and irrevocably; (3) The communal organization enabled the Bar-Giora group to crystallize, strengthen and develop the self-confidence to establish Hashomer as a quasi-legal organization, educating the Jewish community to defend that which it had created and to feel the pride of nationhood. We were, however, unable to bring the Hauran plan to fruition."

News of the successful conclusion of the work year in the collective was received as a triumph by all Galilee workers. For the first time, Krause completed a fiscal year in the black, thanks to the group of workers that farmed two thousand dunams on their own.

It was not surprising, therefore, that Krause implored the members of the collective to continue working the land, hoping that their influence would lead to Jewish workers farming other areas. Despite their farming success, the members of Hashomer saw as their primary goal the watch issue, and they were not satisfied with its existence only in Sejera and Mescha. Their goal was to expand the Jewish Watch throughout the Galilee, as well as in Judea and Samaria.

Despite the fulfillment they felt from the work in the fields, it was decided not to renew the agreement with Krause but rather to disperse the Watchmen—for now only to the I.C.A. farm, to the Sejera settlement and to Mescha.

At the end of the summer of 1908—I had been in the land for only a few months but already felt like a native—we sat in Ben Zvi's room in Jerusalem with a number of members of Bar-Giora. Suddenly Manya made her entrance. We were all delighted to see her, but she had no time to sit around with us. Manya asked me to come with her to the terrace. I remembered her well from the Congress in Basel, but now she was not as elegantly dressed. With a strange expression on her face, she turned to me as though I was already a full-fledged member of the group, and in her deep and soulful voice stated that we could achieve great things with our men; after all, we had already established the first collective on the soil of the Galilee, and now the Watch was being accepted in the settlements. However, she continued, there was a pressing need for arms, and a great deal of money was required for this purpose. Manya raised her big eyes and whispered that it was possible to raise the funds within Eretz Israel, perhaps in Jerusalem, because much money was streaming to the churches and monasteries there. Perhaps, she said, we could intercept one of those shipments. I didn't understand. To take the money by force? This was terribly dangerous, I said, and could even lead to governments getting involved in our business, both the local authorities as well as those who were sending the money, and who could pull the plug on Jewish immigration and perhaps endanger Jewish communities abroad. Immediately Manya's face changed; her eyes shrank as though she was gathering their light within her. She got up and told me to keep the secret to myself, to repeat it only to Ben-Zvi.

A few months after this strange visit, we heard rumors and news about the accomplishments of the collective in farming and in the watch: not only in the fields of the development, but also in those of other farmers in Sejera and Mescha. Ben-Zvi and I were then deeply immersed in teaching our few classes at the high school, but in our hearts we were with our friends in Sejera. We received word that during Passover, the first Hashomer convention would take place in Kfar Tavor. We were invited: Ben-Zvi as a member because he had been one of the founders of Bar-Giora, and myself as a candidate.

On the first day of the Passover vacation of 1909, we started out by foot to the Galilee, Ben-Zvi and I. With us were two friends from Jerusalem, Judah Burla and David Avishar.

The next day we reached Haifa and we met Gad, a member of the collective. Together with him, we continued on foot, following his wagon which was laden with necessities. At noon we arrived at Basa, where we camped. Dawn found us at the hills of Nazareth, where we stayed until the sun peered out from between the clouds. At the bottom of the hills, the valley was spread out in all its glory, and from the distance, we could see the reddening roofs of the houses in Sejera. The sight was spectacular: Jewish workers plowing furrows in the fields. When we got closer we saw that not only the male comrades were plowing, but so were the girls wearing kaffiyahs and wide gray trousers—the new fashion for Galilean girls. We sat on clumps of. earth, our eyes riveted on the scene below.

Together, we entered the main yard of the farm. It looked to us like the remnant of some ancient fortress surrounded by an imposing wall. Inside were small rooms resembling monastic cells where the comrades lived. I immediately asked for Manya and was told that she and Yisrael were expected to arrive shortly from Haifa.

As we stood near the gate, we could see galloping horses on the horizon and Esther Sturman and I went outside. "Who were those riders," I asked, "wearing long robes and white kaffiyahs tied on with black cord? Were they Bedouins?"

"These are our friends," answered Esther, "who are putting on a pageant in honor of Manya and Yisrael."

Through the fields, a carriage approached the gate, and out of it leaped Yisrael followed by Manya. Manya noticed me, and on her face was a benevolent smile. Her two hands were extended simultaneously to me and to Esther.

Yisrael was pale and didn't look very healthy. He had the nose of an eagle and black curls like a Bedouin from the desert. He immediately entered one of the rooms while Manya remained in the yard and turned to the group which had gathered. She had something to say to each one, and she could concentrate on several matters at the same time. I walked over to her and she put her hand on my shoulder. It felt good just to be in her presence.

I followed her to the storeroom, where we would be having our

Seder. Already, all work implements had been removed and one of the older workers, Plotkin, was busy cleaning and straightening. He had come from the same city as Ben-Zvi, and although his hair and beard implied advanced age, his gaze was youthful. Manya approached him with both love and respect. Plotkin set up boards for tables, and Manya helped him. The light penetrated through the wide doorway because the storeroom had no windows, and the atmosphere was decidedly dingy. Manya brought olive branches from outside. Hanging on the walls were hoes and rakes decorated with olive branches; we brought Plotkin more and more branches.

Suddenly, we heard excited voices outside. We hurried out and saw Pachter, the photographer, standing near the gate. He had started out with us from Haifa, but on the way had grown tired lugging the camera equipment; had rented a donkey and gone on alone. Not far from Sejera, two bandits had attacked him and stolen his camera. He had defended himself with his pistol and escaped to Sejera. When the group heard about the theft, they set out to pursue the robbers, some on foot and others on horseback. We girls also ran outside the gates, but then we remained standing, slightly embarrassed. We also wanted to rejoin our comrades—but empty-handed, with no weapons whatsoever? Manya gave us a sharp stare, and said reprovingly that had we had weapons we might have helped catch those criminals. She said that we had to learn to handle firearms, and we should see to it that each of us was armed. Then she streaked away, and we remained standing, the unspoken sadness hovering in the air.

The sun set, and the dusk added to our feeling of despondency. The boys who had gone out by foot began to return and only the riders ventured further to chase the bandits. Those who came back told of traces of blood on the road—probably one of the intruders had been wounded. Doubtless they would be looking for revenge, and we should be expecting attacks.

In the darkness of the yard, our depression grew. Suddenly, the sound of gunfire split the air—an ominous beginning to this night. What toll would it yield? The members of the Watch prepared their ammunition and hurried to their posts.

Manya participated in the plans for the watch. Posts were assigned, and the comrades were organized into patrols. And the girls? Esther whispered to me that she had a gun and could get one for me, too. Had she stolen them? I pressed her hand—this night we would stand together. My eyes locked on Manya who was going from comrade to comrade, exchanging a few words with each, but only to the men...she did not approach us. Esther walked me over to the western corner of the yard, and I didn't have a chance for even a brief conversation with Manya before joining Esther on the watch.

This was to be the first time that I stood on guard duty in the Galilee and my imagination transported me to ancient times. As we watched through the window, Esther whispered that she knew every rock, every grave down below. She told me about the cave where the original Bar-Giora group had met secretly. As my eyes absorbed our surroundings, Esther continued to tell me about the beliefs of Bar-Giora, about the dreams, about the visions of the group. Knowing that I was a candidate for Hashomer, she spoke to me openly. Like me, she was especially impressed by Manya's character.

We asked ourselves where Manya might be that night. It was unthinkable that she was not standing guard somewhere. Perhaps she would come to us? We spoke quietly and listened to every rustle of movement. Suddenly someone opened the door. "Manya," I called. I was somehow sure that it had to be Manya coming to check on us. I was right. She came in and looked at us in shock. She was very surprised to see two girls in this place which was the most dangerous corner, she said, and where the trouble was likely to start. It would be easy for the attackers to ambush us from between the cliffs and the graves....

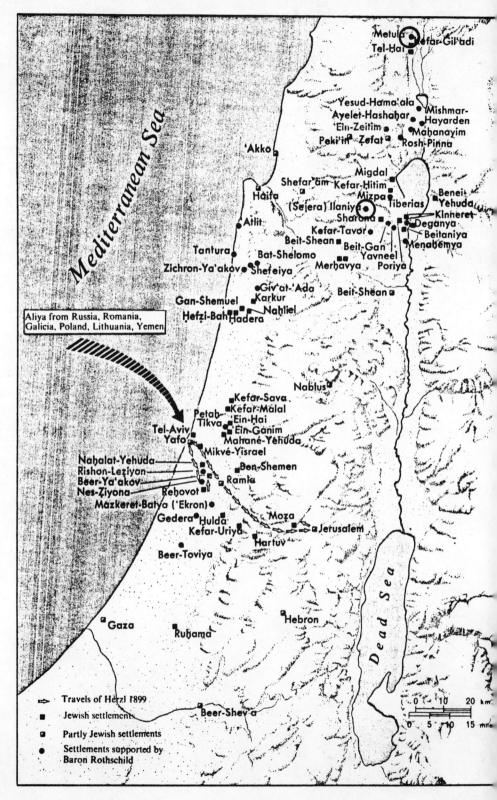

Metula
Kefar-Gil'adi
Tel-Hai

Yesud-Hama'ala
Ayelet-Hashaḥar   Mishmar-
Ein-Zeitim   Hayarden
Peki'in Ẓefat   Maḥanayim
                        Rosh-Pinna
'Akko

Migdal
Shefar'am Kefar-Hitim
Ḥaifa   Mizpa   Benei-
(Sejera) Ilaniya Tiberias Yehuda
           Sharona   Kinneret
Aṭlit   Deganya
           Kefar-Tavor   Beitaniya
           Beit-Shean Beit-Gan Menaḥemya
Tantura   Bat-Shelomo   Yavneel
Zichron-Ya'akov Shefeiya Merḥavya Poriya
                 Giv'at-'Ada
                 Karkur   Beit-Shean
Gan-Shemuel
Hefzi-Bah Hadera   Naḥliel

Aliya from Russia, Romania,
Galicia, Poland, Lithuania, Yemen

Nablus

Kefar-Sava
Kefar-Malal
Petaḥ Ein-Hai
Tikva Ein-Ganim
Tel-Aviv
Yafo   Maḥané-Yehuda
       Mikvé-Yisrael
Naḥalat-Yehuda
Rishon-Leziyon   Ben-Shemen
Beer-Ya'akov
Nes-Ziyona   Ramla
Rehovot
Mazkeret-Batya ('Ekron)
Gedera Hulda   Moza
Kefar-Uriya   Jerusalem
        Hartuv
Beer-Toviya

Gaza   Hebron

Ruḥama

Mediterranean Sea

Dead Sea

Beer-Shev a

Travels of Herzl 1899
Jewish settlements
Partly Jewish settlements
Settlements supported by
Baron Rothschild

0 10 20 km.
0 5 10 15 mile

A-2

B

C

איער אלטע-לאנד דארף איך האבען!

בת-ציון

שלוסט זיך אן אין דעם אידישען רעגימענט.

מניה שוחט 1961-1878

ISRAEL · MANIA SHOCHAT

ישראל

0.40

60 שנה „השומר"

60TH ANNIVERSARY
OF "HA-SHOMER"

E

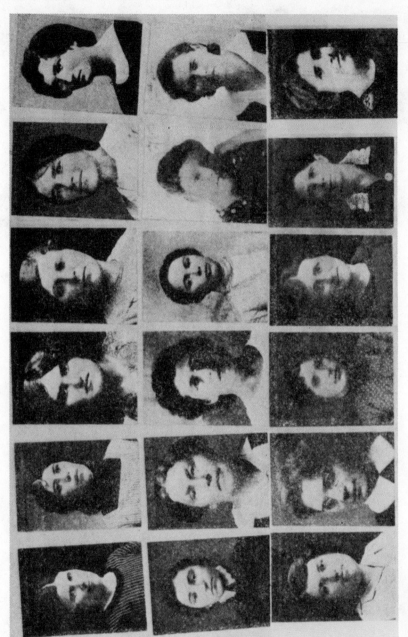

D

F-1

G

F-2

H

I

J

K

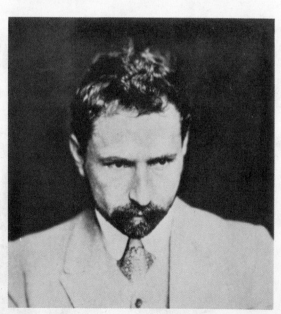

A-1

A-1 Georgi Apollonovich Gapon (1870–1906), also known as "Father Gapon" to Manya Wilbushewitz and other Russian revolutionaries. (It has been established by researchers that no picture of Zubatov exists)

A-2 Kfar Giladi, in the upper Galilee, and Sejera (now known as Ilaniya, the Hebrew name for a tree) are circled; two places most associated with Manya Shochat. Other settlements mentioned can also be found.

B A Shomer member guarding a settlement in 1910.

C A Yiddish newspaper in the U.S. in 1918 uses the allegorical "Daughter of Zion" (the Jewish people) with, "I Want Your Old New Land! Join The Jewish Regiment," referring to the establishment of a Jewish Legion in the British Army.

D Women in the Shomer (Watch). Top row, r. to l.: Pesia Abramson, Yaffa Gad (Avigdorov), Dvora Drechler, Chava Issushkin, Esther Bakar, Kayla Giladi. Second row: Yehudit Horowitz, Zipporah Zeid, Chaya Sara Hankin, Rachel Yanait (author), Vera Nissnov, Rivka Nissnov. Bottom row: Chaya Yigal, Tova Portugali, Chaya Krol, Sara Krinser, Manya Shochat, Atara Sturman.

E Stamp issued by the State of Israel in 1961 showing Manya Shochat, to mark the 60th anniversary of Hashomer. (Note her date of birth is shown as 1878. Our author records it as 1879. The spelling, "Mania," is Shochat's own.)

F-1 Manya Wilbushewitz at the Seventh Zionist Congress, Basel, Switzerland, in the summer of 1905.

F-2 A group of Shomer members in
Damascus, 1915. l. to r.: Manya,
Yisrael Shochat, Rachel Yanait.
Seated is Yosef Strumza.

G Manya Wilbushewitz in her
20's. (Either in Russia or on her
arrival in Eretz Israel)

H Manya Shochat in the
mid-1920's, apparently in the
environs of Haifa.

I Manya Shochat in the early
1930s.

J The Shochat family: l. to r.: The
children Geda and Anna;
Yisrael and Manya, upon their
return to Eretz Israel from exile
in Turkey.

K The Shochat family in the
1940's: l. to r., Anna, Yisrael
Shochat, Manya and Geda.

Photo Credits

A-2 From *The New Israel Atlas*, Zev Vilnay, courtesy Keter Publishing
House, Jerusalem, Israel.

D From *Kovetz Ha-Shomer*, p. 137, courtesy The Lavon Institute for
Labour Research, Tel Aviv, Israel. (Photo by Zionist Archives, NY)

E Courtesy Paul Rothman, NY.

F-1, F-2, G, H, I, J and K. Courtesy Yad Ben Zvi Archives, Jerusalem,
Israel.

10. Hashomer—The First Convention

The Hashomer convention was scheduled to begin the next morning. Toward evening, Ben-Zvi, Gad and I went from Sejera to Mescha. The distance was not long, but this time the road seemed to stretch out endlessly. I could feel eyes peering at us from behind every bush, unknown assailants waiting to pounce on us from behind every rock. Gad tried to distract us with accounts of attacks by local bandits as well as Bedouins from Transjordan.and about how the Watch had become established in Mescha.

An Arab guard had shot at a farmer; the bullet hit a rock and ricocheted, hitting the assailant himself. The tribe of the wounded man, the Mograbis, sought revenge on the settlement. During this life-threatening period, the Watch was handed over to the Jewish settlers. A superhuman effort was required by all the settlers to guard Mescha, because the surrounding villagers also resented this change. In order to be prepared, a number of additional workers from the Galilee had come to their assistance, preventing several attacks. Finally, an uncertain peace was made with the neighbors, but it was impossible to predict how long it would last.

Gad looked at my frightened face, and presumably to instill some confidence in me, continued to tell us about the time when the men left to guard Mescha, Esther and Zippora Zeid had silently followed them on foot, despite having been turned down for guard duty. When they arrived anyway, fears for their safety weighed heavily upon the conscience of the boys. Manya had looked at them and said, "Actions speak louder than words..."

Dust billowed up around us as we entered Mescha together with the flock. The settlement consisted of one long, unadorned path flanked by black stone houses. Gad escorted us to the home of Judah Antebi, the teacher, who lived near the school. Our mood lifted when we happened upon a bunch of boisterous, active children. We stopped for a moment and listened to the Hebrew language that flowed so melodiously from their tongues. These little ones, I thought, will change the facade of this dreary place; they will work the fields and they will guard their settlement. We visited for a while with Antebi, who entertained us with his stories—a compelling mixture of reality and legend—about the neighborhood in the present and in the ancient past. The next morning, we hurried to the small house of the Watchmen at the edge of Mescha, where the assembly was to take place. From the house, we could hear the noise of conversation taking place in a medley of languages. We entered and faced dozens of shining eyes. These members of Hashomer appeared bizarre: unkempt, straggly hair, combined with a demeanor of absolute confidence. They had come from the Galilee and from Judea. They were few in number, but they gave you the feeling that they were many. I had met each of them before. Manya followed me in, placed her hand on my shoulder and led me across the way. We stretched out on the ground, surrounded by the fragrance of desert flowers. I had been anticipating this conversation and was totally attentive. She began talking, warmly and simply, as if she had all the time in the world. She spoke about the work, the Watch, and the members of this group. As she spoke, her words seemed less directed at me, and more at some distant cloud that only she could see. She started describing all the future settlements and how they would grow and develop. She looked right at me and grabbed my hand, but I felt that her thoughts were miles away. Nevertheless, every word she uttered found its way straight to my heart. True, I had already heard about the beliefs of Hashomer and Bar-Giora, but now everything became crystal-clear to me, illuminated by Manya's inner light. The members themselves formed the content of the movement, she said, their entire reason for being was to give of themselves—even their lives, if necessary. Manya's approach was not based upon some abstract theory, but was rather a personal, heartfelt plea to live a real and productive life.

Then we were called indoors; the assembly had already commenced. As we crossed the threshold, I was greeted joyously by the news that I had been accepted as a member of Hashomer. In those days, there was no elaborate ceremony. There were only two candidates: Mordechai Yigal and myself. The members sat on narrow benches along the walls and on the floor, and I sat at the end of a bench. I felt enveloped in warmth and blessings, feeling truly accepted. Manya rose to speak, as though continuing our previous conversation. Although her words were directed to the group, each of us felt as though we were being personally ad-dressed. Her speech, which emanated from the depths of her soul, expressed the feelings of all those present. We would no longer be called "death children" by the Arabs; the Jews would form a solid, indestructible wall with Hashomer, and this would be the direct path to our survival as a people.

After Manya finished, Yisrael Shochat spoke, greeting all warmly, especially the new members. He said that though we were few, the vision of the Watch would pierce the consciousness of the masses arriving in the country. Our readiness to fend for ourselves and sacrifice would heighten the respect of our neighbors. Our Watch would lay the foundation for Jewish might and for Jewish independence in our homeland. To work and guard ourselves, to rely upon ourselves and only ourselves, this was the purpose of Bar-Giora, the secret society which would now be officially re-placed by the open organization of Hashomer.

I was so absorbed in his words, that it took me a few minutes to notice that he was receiving a standing ovation. I rose too. Were we only nineteen strong? I had the feeling that Yisrael Shochat had just been addressing the entire nation of Israel. We stood silently for several moments, his words still resounding in my ears. As I stood there, Manya came over and embraced me, and I felt as though I had been sanctified for Hashomer.

Then Izhak Ben-Zvi spoke. You could see the emotion churning within his eyes, but his words were tranquil and soft-spoken. He discussed the past as a portent for the future.

During intermission, all surrounded Manya. She seemed to en-ergize everyone with the desire to give their all for the cause.

Yes, that day of the first Hashomer assembly, on Passover of 1909, was a great moment in all of our lives. The final decisions were to be made by a committee of three: Yisrael Shochat, Yisrael Giladi and Mendele Portugali—but it was apparent to all that Manya was to have an equal say in all decisions.

The meeting adjourned late at night and the Sejera contingent hurried back to its posts.

Years later, Manya summarized the accomplishments of Hashomer thus:

"Tremendous obstacles and personality clashes were faced by this tight group of individuals, but three factors enabled us to overcome all problems: (1) the power of the organization which gave us the ability to exercise our wildest fantasies in reality; (2) the power of devotion to an ideal which was great enough to sweep away personal considerations; (3) the power of the women of Hashomer—the women who, despite remaining in the background, knew how to bear the burdens of wandering, the suffering and the illnesses that were an integral part of their lives, and to exude strength at the same time."

Once Bar-Giora left the realm of imagination and the Jewish Watch was begun in earnest, it was immediately confronted with the age-old Arab question: How could Jews live in the midst of the masses of Arabs who had an entirely different culture and who had been brought up to revere the gun and the sword? This dilemma motivated the Hashomer people to learn the Arabic language, culture and tenets, believing that the ultimate success of Hashomer would be directly correlated with neighborly relations, based upon mutual respect.

The Arab tradition of immediate retaliation taught the Watchmen to be particularly cautious, to practice self-defense and to avoid bloodshed, because the death of one Arab would inevitably put the entire settlement at tremendous jeopardy.

The attainment of land and the Watch brought the Watchmen in frequent contact with their neighbors and they soon learned that while moments of conflict required courage, more important was the everyday contact, which would be the only way to insure an atmosphere of trust and harmony.

Thus, the Watch gave its members a feeling of confidence and caution simultaneously, and brought them to realize that the Watch itself was not primary, but rather a means to the attainment of more exalted goals.

The Watch and land liberation efforts also had consequences in the areas of collective work and living, even though these concepts were not yet formalized. The problems of collective family life and education had not been resolved, but these early attempts paved the way for the kibbutz movement as a permanent fixture of Israeli life.

From its inception, the Hashomer members were aware of the need to think about more formal settlements, but this need was placed on the back burner because of the exigencies of the moment. Once members undertook marriage and began the experience of continual transiency, it became clear that it would be impossible to continue thus. At that point, it was necessary to stop and consider seriously the question of communal settlement in which family life could be centered, in which children would be trained for their future in Hashomer, and in which the women would feel more central and necessary. It was not until the years of World War I, two years before Yisrael Giladi's death, that he began to realize the dream of actual Hashomer settlements.

Students of the Hashomer era will find that it had a psychological impact on all the disparate elements of the Jewish settlement, particularly on the Jewish youth. This influence was not a result of any propaganda effort, but rather from the essence of its existence and its actions.

The nature of the Watchman's work did not allow for publicity, since one of the requirements of membership was a vow of secrecy. It is not surprising, therefore, that the general population was not aware of the acts of courage and self-sacrifice that were an integral part of Hashomer life, and that there were those who saw in their efforts nothing more than militaristic bravado. For this reason, the ranks of Hashomer remained small and when a member was lost, it was difficult to find a replacement. The Hashomer organization was composed of trail blazers, who tried to adjust to the needs of the time, expressing those efforts in a myriad of ways—from guard duty to independent farming, and even to enlisting in the British army.

At dawn, we began our return trip to Jerusalem, crossing the Valley of Jezreel to Bat-Shelomo. Despite the night of guard duty and the high voltage of the Hashomer meeting, we strode energetically, joyful and enchanted by our surroundings. We started quoting from the Bible, from the words of Deborah the Prophetess, and I felt as though I was part of an ancient dream. We hardly felt the passage of the humid hours when the sun receded westward. Suddenly the sun had set, and we found ourselves standing on the banks of the Kishon. The boys removed their trousers and started crossing by foot; as for me, an Arab with his donkey happened by and my few remaining pennies bought me passage across the Kishon on the donkey's back. We arrived at Bat-Shelomo, still glowing from the lovely day in the valley. We went to one of the farmer's homes, and he greeted us with milk straight from the barn. But even before we finished drinking it, we were told the devastating news that there had been an attack on Sejera and there had been two sacrifices: Korngold and Shimon Melamed.

We were completely shaken. The excitement and brilliance of the Hashomer meeting was extinguished. We were so few, and we had already lost two. Korngold had been a student from Yekaterinoslav (now called Dniepropetrovsk) who had breathed into us the hope that many others like him would follow. Melamed had been the youngest farmer of Sejera. We felt personally wounded; our fate was so intimately tied with each one of us.

We continued the rest of the way in a state of shock. Only when we got to Jerusalem did we pour out our rage and grief to our tiny group there, feeling entirely shattered and hopeless. The distance between Jerusalem and Sejera was only geographic. Although we wanted nothing more than to be with them physically, Ben-Zvi and I had already signed up to teach in the Hebrew high school in Jerusalem. We always kept very close ties with our dear friends in Sejera. From time to time, they came to visit us. Once Manya came, although she was very immersed in her work. The echo of the Hashomer success started to resound southward to Judea, and once again the slogan "To the Galilee" blossomed, as new members started to move northward as well.

We impatiently counted the days until our long vacation. We were looking forward to traveling to the northern Galilee after stopping in the Jordan Valley.

Vacation arrived. We started out by foot—Ben-Zvi, his brother Aaron Reuveni, Yosef Nachmani and myself. This time, it did not take long. After walking for two days and a night, we arrived at Umm-Juni, our first destination across the Sea of Galilee.

We were delighted to find Manya there, perched on a windowsill, sewing patches on shirts. Next to her sat Zvi Nadav with a ripped shirt. Manya always had her sewing tools with her like a first aid kit. She was like a mother or a sister to every member, a focal point of tranquillity and encouragement. Manya raised her eyes to me in a warm greeting and at the same time continued her sewing.

I had already heard from Manya about the group at Umm-Juni, which was an outgrowth of Sejera. The Keren Kayemet* had donated the land, and the land office had paid an advance until after threshing time. This was the first time that such a large piece of land had been worked by an independent group of Jewish workers. It was already threshing season, and one could see the golden wheat piled in abundance; the year had ended profitably.

Manya was still preoccupied with her dream of Hauran, but she was happy with the success of this settlement across the Sea of Galilee. Soon the Hashomer contingent would leave Umm-Juni, to be replaced by members of the collective in Hadera. Meanwhile, a new name for the settlement had been proposed: Degania.

From Umm-Juni, Manya travelled to Haifa, while we toured the length and breadth of the land for three weeks. We absorbed the sights and sounds and encountered new people and new places.

On Erev Rosh Hashanah of 1910, we went from Nazareth to Manya and Yisrael's new home in the German settlement of Haifa. We climbed wooden stairs, entering a long room with a wooden floor, in the center of which was a table and two benches. Everything sparkled with cleanliness. When did Manya have time to do housework?

That evening marked the second convention of Hashomer. Among others attending was Yisrael Giladi, whose voice and eyes radiated his dream, and the effervescent Mendele Portugali, whose broad shoulders complemented his jolly laugh.

The discussion encompassed the redemption of the land of Fula in the Valley of Jezreel. Manya spent the whole time in the kitchen, bringing tea and food to the members, while continuing to participate actively in the dialogue.

The door to their home in Haifa was never closed. Day and night, Hashomer colleagues came from their various guardposts. Yisrael was busy doing clerical work for the building of the Technion, and Manya served as hostess for all. She had a particular talent for listening to each person and giving him the feeling that she was on his side, and yet having him leave with her viewpoint firmly established as his own. Yisrael lived and breathed the work of Hashomer and there was not a single matter upon which he was not advised and encouraged by Manya.

11. Settling the Valley of Jezreel

In September of 1910, Hashomer arrived at Fula. Manya and Yisrael were there when the Watchmen arrived with twelve donkey teams and began plowing. A feeling of wonderment seized Manya as she watched her friends who first furrowed the land of the valley. From that moment in time, the valley was theirs. Manya participated in its colonization; its glorious moments as well as its times of threat, ceaselessly concerning herself with her friends in their ramshackle huts. The Hashomer members settled that land with superhuman self-sacrifice. Their first dwellings were of clay, only windowless huts, crawling with mice. Near them, was the communal oven where the sisters Shifra, Sara and Esther Sturman labored, baking bread and preparing borghul. Later on, with Hankin's help, shacks were constructed, and the place was renamed Merchavia.

Manya's home in Haifa was suffused with the atmosphere of Merchavia. Continuously, streams of friends from Merchavia would arrive—by foot, by train or on horseback. Manya, in her role as the quasi-Foreign Minister of Hashomer, took care of the bookkeeping, collected contributions and obtained loans until the conclusion of threshing season.

The Watchmen guarded the land day and night, becoming so exhausted that they appeared to be sleepwalking. In the beginning of 1911, one of the Watchmen, Yigal, was summoned by Yisrael Shochat to Haifa. Upon his arrival, only Manya was at home. When she saw how spent he looked, she hurried to the kitchen to prepare some food for him; in the meantime, he fell into a deep, exhausted sleep. After twenty-four hours, he awoke in the hospital; Manya, believing him to be unconscious, had called an ambulance. For three days he remained in the hospital, renewing his strength, and only then was he able to speak about the situation in Fula.

That year had exacted a heavy toll from Hashomer. After the first rains, Yechezkel Nisanov and Zvi Nadav had gone from Merchavia to Yavneel on a mission. The wagon ride through the swampy meadows was tortuous. Zvi led the mules, while Yechezkel rode in the rear with a shotgun. At the approach to Bet-Gan, a shot was heard and Zvi urged the mules on. Only after entering the settlement, did he realize that Yechezkel had breathed his last. Rivkele, Yechezkel's wife, was in the hospital at the time about to give birth and someone had to tell her the terrible news. Manya, who always volunteered for the most unpleasant assignments, undertook this task. She went to the hospital, sat by Rivkele for long hours, talking about the dreams and dangers of Hashomer, until Rivkele finally understood that she was being told that her husband was dead. The little girl that she bore was named Yechezkela after her murdered father.

At the conclusion of the summer of 1911, the third convention of Hashomer was held in Hadera. Its many accomplishments were reviewed, among which was a new invitation to guard in Rehovot, thus making it essential to obtain the means to widen the range of activities of Hashomer. Yisrael was ill at the time, and Manya wrote this letter on his behalf to the Chovevei Zion Foundation* in Russia:

Most honored Mr. Ussishkin:

On the 13th of October, we sent you a balance sheet of Hashomer for the past year. Last week in Jaffa, we met with Dr. Chissin (who was then the Russian Zionist delegate to Israel) and discussed our critical financial situation, and we join him in asking you to wire us 2,000 francs.

In response to your telegram, we are sending you a short analysis of Hashomer—about its meteoric rise, its multiple needs, and about the urgent requirement to set up a foundation which will free us from our constant supplications to the government. We will speak more of this in the future, but for now we will address the issue of how vital these 2000 francs are for us, which we entreat you to wire us immediately upon receipt of this letter. From the money which Hashomer received this year, we have the following balance:

Surety Fund	4000 F.
Arms	1400 "
Assistance Fund	1300 "
11 horses	30000 "

(One horse was shot in an Arab attack)

From these funds, we owe banks and private individuals more than 3000 francs, which we must pay immediately. Thus, you can see that our entire holdings are 5300 francs, i.e. fewer sources of funds than last year, at a time when Hashomer is expanding throughout the land.

In the preceding year, Hashomer was present in six settlements in the Galilee as well as Hadera. Now, it encompasses the entire lower Galilee, that is, in ten settlements, as well as Hadera and Rehovot. The distance from Tiberias to Rehovot increases the organizational expenses, because of the necessity of travel, relocation, etc. But we are not asking for organizational expenses. Those we will try to cover ourselves as we have in the past. The main issue is that last year we had only 35 Watchmen (23 infantry and 12 cavalry). This year, it will be necessary, within the next three months to enlist at least 100 additional people.

At this moment, we must immediately send 40 infantrymen and 20 horsemen. We also have to outfit an additional 17 foot soldiers and 8 riders. Able and experienced Watchmen are waiting; farms and settlements are demanding guards, but there is no way we can supply them without the funds for weapons and horses. The Watchman is a worker who cannot begin his work without the tools of the trade. The weapons of each foot soldier cost 120 francs (a rifle and pistol). Each cavalry man costs 600 francs (400 for the horse, 50 for feed, weapons 150). Even if we undertake the smallest possible growth, the result is clear:

17 infantry	2040 F.
8 cavalry	4800 F.
Total:	6840 F.

From this you can see, that at this moment, we have to obtain close to 7000 francs to continue to exist.

It would be easy for you to say that "you do not have to extend your efforts if you cannot." However, the critical disadvantage (and in some ways it is an advantage) of Hashomer is that it cannot stop its own growth, just as a young, healthy child cannot stop growing simply because his parents can't afford bigger shoes to replace the old ones that no longer fit. There are conditions present which affect our national honor and our national existence, and you cannot turn your back and tell us there is no money. You have to tell yourself, "I must do this; we have to find the money." You, Mr. Ussishkin, who have adopted as your slogan, "Nothing can stop us if we have the will," will surely understand us.

Despite all this, we are asking for only 2000 francs, although we need much more, since, according to Dr. Chissin, the Odessa Committee will not authorize more, so there is no point in asking for more. These 2000 francs will serve as an advance payment for horses and ammunition. We can pay the balance in 3-4 months, and we will have to obtain those funds somehow.

This is the reality. We are awaiting the money by wire. Otherwise, we cannot fulfill our obligations and we will be silenced. Please understand this, Mr. Ussishkin.

With the deepest respect,
Manya Wilbushevitz
for Yisrael Shochat who is now ill.

12. In Constantinople

In the meantime, I learned that it had been decided that Yisrael travel to Constantinople, as had Ben-Zvi and Ben-Gurion, in order to learn Turkish law. This way they could avoid the costs of attorneys for every land issue and for freeing imprisoned colleagues. Manya was to travel with Yisrael; it was difficult to imagine Hashomer without the two of them, its living spirit.

I myself was about to travel to France to study agriculture, and before my departure, I visited Manya in Haifa. I climbed the wooden steps and opened the door. Manya, who was alone, did not notice me at first, and continued whistling a tune from a classical aria. She even whistled well! Suddenly, she became aware of my presence and spread out her arms to me. I immediately brought up the subject of the trip to Constantinople. She looked at me, wide-eyed, as though she was amazed at how quickly I had heard the news, and informed me that it was Hashomer which had made the decision that Yisrael should study Turkish law, and that she had no choice but to accompany him. They would be taking their son, Geda, with them. They had no financial means and would subsist from lessons in German that Manya would offer. Her voice was sad; parting from her friends would be difficult. But she perked up quickly, assuring me that she would write frequently. From time to time, she would visit Eretz Israel—it would take several years before they would be able to return to the "womb of Hashomer". About my trip to France, she felt that it was necessary to fundamentally prepare a generation of pioneer women in the field of agriculture, so that they could work side by side with the men.

During summer vacation, on my way home to Eretz Israel, I visited Manya and Yisrael in Constantinople. The three students—Ben-Zvi, Ben-Gurion and Shochat—were immersed in their studies. Manya was absorbed in student associations, which included youths from Eretz Israel as well as diaspora youth on their way to Eretz Israel. Her home was the headquarters for the Jewish students in Constantinople, and there I met among others, David Remez, Aharon Binyamini and Gad Frumkin. The Shochats became close friends with Dr. Neufach, a graduate of the University of Constantinople, and with the student Strumza from Salonika, who helped the three in their study of Turkish law, and particularly in their study of the language. Manya had already begun to master the spoken language.

Hashomer matters continued to absorb Manya and, together with Yisrael, she kept up a steady correspondence with Yisrael Giladi and Mendele Portugali from the executive committee of Hashomer. She regularly took part in clarifying the problems of the Watch, and she understood only too clearly the complicated relations that existed between the Watchmen and the neighboring Arab villagers.

About their home in Constantinople, Ben-Zvi wrote:

"Their house was like a club in Eretz Israel; like a living slice of life in Eretz Israel that had somehow rolled into Constantinople. The hours that I spent with them erased the distance between Constantinople and Sejera, between the Bosporus and the fields of the Galilee. In the home of Manya and Yisrael, it was impossible to forget for a moment all that was happening in Eretz Israel, particularly in matters of Hashomer and the party. Their apartment was a kind of liaison office between Constantinople, the Ottoman capital, and Hashomer in Eretz Israel."

While in their home, Ben-Zvi observed an incident which reflected Manya's nature. He saw Geda, their baby, leaning over the apartment window ledge, several stories up and only one step between him and the distant road. Yisrael turned pale and froze on the spot, while Manya jumped up immediately and grabbed the baby by his feet.

Yisrael and Manya saw themselves as emissaries of the settlements of Eretz Israel in this important center, whose task it was not merely to study in the university, but also to develop plans for the future and to build political and personal connections with Turkey. Although Manya was not a student herself, she was well aware of all student affairs and participated in all her guests' discussions. On their table, a map of Eretz Israel was perennially spread out, with arrows pointing to all the governmental land holdings. Together with Jacobson, the director of the Anglo-Palestine Bank in Constantinople, they expended tremendous effort to obtain this land, which consisted of millions of dunams. The negotiations with government officials were long and arduous. Turkey was then at war in the Balkans and needed money itself, but it was not possible to find Jewish money to buy the land. Jacobson made a personal appeal to the Chovevei Zion in Odessa, but it was to no avail.

As the war began between Turkey and the Balkans, Yisrael Shochat reached Anver Pasha, the defense minister. Together with Manya he wrote a memorandum proposing the establishment of a Jewish unit in the Turkish army in order to protect Eretz Israel in emergencies. Although Yisrael was granted a private audience with Anver Pasha, his request was not granted.

During their stay in Constantinople, Manya and Yisrael made contact with "Donmeh," remnants of the Sabbateans*, a group in which both had been interested even while still in Eretz Israel. At the couple's recommendation, one of them was given the Turkish language chair at Hebrew University. Also, a group of English Jews in Eretz Israel bought up the lands of Karkur, and Manya and Yisrael saw to it from afar, together with the other members of Hashomer's executive committee, that Hashomer would take upon itself to guard this land also, with the guarantee of a land settlement of their own.

At the end of 1912, Hashomer took over the watch in Tel-Adash in the Valley of Jezreel. Merchavia had been transformed into a cooperative under the Oppenheimer plan, but our Hashomer members were still responsible for guarding it.

13. Return, Imprisonment and Exile to Turkey

In 1913, Manya and her child returned to Eretz Israel to the bosom of Hashomer. This time, she settled in Rishon LeZion, which had just been taken over by Hashomer. Manya was absorbed day and night in their activities.

Toward the end of 1913, Yisrael also returned, though he had not yet completed his studies. His colleagues had demanded his return and he had responded without hesitation.

The second Hashomer unit in the Valley of Jezreel, Tel-Adash, was an hour's walk from Merchavia. Adjacent to it were Arab huts, separated only by a low, stone wall. The Watchmen brought their supply hut with them from Merchavia, hoping that this new unit would become a village of Watchmen—a kind of central headquarters for Hashomer in which they could work and from which they could go out on guard duty. The first families of Hashomer moved into Tel-Adash, among them Manya and Geda.

In a women's meeting, Manya argued that since their situation required that mothers must work outside their homes, there was a critical need for collective care of the children. Manya was thus one of the first advocates of communal child care.

In that same year, 1913, we were witness to an exciting event: Before Passover, a group of nearly 12,000 Russian tourists arrived to celebrate the holiday in Eretz Israel. We imagined them to be the forerunners of the waves of future immigration. All that year I corresponded with Manya. We were full of dreams and strategies for the new developments which we anticipated. Then World War I erupted. Before the war broke out, I was in an experimental agricultural station outside Paris, but feeling the winds of war, I hurried to Marseille. While at sea, I heard the news that war had been declared between Germany and Austria and between England, France and Russia. Turkey was still neutral.

After overcoming many obstacles, Ben-Zvi and Ben-Gurion were able to return to Eretz Israel, and together we continued to publish our newspaper, *Unity*. The atmosphere in Eretz Israel was tense. From Constantinople, we heard worrisome reports about the expected participation of Turkey in the war and we trembled about the fate of the Jewish settlement, particularly since most of the Jews were subjects of hostile nations. Ben-Zvi, Ben-Gurion and I began a massive effort to naturalize the Jews of Jerusalem, in order to prevent their expulsion as enemy aliens. I worked mostly with women. In Haifa and in the Galilee, Yisrael Shochat, Yehoshua Hankin and Manya devoted themselves to this effort. In Tel-Aviv, Eliahu Golomb and Dov Hos carried on the work. At that time, the idea was conceived to form a national militia. Manya was stimulated by this idea, seeing the possibility of creating seeds of Jewish might in the tradition of Hashomer. The Turkish authorities, however, rejected this proposal and the whole matter went up in smoke.

In October, Turkey joined the war, and a pronounced feeling of hostility emanated from the local Turkish authorities toward the Jewish settlements. In Turkey, there was a massacre of Armenians. In Eretz Israel, rather than encouraging nationalization and establishing a militia—and, in fact, we had proposed one that would consist of Jews and Arabs—waves of decrees fell upon us, followed by imprisonments and deportations. Searches were organized in Tel Aviv for any reason: money, valuables, weapons, food. Prohibitions were placed on the use of Hebrew in the Turkish mails, the display of Hebrew signs and on the use of the stamps of the Keren Kayemet. It appeared that shortly all our organizations would be destroyed and our schools would be closed, as would the Anglo-Palestine Bank. Jamal Pasha, one of the ruling triumvirate of the "Young Turks," was sent to Damascus as Commander of the Suez Front and he became a de facto military dictator over Syria and Eretz Israel. Quickly, the settlements felt his heavy hand and his autocracy threatened their very existence.

During this period, Manya was living in Jaffa with her brother, Gedaliah. When the government agents appeared at the farms and demanded that all weapons be turned over, many frightened farmers complied, but the members of Hashomer went underground and hid their arsenals.

In early December, 1914, Manya was arrested and imprisoned in the French monastery in Jaffa. It turned out that a Jew from Rishon LeZion had informed on her. An Armenian friend, an official in the Turkish government, showed the letter to Manya and warned her to be careful. He would not deliver it to his superiors. But a few days later, a second letter arrived and he told Manya he could no longer avoid passing on the letter.

(Years later, when Manya returned from her exile, the man from Rishon LeZion tried to apologize to her. He said that he had believed that by informing on her he would save the rest of the members of Hashomer).

Her brother Nachum accompanied her to jail in order to protect her from her cellmates. Manya was accused of possessing concealed weapons for Hashomer, and they demanded that she reveal her hiding place. Baha-Al-Din, the recently-appointed regional governor in Jaffa, was a new type of Turkish official, a patriot from the ranks of the "Young Turks," who tried to lessen the Zionist impact on the land, particularly that of Hashomer, hoping in this way to fulfill the new approach of the Turkish government—to pull Zionism out by its roots.

Manya's imprisonment set shockwaves throughout the community and there was much concern for her plight. Not only the ranks of Hashomer and Poalei Zion loved and respected her—the entire populace admired her and had spun legends about her. Their devastation was sevenfold greater when it became known that it was one of their own, a man from Rishon LeZion, who had sent her to this fate. Those involved feared that Manya's incarceration would seal their own fate as well, knowing that she would not hesitate to speak her mind openly regardless of the consequences.

After a number of days, Manya was summoned to the office of Baha-Al-Din to be interrogated. First he started conversing with her in apparent camaraderie, telling her that he had lived in Switzerland during the Russian uprisings, giving her the implicit impression that he might even be pro-Zionist. In her great naivete, she began to get excited and started talking to him as though he were a friend, about her aspirations and those of Hashomer. Since she saw no contradiction between the desires of the Jews and the interests of the Ottoman government, she spoke with total candor, and he listened with complete absorption, encouraging her to continue. Thus Manya broadened the scope of her remarks to include the two thousand years of suffering by the Jewish nation, striving to return to Eretz Israel and rebuild it, and how Hashomer was helping accomplish those goals.

Suddenly, his face seemed to explode with rage, and with clenched fists he shouted: "What? A nation within a nation?!"

On the writing desk was a dagger, and, in a flash, Manya

grabbed it. The official jumped to his feet as though bitten by a snake and dodged about the room in terror. Manya threw the dagger to his feet and exclaimed that he was both a bigot and a weakling. Then she walked out.

News of this episode was widely disseminated throughout the community, but the reviews were mixed: there were those who admired Manya's courage, but there were others who worried that her frank words would serve only to fan the fire of hatred.

An editorial appeared in *Unity* against the new governmental decrees. In its wake the newspaper was shut down, and its two editors, the Ottoman students Ben-Zvi and Ben-Gurion, were imprisoned and sentenced to exile. Other community leaders in Jerusalem, Tel Aviv and Haifa were arrested and sentenced to deportation, including Yisrael Shochat and Yehoshua and Olga Hankin. As for Manya—her trial was to be held in Damascus.

On the day before their deportation, Ben-Zvi, Ben-Gurion, Manya and Yisrael had 24 hours out on bail and, with an escort of policemen, they travelled to the Hotel Amdursky near the Jaffa Gate, inside the wall, to a meeting with the executives of Poalei Zion and Hashomer. During the meeting, the officers stood outside the room. We all felt that this was a fateful session in which we would have to determine our plans of action for the entire period of their banishment. The central members had been sentenced to exile and we who remained would have to focus all our strength to maintain our existence and continue our work. Ben-Zvi and Ben-Gurion were to be sent to Egypt and their intent was to make their way to the United States where they would establish a pioneering volunteer movement. We proposed strategy both for those who would be expatriated and for those who would be left behind. The fragments of conversation and thought in that room led us to a unanimous conclusion that from now on there would be complete harmony between Poalei Zion and Hashomer. And as for our exiled colleagues, they would put all their efforts into obtaining more outside support. We spoke at length about the urgent need for Jewish national strength, laying the groundwork for the Jewish Brigades.

I can still envision Manya's excited expression when we walked out. Encouraged by the proceedings, she hugged me. In the morning, she was visited by her sister-in-law, Gedaliah's wife, who brought her a velvet dress as a parting gift. "You know," Manya said, "that I never pay attention to clothing; I've never cared what I wore. I will admit that I once yearned for a velvet dress, but I was embarrassed by this wish and never mentioned it to anyone, not when I was young or later. Isn't it ironic that today, when I am being exiled, I get my wish for a blue velvet dress!"

The next morning, at dawn, Manya and Yisrael, Olga and Yehoshua Hankin, Strumza and I travelled by wagon to Haifa and from there we continued by train to Damascus.

In Damascus, we stayed in the Continental Hotel. Since Manya and Yisrael were restricted to their room, we stayed with them. Hankin tried to prepare Manya for the trial. Until late at night, he quizzed her, bombarding her with questions she might expect from the Turkish judge. The Arab policeman that accompanied us stood mutely by, understanding nothing.

Strumza strolled through the courtyards of Damascus in order to gather information, and thus he heard that one of the judges was a Turk from the Caucasus who understood Russian. Strumza suggested that we go and speak to him—he in Turkish and I in Russian—in order to try to lighten Manya's sentence. She was accused of three major crimes—treason, possession of Keren Kayemet stamps, and last, but surely not least, possession of the Hashomer weapons.

Strumza discovered the judge's address, where we went. An old woman opened the door and we entered hesitantly. Strumza explained softly that the matter had to do with the rescue of a mother. We found out that the judge was ill and in bed. Perhaps this is good, I thought, maybe he will have a more humane attitude. We asked to be allowed upstairs to see him, and with trembling hearts entered his room. The man looked at us questioningly, raising himself up slightly. I immediately began to speak very quickly, so as not to be interrupted. I presented our request and explained briefly that the accusations against Manya were fabrications, that she had been framed. It was peculiar to be talking about Manya to this stranger—how could he understand? My own voice sounded unfamiliar to me as I spoke to him, as though I had been split in two and was listening to someone else. First I spoke about our resettlement in our desolate land, the land of our ancestors, and I asked him what was Manya's crime? Midstream, I changed my argument. I decided that it would be better to speak to his heart than to his mind and I begged compassion for Manya as a mother, pleading that she should not be sent to prison, but rather to Anatolia with her husband. I looked closely at the judge's eyes and it seemed that his gaze had softened a little. Suddenly, Strumza stopped me, and in elaborate Turkish, begged the judge's forgiveness for this intrusion, expressing his confidence that he would understand our predicament.

When we returned to the hotel, we found Manya sitting serenely. Yisrael and Hankin, by contrast, never stopped haranguing her, testing her repeatedly up to the evening before the trial. For who knew what her fate would be?

The Ides of March, 1915. The day of judgment had arrived. Dawn found us all wide awake, as though we were all to stand trial. Strumza left first, and I went with Manya, accompanied by the policeman.

On our way to the courthouse, Manya started to talk about her past. The same Manya, who never spoke about herself, began to recount her life softly and peacefully. With her unique simplicity, she told us about her childhood, her beloved brothers, her adolescence and her desire to be a proletarian, and about the most bitter and tempestuous chapter in her life—the days of Zubatov. It was as though she were reliving those distant days and a kind of sadness enveloped her as she talked about the depression that had come over her because of her terrible disappointments—until the time she dedicated her life to the protection of an independent Jewish nation. Paying no heed to the surroundings, she descended into the past, thus separating herself from the current reality. We, too, forgot time and place, and were surprised when the policeman informed us that we had arrived at our destination.

Manya was called upstairs. Before very long, she returned and told us with a smile that there had been practically no interrogation. Her sentence was exile—together with Yisrael and the Hankins, she would travel to the Sivas region, not far from the Turkish-Russian border.

The next morning, we parted at the Damascus train station. Uppermost in my mind was the question, how would Hashomer continue to exist without them? After all, from the day of its inception, the work of Hashomer had never been as vital as it was then. It was inconceivable that these people would not be with us in our most desperate time....

Manya was pale and subdued. Here she was, leaving all that was dear to her—Eretz Israel, Hashomer, her little boy—and who knew for how long? This question filled the air around us. Yisrael's face was drawn, but he managed to control his grief. Again he asked me to join the Hashomer leadership and to help uplift the morale of the members. In my heart, I felt that these two were simply irreplaceable.

The entire way home, to the train station in Tzemach, and from there to Afula, I was mired in self-doubt, and Strumza and I exchanged few words. In the evening, I arrived at Tel-Adash, at the home of Hashomer. It was a rainy and chilly spring night, reflecting the gloom within me. Ben-Zvi and Ben-Gurion had set sail from the port of Jaffa while I had been in Damascus. Without Ben-Zvi and Ben-Gurion in the Poalei Zion movement and without Yisrael and Manya in Hashomer, where would we all end up?

The members gathered in the dining room to hear about the trial. The walls were still not completely up, and a divider of boards separated the eating area from the storage shed. Rain leaked in and the wind blew between the cracks. We sat along narrow tables. Smoke rose from the kerosene lamp, making it hard to distinguish the faces of the people. But there was, despite the general air of gloom, a light that shone from the members' eyes that brightened up the darkness of the room. The whole Hashomer family was there—not just from Tel-Adash but also from the Galilee. There was not enough room to seat them all and many stood. They drank sweet tea from tin cups and chewed on hard bread which was sort of greenish because of the desert grass in the valley's wheat fields. Shmuel Hefter showed no patience and nudged me to speak. Immediately, they all put down their spoons and stopped chewing. All wanted to know about Manya's trial, thirsting after every detail. I omitted nothing, including our trip to the judge's home. "Wasn't that likely to be dangerous for Manya?" asked one of those assembled. I reviewed the entire chain of events, including the pretrial preparation that Yisrael and Hankin had given Manya. When I finished speaking, there was total silence and lingering in the air was the unanswered question: So what if Manya's sentence had been commuted to exile? The main thing was that they could not return!

After midnight, the members scattered and in the corner, surrounding the kerosene lamp, remained the Hashomer executive committee: Yisraelik, Shmulik, Mendele, Zvi and I. Only then, when we started dealing with immediate problems, did we feel the enormity of the responsibility that rested on our shoulders.

When Yisrael, Manya and the Hankin family arrived in Constantinople, they discovered that through the efforts of Henry Morgenthau, the U.S. Ambassador, their expulsion to Sivas had been cancelled, and after a number of days, they were sent to Brusa, only eight hours from the capital. Correspondence with them was spotty at best. We were upset to find out, that while at first Ruppin* had sent a monthly stipend to Yisrael and Manya, suddenly it stopped coming and they had to support themselves with the German lessons that Manya gave to generals' wives. We tried to send our colleague, Isaac Hos, with some money for them, but he never managed to get past Constantinople. Then a similar attempt was made with Dr. Binyamini, who was serving in the army, but he also failed to connect with them because he received no furlough. It wasn't until the early part of 1918, that Yisrael and Manya managed to meet with Hashomer prisoners from Eretz Israel who passed through Constantinople on their way to exile in the Caucasus. It is difficult to imagine the torrents of emotion on this occasion, with all concerned having been the victims of decrees and persecutions. Manya lifted her colleagues' spirits, as usual, even managing to convince Zvi Nisanov, who knew Turkish, to accompany the exiles. Despite their troubles and their state of near-starvation, they somehow managed to keep their hopes up. Manya and Yisrael were also fortified by seeing their friends even in these depressing circumstances.

The four of them spent three years in Brusa. The months became years, and still they were in Brusa. During this period, Manya gave birth to a girl—Anna. From the meager information they received and from the few letters, they learned that the war was still in full force, and that the first to suffer, as usual, were the Jews. Particularly grave was the condition of the Jews in Eretz Israel: starvation, persecutions, decrees and plagues. Yisrael and Hankin were like two lions in a cage, said Manya, yearning fruitlessly for freedom and full of endless schemes for escaping from this crushing exile in order to rededicate all their strength to their land and their people.

In the military hospital in Brusa, there worked a Jewish nurse, a friend of Manya's, whose name happened to be Manya, Manya Zionska. With her help, Yisrael was able to write a letter to the Dutch legation in Constantinople, requesting aid for the British prisoners of war in Brusa, whose condition was unbearable because their food supplies never reached their destination. Following this letter, their situation improved somewhat, and, as a by-product, Manya and Yisrael benefited as well. Thanks to the connections that they developed, the British legation in Constantinople helped them to go to Stockholm as representatives of Poalei Zion of America at the second Poalei Zion convention.

In August of 1918, Yisrael and Manya travelled to Stockholm and in the spring of 1919, after much wandering, they managed to return to Eretz Israel.

14. Return from Exile

I will never forget my reunion with Manya and Yisrael when they finally returned home! At Manya's request, I described in detail the sufferings of the community and, in particular, the hardships of Hashomer during the war years. She was not satisfied until she had heard about each one of the members individually—after all, they were family to her. She was pleased by the fact that the work of Hashomer had been extended from the framework of the Watch to a full-fledged self-defense movement. Manya understood full well the dangers presented by the spread of the Bedouins from the Transjordan, as well as from Turkish army deserters.

With barely suppressed emotion, she listened to our past plans and machinations to retrieve them from exile. I could feel her tension when I recounted how Hashomer worked, inspired by her and Yisrael, ceaselessly preparing the settlements for defense, and how, when Judea was cut off from the Galilee, Hashomer had redoubled its efforts to create the first Shomer division in Judea.

During her temporary stay in Haifa, Manya was devastated to hear about the sudden death of Yisrael Giladi. This is what she wrote to Kaila, his widow:

Haifa, 1919
Kaila, my beloved, dear sister,

I have no words. I cannot comfort you and I cannot speak about other things.

I just found out that your Yisrael is no longer among the living. They kept it from me until now. I am longing to see you and Faigele and to talk with you about your lives now and in the future.

I keep trying to find the time to come to you in Jerusalem, but here Yisrael got sick and after him, our daughter. She has only been feeling better for two days. I have been told that you will be returning to Metullah. Perhaps you can stop by in Haifa on your way? Stay with us for a few days so we can talk with each other and feel close to one another; I probably won't be able to go to the Galilee now.

My darling Kaila and Faigele, what can we do to get together? I embrace you warmly in my grief-stricken heart and love you dearly. Manya

(From the archives of Hashomer, Kfar-Giladi)

In those days, an atmosphere of tension enshrouded the settlement. We had been disappointed in our hopes to liberate the Galilee, and were even more bitterly disillusioned when we discovered that the officials of the British government were working in direct opposition to the Balfour Declaration. Once again, it was perfectly clear to us that the land would be liberated only through our own efforts.

Manya became very involved with obtaining arms for the movement. Her strong stand on this issue influenced our future more than any rhetoric. Hashomer members would travel by train with the regiments from India and, when the passengers would fall asleep, they would hurriedly toss the Indians' weapons out the window and then jump off the train to collect them.

Gershon Fleischer was one of those who worked to redirect the weapons from the Jewish Brigade into the hands of Hashomer. He was in constant contact with Manya who received the arms and took care of their transfer. One day, Yisrael and Manya came to him with a request for a machine gun—not simply a rifle or grenades. This request was as preposterous as asking for a slice of the moon, said Fleischer, considering that in the entire unit there were only four, and those were meticulously guarded. Fleischer was at his wit's end, but he finally decided to meet with two of his cohorts, Motti Braverman and Isaac Altshuler to discuss the problem. The two came to his assistance and told him to bring an army blanket. Fleischer met them in the field and they somehow had brought him the weapon. He wrapped it like a baby in a blanket and rushed to Manya on the small train that ran from Lod to Tel Aviv. Manya told him that she knew who to count on and that his faith in her judgment would now help to insure their security.

Then as always, Manya tried to reach an understanding with the Arabs, but she still felt that the settlement must be prepared to defend itself in any event. The English deceit in the matter of the Balfour Declaration served to encourage the Arabs to oppose Zionism, and the weapons that the British sold to the Arabs strengthened considerably the terrorist movement within the Arab ranks. Manya saw in Hashomer the potential for obtaining armaments for the Jewish community, and in meetings with the Jewish

army unit, devised plans for the risky task of accumulating weapons. It was she who convinced Yitzchaki from Beer-Yaakov to let them use the shack in his vineyard as a cache for weapons. Under Manya's influence, Zipporah Drucker volunteered to guard this storehouse day and night.

15. The End of Hashomer: The Haganah

In March of 1920, Manya and Yisrael viewed with trepidation the situation in Tel-Chai, enlisted volunteers from Tel Aviv and prepared for the terror that was expected in Tel Aviv and its surroundings. She could never reconcile herself to the fact that so few had volunteered to come to the aid of their comrades in Tel-Chai.

A year later, during a memorial for the victims of Tel-Chai, Manya characteristically expressed her opinion. In clear and ringing tones, she said that in her role as a member of Hashomer, her attitude toward death was simple. Judea would not be built with work alone, but with blood, with death; our defenders had fallen and it did not matter where they were buried—what was important was that their death in Tel-Chai had *de facto* delineated our northern border.

The thirteenth convention of Hashomer, held in Tel-Adash on May 18, 1920, was a turning point for the movement.

Members came to this convention from all corners of the land. All were stimulated by their meeting with Yisrael and Manya. I came to Tel-Adash together with Ben-Zvi, who was still wearing his army uniform. We were still dazed by the fall of Tel-Chai and the bloody pogroms in Jerusalem and were on alert for this meeting.

Yisrael and Manya were received with respect and admiration. In their opening remarks, they proposed an idea that took hold among many of our colleagues—that the time had come to gather many more people and to form a broad national defense group. While it was difficult to leave the traditional, secretive framework of Hashomer, Yisrael saw the original Hashomer as the seed from which would blossom the Haganah. Manya regretted losing the intimate atmosphere of Hashomer, but agreed that a broader defense system was necessary.

At the meeting in Tel-Adash, the foundation was thus laid for the formation of the Haganah. Officially, the Haganah was born on June 13, 1920, headed by Yisrael Shochat, Eliahu Golomb, Dov Hos and others. In effect, Hashomer was dismantled at this convention, but, actually, the close connection between this group of comrades remained, some of whom headed the Haganah in Jerusalem, Tel Aviv and Haifa. In all the settlements, the original Haganah leaders came from the ranks of Hashomer.

After the establishment of the Haganah, the third wave of immigration began. The Hashomer leadership, with Yisrael and Manya in the forefront, renewed the concept of a workers' legion, and together with the pioneers of the Aliyah, formed a Workers' Brigade. Manya accomplished much, including obtaining a sizable grant from Hadassah to form a division of the Workers' Brigade in Jerusalem.

16. Terror in Jaffa

During the onset of the attacks on Jaffa in 1921, residents of the narrow streets gathered into groups for self-defense. Their tools of war were very meager: iron rods, stones, bottles, etc.—but no live ammunition at all. On the plus side, the Arab masses were not well-armed either, using mostly knives. It is noteworthy that the Jewish "partisans" compensated in ingenuity for their lack of resources.

Manya was witness to numerous examples of this resourcefulness. She saw, for example, how upon the suggestion of a young boy, the residents of one of the neighborhoods removed all the brass beds from their homes and, within twenty minutes, a fortress was built at the entrance to their alley. Poised on top were youths holding bottles of sulphuric acid which they had removed earlier from a drugstore. When the attacking mob approached them and began to charge, the boys threw the bottles at them. The crowd was seized by panic. Screams punctuated the air and, within minutes, the attackers fled the scene.

In the entrance to another alley, Manya observed a tall, skinny old woman, with a headful of dishevelled, white hair who swung an ax above her head and shouted in Arabic, "Don't come here! Death is here! Plague is here!" The Arabs who had been preparing to break in, became confused and frightened and reversed their direction.

In one of the courtyards, Manya watched as two elderly Jews broke the water pipes which passed through the yard, causing a fierce stream of water to surge at the street. The attackers did not dare enter and fled.

But this kind of unified effort was possible only in streets that were inhabited solely by Jews. In most of the neighborhoods of Jaffa, such as Ajami, Jews and Arabs lived side by side; there, self-defense was impossible. Many of the residents fled to Tel Aviv, others hid out with Arab friends, but the rest were fodder for the rioting mobs.

A Sephardic Jew told Manya an encouraging tale: For many years, he had dwelt with his family in Ajami, next door to a respected Arab family named Abu-Salach. The Jew and the Arab were both small shopkeepers as well as dear friends and their children had grown up together. When the terror began, Abu-Salach hid the adults of his neighbor's family and placed their valuables in a secret place. The children he took home and dressed in his own children's clothing, nailing shut all the entrances to the Jew's house. When the attackers burst into the Jews' yards, zealous neighbors informed them that Abu-Salach was concealing a Jewish family. The terrorists demanded that he hand over the family, but Abu-Salach refused. They beat him with clubs and threatened to kill him, but he simply wept and kept silent. His own wife pleaded with him to tell them the hiding place for fear they would all be killed. His relatives came and begged him to have pity on his own family and even threatened him with excommunication. But Abu-Salach remained silent and when the tide of the attack abated, he managed to secrete the Jewish family out of the neighborhood and into Tel Aviv.

As for Manya, dressed like a nurse and wearing a red cross on her sleeve, she roamed freely through the Arab sections, finding out the latest developments and reporting to the members of the Haganah. Thus, on one occasion, she found herself in the midst of a gathering of thousands of Arabs in a field near the government office buildings in Jaffa. Several held the speaker on their shoulders while he proclaimed that a Jewess had entered the Dome of the Rock Mosque in Jerusalem during prayer time, had thrown a bomb and killed 800 Moslems. (This was a lie, one which the Arabs used again in 1929). The fire of revenge was kindled in their eyes and they burst into the streets near Ajami with the cry "Slaughter the Jews!" Manya was dragged by the crowd for quite a while before she was able to extricate herself.

In the chaos that reigned, several people from the outskirts of Tel Aviv turned to Pinchas Rutenberg, asking him to intercede between the Jewish community and the government and to convince British officials to send some military assistance to the Jewish areas. Rutenberg was the only person who had both the confidence and the courage to negotiate with the government, not as a supplicant but with a sense of national pride. But no tangible results were produced by this negotiation. Promises were made, but help was long in coming and was minimal when it came.

Rutenberg joined the Haganah division in Tel Aviv and its outskirts which was headed by Yisrael Shochat in order to establish some connection between the Haganah and the government. His main request was to evacuate the residents who were unarmed and could not protect themselves, and to relocate them in Tel Aviv. In truth, the members of Hashomer, among them Manya, had no desire to leave and were busy organizing volunteers to help the residents of these desolate areas hold their ground. They had one overriding principle: Do not leave any settlement. In order not to offend Rutenberg, they did not argue with him and pretended to heed him, while in fact they continued their own plans.

They decided to bring ammunition to the camp of the Workers' Brigade near Petach-Tikvah, which was facing imminent danger. Weapons were unavailable at the time, so Yisrael sent them an interim supply of grenades. To help organize a self-defense unit he sent Zvi Nadav, Aryeh Abramson and Motti Braverman. Manya was assigned the task of delivering the grenades. She filled two large baskets with the grenades, camouflaging them with eggs and vegetables. It was very difficult to get a car, because drivers were afraid to travel on the dangerous roads. There was not even a paved road which led directly to the camp and part of the way was extraordinarily bad. Finally, she managed to secure a driver, Abrashka. After the situation was explained to him, he agreed to help, despite the fact that he was literally trembling with fear. His car was small and undependable, but there was no alternative. They set out early in the morning. As long as they were on a paved stretch of road, all was well. But near Petach-Tikvah, the car sank in the sand and all efforts to free it failed. Suddenly they noticed horseback riders approaching. It was a patrol of about eight Indian soldiers— part of the English units that remained in the land after the war— their task being to prevent the smuggling of arms. The friends understood that all was lost if they were searched. In panic they became immobile. Suddenly, an idea grew in Manya's mind. She ran towards the riders and, speaking to the officer-in-charge in halting English, told him a heartrending fabrication that concluded by asking him to help pull the car out of the sand. Sure enough, the officer believed the story and instructed his men to dismount and extend their help. At first, the soldiers worked grudgingly and made little progress, but after Manya treated them to the cigarettes and candy which she had brought for the members of the camp, they began to work enthusiastically and earnestly. Within a short time the car was extricated. Meanwhile, Manya watched over the two baskets, making sure that the "eggs" would not break. The members of the patrol escorted them until they reached level ground and they all parted as friends.

In the afternoon, the group reached the camp and the baskets were brought into the kitchen. Most of the residents had not yet returned from work. They soon learned that half an hour before the group had arrived, there had been an attack on the camp. Bullet holes could be seen on the walls of the kitchen and dining room. They were quite sure that there would soon be a repeat attack.

The dining room was constructed completely of wood except for one corner which was built out of large stones—a remnant, no doubt, of some ancient structure. In this corner was an oversize, belching stove, from which smoke emanated. Standing next to it was a charming girl of about seventeen making pancakes out of some unrecognizable ingredients. Her bright eyes were darting; her nose and cheeks completely covered with soot. As she served the pancakes, Manya told her that the attack was likely to be renewed any moment and that she should stand somewhere else, pointing out that bullets had already pierced the walls on all sides. The girl answered her proudly, in Hebrew laced with Russian, that there was no place that was more secure. She herself had found this spot and had moved the stove to it. This corner was a fortress; soon the boys would be returning from work, and as they would be starving, it was necessary to prepare something for them to eat. She was now responsible for the kitchen since the first cook was sick, she would not move from her place until her work was completed. Then she asked Manya her opinion of the pancakes, insisting she still did not know how to cook well. You, thought Manya, are our fortress; if we had many like you, we would conquer all our enemies, without and within.

The three friends remained in the camp, while Manya returned with Abrashka to Tel Aviv. That day, Arabs attacked the Jews in Ajami. Immediately, Manya turned to Rutenberg, asking him to obtain for her an army transport van in order to remove the wounded from Ajami. She thought it would be impossible to send a Jewish vehicle, as the frenzied crowds would surely attack the wounded and finish them off. Rutenberg was somehow able to obtain a large army transport and two stretchers. The driver and his assistant were English soldiers. Four boys wearing khaki clothing volunteered to come along to help find the wounded and transfer them to the car. Before noon, the group set out with neither a doctor nor a nurse. The drivers had received orders to return to camp by seven o'clock in the evening. At first they were able to progress quickly since most of the wounded were close to the streets where a car could pass (most of the alleys in Ajami were traversable only by donkey). The car filled quickly, even though most of the injured had to be loaded on by stretcher. Meanwhile, Arabs started to surround the car, and since the drivers were becoming extremely nervous, they lay down the wounded quickly, one on top of the other. The car went to Tel Aviv and returned, but then the troubles began: Two of the four boys that had volunteered that morning did not return, and one of the stretchers was broken. Manya gave baksheesh to an Arab boy who brought her to a place far from the main street, in the heart of Ajami, where men and women were stretched out on cellar floors, writhing in pain. Moving the wounded exhausted their strength and patience because the place was so remote. The driver needed to return to camp and it became clear that he would not wait.

Suddenly someone noticed an old couple lying in a filthy corner of the courtyard. Both of their legs were broken and they had suffered many knife wounds. Manya told the old woman that first she would be removed with the stretcher and that afterward they would come back and get her husband, but the old woman stubbornly refused—they both must be removed together, at the same time, or both be left to die together. They had been together for forty years and would not be parted now. Manya explained that the stretcher was weak and it was impossible to take them both together and she asked the old man to agree to go first. But he too refused. Manya's assistant, a tall, strapping boy who seemed to have a permanent smile fixed to his face, became nervous and began to yell at the old people, but to no avail. Finally, he thought of an appropriate Biblical verse which influenced the old man. The helpers swore to him that they would immediately return to get his wife and he finally agreed to go first. When they reached the car with the old man's stretcher, the driver refused to wait for the old woman. Manya and her assistant pleaded with him to wait just a quarter of an hour and they ran back to fetch her. Suddenly, they realized they were lost. Neither of them was familiar with Ajami, and for a long time they wandered in the narrow alleys, with an iron determination to find the old woman. When night fell, they decided to separate, agreeing that if one of them found her, he would stay with her so that she should not feel she had been betrayed. In the morning, they would somehow find a solution. Manya wandered alone for some time. Along the way, the only living creatures she passed were a few cats. Finally, having no more strength left to walk , she sat down on the ground, leaned against a wall and fell asleep. When the sun rose, she awoke, and to her amazement found that she was in the vicinity of the yard in which they had left the old woman. She entered the courtyard and found her there huddled in the same position she had been, but with the breath of life gone. Manya gave a few pennies to an Arab boy who helped to bring her to the main street, from which they would be able to return to Tel Aviv. Once there, she began to search for the old man among the wounded, but soon discovered that he too had died during the night.

Meanwhile, an Arab mob was storming the immigration center. This was serving as a temporary shelter for about eighty immigrants who had just been released from the quarantine which all were required to undergo so as not to bring contagious diseases into the country. The workers at the immigration building managed to secure it with the iron gates which surrounded it, and the attackers were foiled. After a little while, Tawfik Effendi, the Arab chief of police from the Husseini family, knocked at the door, ordering them to open the gates so that the immigrants could be removed to a safer location. The Jews believed him, and opened the gate. As soon as he entered, he gave the signal to his ambushing men who burst into the building and began their slaughter.

Manya heard about the occurrence from an Arab woman. Through unfamiliar roads, all resembling a warring camp, Manya managed to find the building. When she arrived, she found the gate broken. Inside was the stillness of death. The bodies of the dead were strewn all over the house, and nestled among the dead were the living wounded, who had pretended to be dead in case the Arabs would return. In the coal cellar, she found a girl of 12, well and healthy. From her hiding place, she had seen the entire massacre, and it was she who reported to Manya all the details of the event, which had taken place over several hours, including the girl's mother's murder at the hands of the Arab officer.

Manya hurried to Tel Aviv and poured her heart out to Chaim Feinberg who had been appointed to head the immigration center and who had not yet been informed. The dead and the wounded were brought to Tel Aviv and Manya swore to take revenge on the Arab officer. The members of Hashomer took it upon themselves to bring him to justice; in fact, it was not until two years later after an intensive investigation that Tawfik, the chief of police, was executed.

The massacres continued for nearly three weeks. Thanks to actions by the Haganah, occasional interference by the government in some incidents and the natural waning interest of the tired mob, the tensions began to dissipate. Many sobered up, and slowly the mobs dissolved.

Following the events of May 1921, the leadership of the Haganah came to the conclusion that they could not rely on the government. It would be essential to obtain large supplies of arms and to prepare the community for serious defense. The national committee of the Haganah, which had been established in 1920, began to redouble its efforts and in every location defense committees were formed. The central committee was presided over by Yisrael Shochat, Eliahu Golomb and Dov Hos. Manya was involved in obtaining arms and ammunition. Although she refused to participate officially in any of the central committees, she was everyone's inspiration and she devoted all her efforts to the cause.

At the end of summer 1921, Manya appeared in the garden of my school, where I was busy planting seedlings. She was so intent on speaking to me that she did not even let me wash the dirt off my hands, but insisted that I come into the yard with her. The executive council meeting of the Haganah had just been held and she approached me to demand that I travel to America in order to raise funds for the Haganah. Manya spoke with conviction and excitement, but I replied just as heatedly that we should be first collecting money in Eretz Israel, before asking for help from the diaspora. We did not realize how loudly we were arguing and friends who were working in the nursery looked up in surprise—what was happening between Rachel and Manya? What were they fighting about? Manya was so intent on presenting her point to me that she did not notice their smiles. When she did, although she was in a hurry, she spoke briefly with them, sitting on the ground near them, arms outstretched. Who would have believed that some day some of them would desert the land and follow the false idols of Russia, of the communist world....

Manya enjoyed watching their work in the nursery. Feeling suddenly gregarious, she started telling them about the work of Hashomer and its attitude toward women.

It was very difficult to be accepted into Hashomer, especially for girls. Each candidate had to guard for two years and to undergo numerous trials before being accepted for membership. Thus, for example, a prospective member would be asked to deliver a letter; on the way they would shoot at him (above his head, of course) to determine how he would behave in facing an enemy. Girls, too, were given difficult tests.

Because of the secretiveness of the organization, it was not possible to accept every girl, because some could not be trusted to keep quiet. When Manya had been only a small child, she had learned the art of silence when illegal books were hidden in her room. She did not want to know what was being hidden so that she could profess ignorance in the event that she were caught and even tortured. But the secretiveness of Hashomer knew no bounds. A wife of a Watchman knew only that her husband had gone out on the Watch, but she never knew where he had gone or when he would return.

In the early days of Hashomer, there was a feeling of partnership between the young men and women and the women were accepted as self-standing Hashomer members. However, as the number of couples multiplied and women became accepted into the ranks only because of family ties and without any demonstrated talent, a difference in attitude began to prevail. A wife of a Watchman was discriminated against, by not being included in the discussions and decision-making process that determined the course of their lives. Every annual gathering of Hashomer was an important event, a kind of holiday to the members, but the women were not invited to the meetings, only allowed to escort their husbands to the door, while they themselves seethed with humiliation.

Manya could not rationalize this discriminatory attitude toward the women, and many times she raised the issue at their meetings. Still, she could not change the ways of Hashomer.

The lives of the Shomrim were poverty-stricken. They were never paid on time by the farmers, and they often moved from place to place, filling in for their colleagues who had been wounded or killed.

In retrospect, Manya regretted that she had not been able to do more for the women, that she had not trained them properly for their role in Hashomer and that she had not fought more forcefully for their full-fledged acceptance.

She laughed ruefully at the irony that it was not until the last assembly in Tiberias, when Hashomer was officially dismantled, that the girls were accepted as full-fledged members....

From the time that the first ideas of Hashomer had taken shape, the Shomrim dreamed of their own piece of land, especially of settling the borders, a dream that was shared by the women. If they could not participate in the Watch, they could certainly be equal partners in the settlement. Thus were born the Tel-Adash settlement and those in Kfar-Giladi. The evolution to settlement status from a mostly nomadic existence effected a fundamental change in the relationship between the men and women. The women finally found a field of endeavor in which they were accepted as equals. Once they were in their own place, working the land as equals, they eventually took shifts in guarding their settlements as well. Thus, changes in living conditions contributed to changes in attitude.

17. Mission to America

In the summer of 1921, a delegation of the Histadrut was sent to the United States to raise funds for a workers' bank. Members of the delegation included Berl Katzenelson*, Baratz* and Manya. Manya had an additional mission because of her personal connections with the Brandeis people*: to establish a secret fund for obtaining arms. Officially, she was an emissary of Rutenberg*. Knowing that the Brandeis people would help her only if the treasurer of the foundation were someone who was totally trusted, Manya proposed to Henrietta Szold that she accept the position, which Szold did. It was agreed between the two that monies received would be sent to Ben-Zvi or Yisrael Shochat. A short time before the departure date to the USA, Henrietta Szold informed Manya that she was cancelling her agreement, that in her role as president of Hadassah, she had no moral right to undertake an illegal assignment, because if the matter were somehow leaked, it could mean the downfall of Hadassah.

Before embarking to America, Manya asked me to help convince Henrietta Szold to give her at least a letter of recommendation. That evening, I visited Henrietta Szold and we spoke at length about the security situation. She had already heard from Manya about the need for defense against terrorists. Now she ⁰listened carefully, from a desire to truly understand our position. After I finished speaking, she broadened the scope of our conversation to include her desire to reach a state of peaceful coexistence with the Arabs. I remember answering her that while we too were seeking peace, until the Arabs agree, there would be a need for self-defense. We argued the point for quite a while, and it seemed to me that I was somewhat convincing. Henrietta sat down and wrote a letter in which she depicted Manya quite accurately and enthusiastically as a person worthy of assistance. Still, when she handed me the letter, I felt that her emotions were mixed: on the one hand, she wanted to help Manya, but on the other hand, she was hesitant about the matter at hand. I returned home, happy that I had the letter in hand. Early the next morning, Henrietta Szold appeared on my doorstep with a tense face. Fearfully, she asked me if I had already sent the letter because she regretted writing it. All night, she had lain awake thinking about it and had finally reached the conclusion that she could not in clear conscience recommend to Brandeis that Manya be assisted in raising money for the Haganah. She was very relieved when I returned the letter to her.

Manya later wrote the following about her trip to the States:

Before I even finished telling our friends about Szold's refusal, I knew that plenty of troubles were awaiting me. Baratz and I arrived in New York first and Berl somewhat later. We were waiting for the opening of the fund drive for the Bank Hapoalim. Meanwhile, I devoted all my persuasive efforts toward the Brandeis group to convince them to support the arms fund. It was difficult to win them over, since they were not accustomed to supporting "illegal" activities, but they, too, had learned something from the terror of 1921. After two months had passed, they pledged $20,000 for the arms fund, but then the question arose as to whom to send the money in Eretz Israel. Alexander Aaronson, who was well-accepted by the Brandeis contingent, started propagandizing intensively against our mission; while the fund was important, he felt that sending the funds to Ben-Zvi and Shochat was destined to cause more harm than good. They decided to address an authority in Eretz Israel in order the clarify the issue and asked me to recommend an Israeli consultant. I suggested Rutenberg, knowing that they already respected his opinion. And then, the most aggravating thing occurred. The link between the Brandeis group and Eretz Israel was Emanuel Mohl, and he delivered a telegraphic response: 'Personal confidence in Manya Shochat. Stop mission. Await letter.' Several more weeks passed before a letter was received by a special messenger. The letter explained that for political reasons, any action connected with arms was most dangerous at this time. Until the Balfour Declaration would be ratified, should any of this leak out, it could be most harmful. I was not told who wrote the letter. I was most agitated. I felt that Aaronson's hand was in this somehow and wrote about the whole matter to Rachel Yanait. From her answer, in which Rachel described the successful action of the Haganah in Jerusalem on November 2, I finally realized that it was Rutenberg who had pulled the plug on us. I was shocked. What had happened to Rutenberg? After a while, the whole matter was cleared up by Henrietta Szold. When Rutenberg had returned to Eretz Israel, he had heard that we had reached

Henrietta Szold (he did not know that she had changed her mind at the last moment). Insulted and angered that an agreement was made with Szold without asking him and that he had not been asked to be the treasurer of the foundation, believing that the effort could succeed only if he was at the helm, he had chosen this subterfuge to undermine the entire effort and had sent that letter. The whole mission was thus brought to an abrupt halt. The money was frozen in the bank, and only at the end of the year did Alexander Aaronson (Aaron's brother) succeed in convincing the board of the fundraising group that Rutenberg had been incorrect in his political assessment. There was a definite, pressing need to arm the settlements, and there were no better candidates for this job than the settlers themselves. The money was ultimately transferred to the young members of Zichron Yaakov. After these events, I did not speak to Rutenberg for many years. Despite his letter, however, I managed to personally collect several thousand dollars from friends who were apolitical. I sent the money via Vienna to Yisrael Shochat, and he and his friends, Fleischer and Shmulik Hefter bought the weapons and took care of their delivery to Eretz Israel. In the fall of 1922, we completed our assignment for Bank Hapoalim...Dr. Magnes helped a lot. I returned home to Kfar Giladi.*

Fleischer recalled that when he had travelled to Vienna, he had received only 18 liras for travel expenses, and that when he arrived at his destination, he was literally penniless. He had Manya's address in America and to whom would one turn if not to her? And, true to form, she quickly wired him a thousand dollars, and he was thus able to begin funding his procurement activities in Vienna.

18. Kfar Giladi: Personal Life and Love

In 1921, The members of Kfar Giladi returned to rebuild their homes out of the rubble and Manya hurried to join them with her children; Yisrael remained alone in Tel Aviv. Despite his basic respect for Manya, a deep sorrow gnawed at her soul because of his relationships with other women.

Manya suffered a great deal from Yisrael's change in attitude and from their loss of intimacy, but she bore the situation stoically, never uttering a word of complaint. One day, in the early 1920's, she suddenly took to bed in Kfar Giladi. Although she was sure that no one knew the reason, her close friends were quite aware that this had been a case of attempted suicide. One of her friends heard from the doctor that she had swallowed a massive dose of poison pills, and that she had been saved only by her own strong constitution. Apparently, the dissolution of her family life had created such a void in her that, at the time, she felt she had no other recourse. But her life in Hashomer and in the Haganah and her love for others stood her in good stead and eventually enabled her to find new strength.

Ironically, before she had completely recuperated, Manya received a message that Yisrael was ill. She immediately left her bed and her home, travelled to him and nursed him back to health. There was no other woman in Yisrael's life at that point; he was then living alone. It was Manya, only Manya—until he got back on his feet. Once he was fully recovered, Manya returned full time to her activities for the fulfillment of her dreams. It was no family life, yet it was a firm partnership based on mutually held aspirations.

Manya loved Yisrael deeply, not only as her husband, but also in his public persona. She respected his every utterance, his every idea, and she often credited him with initiatives of her own.

When she would come to Tel Aviv from Kfar Giladi on community business or for the Haganah or Aliyah Bet, she did not always go to see Yisrael. But whenever a new idea came to him, he would immediately call Manya and she would go to him. Thus compromises were made, but her suffering continued.

Kibbutz Kfar Giladi was the home of Manya and her children and when it came time for her son Geda's bar mitzvah, Manya held a big party. For this event, Yisrael also attended. Manya spoke warmly and simply and then presented to Geda a set of tefillin and a revolver. To this day, this ritual is followed in Kfar Giladi.

Manya was the spirit incarnate of Kfar Giladi. For many years, she kept the books as she had done earlier in Sejera. In addition to her work with the finances of the kibbutz, she also kept up ties with all the settlement institutions—the Zionist Executive and I.C.A. In her role as representative of the farm, she demanded additional land and a guaranteed stipend. She developed a relationship of mutual understanding with the FICA official, Frank, from Alsace. Rumor had it that Manya had turned the icy-tempered Frank into a Zionist. Frank would advise Manya on general problems of settlement and he extended a great deal of assistance to Kfar Giladi.

In those days, there was no division of labor, and it was not until 1933 that the accounting was done in a more organized manner. Manya served as the accountant and the external affairs liaison and a bit of everything else as well, while continuing to compile data on every branch of the settlement, often working until late at night. While she was no agronomist, she grasped the heart of a problem, and with the help of her mathematical proficiency and her friends, she was an integral part of all strategic planning.

While she was deeply involved in long-range decision making for the settlement, she was at the same time a full participant in the day-to-day work of the kibbutz. Although Manya was already overburdened with her clerical chores, she felt obligated to be a part of the "real" work as well. As soon as she would finish her office work or when she would return from a trip, she would immediately join the others, sometimes in the kitchen, but more frequently in the laundry shack. Every friend who happened to come to Kfar Giladi knew that that was the most likely place to find Manya.

Manya worked in the kitchen like the other girls, changing from her business clothes to the standard work uniform: corduroy trousers and a colored blouse from the storeroom. Together with the other girls, she would worry about what to cook. There were fifty people at that time in the kibbutz. Bread was scarce. There was no cooking oil. Manya invented a new delicacy: She would clean the crumbs off the table and, when she could get hold of a little oil, she would fry the bread crumbs with onions and eggs and make a sort of pancake. She made these pancakes so often that people got sick of them. But Manya was proud that she had devised a way to use every crumb of bread. She had her own inimitable style in every task; every menial job was a challenge to her. In the kitchen, she was constantly trying to prepare less expensive dishes and in the laundry, she would experiment on ways to save soap and water.

As to her living arrangements, she shared rooms with the other women. Until the day she died, she never had nor wanted her own room; she was a true kibbutznik to the end.

In its early years, the economic conditions of the kibbutz were very poor. The lands received from the I.C.A. were infertile and the crops were meager, particularly so because the settlers did not yet fully understand the influences of the climate on agriculture. The farm was in the very early stages of development after its destruction in the terrible days of 1920 and the saplings did not yet bear fruit. Scarcity reigned in every area and the settlers were in a state of near-starvation. There were practically no vegetables; fruits were completely nonexistent and there were not even enough milk and eggs for the children. As treasurer, Manya combed the streets of Haifa, Safed and Jaffa searching for loans and wrestling with suppliers for the staples of existence.

She would never forget one particular day in the kitchen. It was winter and rain was falling. The kitchen workers were waiting for a delivery of staples from Haifa, already two weeks overdue. The pantry was completely depleted—no beans, rice, oil, tea, or sugar. There was one last serving of bread and onions: many onions, because that had been the only successful crop that year. No one cooked that day because there was nothing to cook. Sadly, they spent their time scouring the kitchen and the dining room. Manya placed the bread and onions on the table. It was almost noon and the men would be returning from the fields, tired and hungry, and there was practically nothing to eat. The girl in charge of the kitchen ran out, crying, while Manya remained sitting there, her eyes bright with unshed tears.

Just then, Yerachmiel Lukacher-Horzo ("Horzo," because he was from the Horzim, converts long ago in Russia) entered the room. They all called him Luka. He was the youngest member of the kibbutz, a stout-hearted young man, completely devoted and loyal, ready for self-sacrifice without hesitation. As a very young boy, he had come alone from Astrachan in Russia to learn in the high school in Tel Aviv. At the beginning of World War I, he had enlisted in the Turkish army, where he rose to an officer's rank. When the war ended, he joined the ranks of Hashomer at Kfar Giladi. Manya was very fond of him, because he was always ready to undertake assignments, carrying them out quietly and responsibly. It was he who was responsible for implementing the execution in 1923 of Tawfik, the treacherous chief of police from Jaffa.

Luka saw Manya's drawn face, and asked her why she was wearing such a scowl. Manya, full of bitterness, poured out her heart to him: "There is no food! Soon the men will come from work—what shall we give them? The situation is worsening from one day to the next, and it is very hard to go on." Luka looked her in the eye, and in a cheerful voice, as though Manya had just given him some good news, replied that this was no tragedy. Nothing terrible would happen if they did not eat for a few days—they would not die, and they would not even harm their stomachs. "And," he concluded, "don't you know that we are nothing more than the fertilizer for the next generation?" Manya stared at him blankly, and then she burst out laughing. He was right! From Luka's perspective, their daily struggles were hardly earthshaking.

When the men returned from the fields for lunch, Manya stood up before them and, with a big grin, said, "Friends, there is nothing to eat! We have not cooked. The food has not arrived from Haifa. All you have is bread and onions. But don't worry! Luka says that all we are anyway is fertilizer for the next generation!"

There was a moment of stunned silence. Suddenly, one of the boys picked up a large onion from the table, walked to the center of the room, and burst into song and dance: "Luka will build the Galilee! God will build the Galilee!" This turned out to be the merriest lunch in the history of Kfar Giladi.

The terrible financial straits of the kibbutz had been caused by problems other than the poor quality of the land and the settlers' lack of experience: Aliyah Bet and arms procurement. The illegal immigration, Aliyah Bet, had placed a tremendous economic burden on the kibbutz and the work in these two critical areas required that the skills of the most gifted members be diverted from farming.

19. Aliyah Bet: The "Illegals"

From the beginning of 1921 until 1934, nearly the entire illegal immigration passed through Kfar Giladi, while the kibbutz received no outside assistance whatsoever.

The Mandate government had granted less than twenty percent of the permits required for immigration; yet, at the same time, hordes of Arab workers were streaming unhindered through Eretz Israel's open borders. The Jewish Agency had to do battle for each authorization. In Poland, the need to escape was so great that people sought any and all means to enter Eretz Israel. Responding to the exigencies of the moment were groups of "con artists" who perceived the desperate situation and who, for large retainers, sent the would-be emigres to Beirut as tourists, convincing them that their "offices" in Beirut would supply them the necessary visas for entry to Eretz Israel. When they would arrive in Beirut, the "tourists" would discover that they had been duped, having no choice at that point but to hire Arab border runners, who would promise to bring them into Eretz Israel. Their real troubles would then begin. For the most part, the Arabs would lead them in at night through the mountains, rob them of their few remaining possessions and leave them there on their own, telling them that if they continued to walk, they would eventually reach a Jewish settlement.

On the northern border, a special police force of Arabs was posted, whose job it was to capture these immigrants. These guards would receive three liras salary per month plus one shilling bonus for each captive. Clearly, their motivation was great and they guarded the borders day and night.

The situation deteriorated still further when Hyamson, the highest Jewish official in the Mandate, was appointed head of the immigration bureau. Hyamson fought the illegal immigration and there was severe punishment awaiting those who either hid the immigrants or helped them. For this battle, Hyamson assembled a police dragnet and most of the hapless immigrants who got lost in the mountain ranges fell into their hands. They would then be sent to prison where they sometimes remained for five or six weeks until they revealed their country of origin, at which point they would summarily be deported at the expense of their native country's.

Despite all this, there were those lucky ones who found their way to Kfar Giladi. The kibbutz members housed them, fed them and concealed them from the police until they could be transferred to safety. The biggest problem was getting them through the customs station in Rosh Pinah, where the English officials painstakingly examined each passerby. There was no other route south. Much initiative and resourcefulness was needed to overcome Hyamson's decrees. In the government, it was well known that the kibbutz people were importing arms and assisting Aliyah Bet, and inspections were held frequently. The arms cache was never found, but, on a number of occasions, the government agents appeared just at the moment that a group of immigrants arrived and they would be arrested together with the kibbutz manager. It was completely logical that Kfar Giladi would serve this purpose since it was the only Jewish unit near the northern borders, other than at Metullah which served as the seat of the army and the government. The border runners in Beirut, for whom Aliyah Bet was a source of income, knew that the people of "Tachshiba", Kfar Giladi, would not desert the immigrants and would pay for their safety. They took full advantage of the situation.

Sometimes the immigrants would arrive and demand rooms in "Hotel Kfar Giladi" because in Beirut they had prepaid for rooms and good food in this mythical hotel. This, while the members of the kibbutz were still living in the haylofts of the stable.

Among the immigrants were refugees from Russia who came with no possessions. Most died along the way, and only a few reached Kfar Giladi with their last ounce of strength.

Each year the tide of immigration rose and there were many days when the "guests" exceeded the residents who numbered about eighty at the time. Each such immigrant group—and they included families with children—was a heavy burden on the kibbutz. The kibbutzniks themselves did not have enough food, but they were forced to share with the immigrants who sometimes had to be hidden for eight or nine days until an opportunity arose to pass them through Rosh Pinah. Manya waged a continuous campaign with the Jewish Agency for monetary assistance to support the "visitors." The answer was always negative. She and a friend compiled statistics, presented them to the Jewish Agency administrators, but she almost always received a reply of the following type: "We should not encourage unsupervised illegal immigration." Period. Hyamson threatened that every illegal immigrant who became known would only cause the government to issue one less legal visa. The Jewish Agency would simply not get mired in this complicated issue. And when Manya would pose the difficult question, what should be done: the kibbutz was small and its financial condition dire, the officials would reply that the kibbutz was not required to accept the immigrants since they had not been invited. Henrietta Szold was the only one of the lot who expressed sympathy, but she did not have the means to help. Nachum Horowitz, who spent a great deal of time in Beirut obtaining weapons, saw the utter confusion involved in smuggling the immigrants into Eretz Israel and proposed a plan which would have prevented the capture of so many. To put his plan into action, they would need a stipend of 25 liras monthly. Manya presented his plan to the Jewish Agency, but was rebuffed. Only once was help extended when Henrietta Szold donated 50 liras to establish a fund for the new pioneers.

Many kibbutz members became discouraged and began asking themselves if indeed the kibbutz was really responsible for the entire burden. In one stormy meeting, the question was raised as to whether they should continue to help or should terminate their activities. The ensuing debate was bitter and angry and no resolution was reached. Finally, it was said that the question would be dropped if one member would volunteer to care for the new immigrants as a personal assignment. There was a dramatic silence. Then Chaya Krol stood up and said quietly that she would assume this responsibility. There was an embarrassed hush and the members started drifting quietly away as though they were sorry the whole matter had been raised. From then on, Chaya Krol together with Manya took care of the orderly transition of the immigrants and the burden was somewhat lightened for the others.

Once a group of two Russian men and one woman arrived at the kibbutz—the sorry remnants of a group of fifteen people who had spent eight months in transit. The woman was very ill and Manya was determined to transfer her at all cost lest she die in the kibbutz. The woman's brother, also an illegal immigrant, was awaiting her in Tiberias but there was no apparent way to avoid the scrupulous inspection in Rosh Pinah. As luck would have it, a luxurious car arrived at the kibbutz that day in which were two important tourists from America. While these visitors went touring the grounds, Manya spoke earnestly to the driver and convinced him to place the woman in the trunk without saying a word to the tourists. She felt that there would be enough air to last the woman until Tiberias. The trunk was not large, but the woman was small and emaciated, and they finally succeeded in placing her inside. Manya asked the tourists to give her a lift to Tiberias and they gladly agreed. The whole way, Manya told them about the illegal immigration to Eretz Israel. After they passed Rosh Pinah safely, Manya asked the driver to stop the car and open the trunk lid. The woman was completely delirious and with difficulty they managed to extricate her. Manya revived her, begged forgiveness from the tourists and explained the whole matter to them. The tourists became very emotional upon hearing the story and promised to speak to the Jewish Agency about the terrible problems. Unfortunately, instead of going to the Jewish Agency, the tourists decided to go directly to Hyamson to complain about the government regulations. In their naivete, they mentioned Manya's name, in order to prove the veracity of their claims.

A few days later, Manya was summoned to an interview with Hyamson. The conversation was open, serious and one-sided. Hyamson explained his position and claimed that Manya and her friends were nothing more than empty-headed idealists who were undermining the law of the land. Their work in arms procurement and illegal immigration might stem from patriotism, but without law and order it would be impossible to build a national homeland. Things had to happen gradually and deliberately in concert with the government. Manya and her cohorts were destroying faith in the government. Although he respected their motives, Hyamson would fight them at all costs.

Most of the administrators of the Jewish Agency as well as much of diaspora Jewry displayed such a negative attitude that it was not surprising that the members of the kibbutz felt a sense of isolation and despair. Their only consolation was that their children were being brought up in this atmosphere and that for them it was self-evident that their kibbutz had as much at stake in obtaining weapons and reclaiming immigrants as it had in producing crops.

On a cloudy spring day in 1927, Manya came from Tiberias in a wagon loaded with wooden planks and food staples. Passing through Jachula, they met up with another kibbutz wagon driven by Dov Krol, who was then about fourteen years old. They had just begun talking when three wild-eyed men and a woman ran toward them, looking as if they had just escaped from a mental hospital. When they got close to Manya, they collapsed from exhaustion and begged her to hide them from the Arab police who were following them. Twenty-nine people had crossed the border and all had been caught, but these four had struggled with their captors and had managed to escape. Manya did not know what to do because the area was completely open, not even a bush in sight and she wearily turned to Dov for advice. Dov smiled and quickly steered the mules over to one side. The sudden jolt caused the wagon to turn over and all the hay spilled out on the ground. At lightning speed, Dov had the four of them lie down on the damp ground, covering them with a giant stack of hay. Just a few moments later, eight breathless policemen appeared and asked if they had passed four people who had escaped from them. Dov unhitched his mules and replied that yes, four people who looked insane had just run past toward Jachula. The policemen were near collapse themselves and sat down near the haystack to rest, cursing the skies for their misfortunes, their lack of livelihood and the rotten government that paid only one shilling per captive. After a short rest, they continued on their way to Jachula. Dov looked around cautiously and, when he was convinced that there were no more unwanted visitors, he suggested that they put the people into the wagon and get out of there quickly. The hay was removed from the refugees, they lay down in his wagon, the kibbutz friends removed several boards from the other wagon and piled some more hay on top of them. Manya joined Dov in his wagon and within two hours they arrived at Kfar Giladi. Pleased that he had fooled the government lackeys, Dov freed the refugees from their prison and hurried back to the place to gather the remaining hay because evening was approaching and it was beginning to rain.

Soon the Mandate government did not content itself with Arab police and began to send British officers who could not be bought for three liras a month. These police rode horses and did not tire as quickly as the Arabs. To everyone's dismay they came often to Kfar Giladi, wandering in and out of the houses, searching for new faces.

Once a group of frightened immigrants arrived at the chicken coops of the kibbutz. It was Manya's assignment at that time to be on the lookout northward all day and to hide new arrivals in the chicken coops. Suddenly, breathless runners appeared with the news that the police were on their way. What to do? How to hide them? Inside the coops was a big pile of corn, and near it some empty sacks. Quickly, each person was put into a sack, and all the kibbutz members who were there began to cover them with ears of corn. At that very moment the police arrived, stiff-backed and dignified. When they reached the coops, their noses contorted from the unsavory smell, they gave a cursory glance inside and left quickly.

A memorable group of immigrants from Syria arrived after wandering aimlessly all night. The group included men and women who were starving and thirsty, blood-stained from the road and carrying babes-in-arms. Two Arab policemen found them and wanted to arrest them, but some of the girls who were working in the vegetable gardens started to flirt with the police and they were finally able, with the help of some baksheesh, to free them.

The illegal immigration through Kfar Giladi continued for many years. One of the groups that Manya remembered fondly was a Hashomer Hatzair contingent from Belgium, all of whom were diamond polishers. These immigrants, who were smuggled first to Ein Horesh, eventually founded the diamond industry in Netanya.

The kibbutz kept statistics on all the people who passed through. In order not to inflate the figures, those who arrived in the first three years were not included because accurate records had not begun to be kept during that period. In total, eight thousand pioneers passed through the portals of Kfar Giladi until the Haganah took over the responsibility.

20. The Haganah and the Shochats

Yisrael Shochat, Shmulik Hefter and Fleischer spent the year 1921 in Vienna buying arms. This activity, which had been initiated by Hashomer, was carried out with the full knowledge of the Haganah. Despite their common goals, there was some inevitable friction between the Hashomer contingent and the leading members of the Haganah, Eliahu Golomb and Dov Hos, who resented the Hashomer dominance in this realm. From time to time, suspicions arose that information had been concealed, such as the occasion when Shmulik sent rifles and ammunition inside beehives which were dismantled in the Haifa port, causing a great loss for the Haganah. Many such conflicts arose.

During this period, Manya and her children were in Kfar Giladi. She continued her periodic trips to Tel Aviv and Yisrael continued to consult her on Haganah and arms procurement matters.

Under top secret conditions, with only a few members involved, a unique arms cache was constructed in Kfar Giladi—the British police never uncovered it despite frequent searches. Carved out of a cliff, ten meters deep, this was the largest storehouse for weapons in the land. It was a 5 by 5 meter square and it was 2 meters high. Shelves were built into the walls for ammunition and other paraphernalia. Around the dig site were piled large bundles of straw, high enough to conceal the goings-on even from the uninvolved kibbutz members. A hidden entrance through the stable led to the cache, which had been built according to the blueprints of Gedaliah, Manya's brother.

In 1924, with the assistance of David Fish, Manya and Yisrael established the first arms factory in Afula, under the cover of a workshop for the repair of farm equipment. In this factory, bullets and interchangeable parts for weapons were manufactured.

Another project which was implemented by Manya and Yisrael was the birth of an infant air force. With the help of Dov Hos,

Yisrael put into motion a plan for the use of gliders for surveillance. Manya's part in this was to enlist a small group of volunteer pilots, which was called "The Flying Camel" and was centered in Kibbutz Afikim.

In 1926, the members of Hashomer, under the direction of Yisrael and Manya, instituted the first military academy in Kibbutz Tel-Yosef.

By the years 1927-28, most of the settlements had Haganah units, many of whom included the original Hashomer members.

The members of Kfar Giladi obtained weapons by all means possible—from the Bedouins, from Metullah, from Beirut—and the cache grew silently and steadily.

The terror of 1929* broke out suddenly throughout the land and the members of Kfar Giladi were then in a position to send both arms and experienced soldiers to other units throughout the country. Manya was responsible for the shipments, and through her efforts, they successfully reached Haifa, Safed and units in the valley.

21. 1929 in Haifa: New Schemes and New Friendships

Manya's inner tranquillity and her ever-present certainty as to her own rightness continued to give her the strength to brush aside obstacles and devise ever more ingenious schemes.

Astrakhan, a Haganah member from Haifa, agreed to allow Manya not only to use his van for arms transports but also to be her driver. Jenka Wilbushevitz, Manya's brother Moshe's son, was a gifted engineer who converted the van to resemble an ambulance but with secret compartments for weapons. Manya wore a white dress with a red star of David and Jenka played the role of a doctor touring the Galilee settlements. Others acted as "patients", and thus Manya was able to transfer arms from Kfar Giladi.

During one of their trips, the "ambulance" was stopped by a British unit conducting a search of all vehicles entering Haifa. They were carrying a particularly large shipment and the passengers were understandably terrified. But Manya kept her composure; with a razor, she cut the hands and face of one of her escorts. The English soldiers, convinced that there was a critically ill patient aboard, passed them through quickly without inspection.

One of the "patients", Emek Reinin, recalled another adventure. When the "ambulance" reached Machanaim, they found that the boy who was to remove the weapons had been bitten by a snake. It was urgent that he be brought to Rosh Pinah for treatment, the very place where the central police headquarters were located. Just as they reached their destination, the boy died. They had no choice but to return to Kfar Giladi that night with the weapons. Halfway home, the car broke down. It was pitch black outside and there they were, stuck right near the village of the Hamdun tribe which was known for its zealousness in shooting down passersby. But Manya's presence of mind instilled confidence in the others. Jenka began fixing the car while Manya stood by his side holding a flashlight. Finally, the car was repaired and they continued their trip, but when they arrived at the foothills of Tel-Chai, they were stopped by a French armored car. There was, at that time, an agreement between the English and the French that the latter would patrol the area up to Rosh Pinah. They prepared to search the ambulance. Manya turned to the officer-in-charge and in her quiet and sincere manner explained to him that there were two ill people aboard who could not be delayed. After a moment's hesitation, the officer allowed them to pass uninspected—he was just as affected by her complete sincerity as were all who came into contact with her. She believed so completely that justice and truth were on her side that, if the need arose, she could lie as convincingly as she could speak the truth.

Upon completion of the "shipment," Manya traveled to Haifa and presented herself to the Haganah commander on duty, who appointed her as liaison amongst the various Haganah posts in the area. Dressed as a sister of mercy, Manya spent days and nights transporting arms and other equipment from place to place, with no apparent regard for the dangers involved.

22. Land Redemption

In the year 1921, four friends—Manya, Yisrael, Ben-Zvi and I—expressed their idea of settling the Negev. Weizmann and Ussishkin were opposed, so Manya turned directly to agricultural headquarters:

Jerusalem, 25.7.1925

To the Negev Committee of the Agricultural Center
Jerusalem.

Unfortunately, I am ill and cannot participate in this meeting. Nevertheless, I would like to briefly describe the work that now awaits you.

1) Four members of an executive committee should be chosen to be freed from all other tasks and to devote all their efforts to the Negev question. Without a strong commitment to this effort, our plan will be buried before it has had a chance to be born.

2) These four people must be: Ben-Zvi, Yisrael Shochat, Rachel Yanait, and myself because we have already been working on this project for four years; it is in our blood, and we have decided to dedicate ourselves completely to its fruition. We are all intimately linked to this project and are all needed.

3) Rachel Yanait should be sent to the Congress to fight for the fulfillment of the Negev plan. She will be faced by major obstacles, not the least of which is Ussishkin's complete opposition. He is afraid that raising money for the Negev will interfere with his efforts in America to raise money for the general fund of the Keren Kayemet and Weizmann is similarly afraid for Keren Hayesod. There she will be able to meet with Henrietta Szold and others who already have a stake in this question and receive unofficial approval to begin campaigning for this purpose in America right after the holidays.

Travel expenses will be paid for from the money that Mrs. Lindheim* has donated for this purpose. The agricultural committee has thus far excelled in its refusal to allow political bickering to interfere with its work. I hope that this time as well, it will be above such factionalism and assign this work to those people who are most qualified and most dedicated.

In anticipation of a favorable reply and with respect,

Manya Shochat

And thus the Negev committee was formed with the four members as requested.

We tried, as an experiment, to take over the land of Eilat near Aqaba (Umm Rashrash), by establishing a factory for making art objects out of seashells. Several of our Hashomer friends went down there for this purpose, but the British police arrested them. They did not get discouraged and sent a new delegation to Transjordan with the purpose of getting through to Aqaba. In this delegation were Zvi Nadav, Yigal—who spoke a fluent Arabic— and the researcher, Yosef Braslavsky (Breslavi). They got as far as Karak (Kir-Moav) and visited Petra, but there they were detained and managed to return only with difficulty.

I spent much time touring the Negev with Ben-Zvi under the auspices of the Histadrut and, with Manya's help, we interested Henrietta Szold in the Negev settlement issue. In my role as recording secretary for the Negev committee, I was sent in 1927 to the Fifteenth Zionist Congress in Basel in order to further the matter and and in fact succeeded in securing Stephen Wise's cooperation in our plan.

One of the few devotees of the Negev plan was the millionaress, Irma Lindheim. Manya was able to inspire in her the excitement which she herself felt for settling the Negev. Irma helped in the research of the area, helped to fund the travels of the Negev committee and once even joined them herself in an expedition until Chusiba.

Manya first met Irma at the home of her close friends, the Mohl family. She was very impressed with Irma's personality—Irma was one of a handful of pioneers from the assimilated group of Americans of German descent. Manya had the strong feeling that she represented an entirely new type of pioneer woman. Irma recounted how she had met Stephen Wise and had decided to learn about Judaism at his seminary. From him, she had heard about Zionism and had become filled with the desire to see for herself what was transpiring in Eretz Israel.

Manya invited Irma to Kfar Giladi, and the kibbutz children

immediatedly renamed her Rima. Rima was hungry for every bit of information about Eretz Israel, and therefore Manya planned for her a tour of the lower and upper Galilee settlements and Bedouin camps under the direction of Mordecai Yigal. Astride a horse, Rima gazed at the unfamiliar terrain, heard from Yigal about how the land had flourished in ancient times, and she absorbed the ambience of the landscape, the scent of the plant life and the flavor of the Eastern dialect—without knowledge of either Hebrew or Arabic. She began to feel the special, unique flavor of life in the land and marvelled at the accomplishments of the pioneers who had striven to rebuild the land as their life's work.

Rima spent a great deal of time with Manya and eagerly drank in her tales of Jewish history, her stories about her travels with her brother, Nachum, to Hauran, the legacy of Hashomer with its purpose of creating a life of peaceful coexistence with the Arabs, despite ongoing confrontations. The Watchmen, with their gala pageants on horseback, delighted Rima and with great interest she followed the kibbutz members on their visits to the Bedouin camps and observed the return visits of the sheiks and village heads to the kibbutz. Manya felt that Rima grasped the essence of kibbutz life and that she would no longer be able to return to her New York lifestyle.

And thus it was. After a long stay in the kibbutz and a visit with her children, she decided to settle with the children in Eretz Israel. How delighted Manya was to help them.

During the depression of the 1930's, the Lindheim family was stripped of most of its wealth. Rima's husband, in a state of despondency, took his own life. Rima never seemed to lose hope despite a series of catastrophes which struck her time after time: Her son, Norman, who had immigrated to Eretz Israel after marrying a Jewish girl from Italy, also committed suicide after his wife was killed in an accident; her second son, Dan (Donald), who loved the land like his mother and worked on a kibbutz, died as a U.S. Air Force pilot in World War II. Rima then travelled to her remaining children in America—a son and a daughter—but they did not understand her, so she returned alone to Eretz Israel and joined Kibbutz Mishmar Ha-emek. Eventually, two of her granddaughters followed in her footsteps and made aliyah.

The American Zionist community admired Rima a great deal and offered her the leadership of Hadassah. But Rima had deepened in her Zionist aspirations and strove to put those hopes and dreams into practice. Still, she visited America from time to time, doing much to attract the assimilated Jews from Western Europe towards Zionism, particularly the youth, who respected the fact that she was living according to her principles.

At the culmination of each trip, Rima would hurriedly return to her kibbutz, just like Manya. In fact, there was much similarity between the two of them in their lifestyles and their aspirations, and, not surprisingly, they kept close contact throughout their lives.

In the year 1930, we, Manya, Ben-Zvi and I, went to visit Tel-Shuk (this was government land adjacent to Bet Shean) together with Officer Andrews, an Australian friend. The slogan of the time in the Jewish community was "Another dunam and another dunam" and Manya decided that the time had come to settle Tel-Shuk. The area was rich in water, yet completely barren. The place made an unforgettable impression on us. A desolate ruin, a bubbling spring but parched land, looking like its Jewish inhabitants had just left. My eyes were rooted to the pond, my heart echoing with the heartbeats of the ancient settlers. Manya was delighted that we had brought her there.

During our visit, Ben-Zvi spoke a great deal with Andrews and it seemed to me that even he felt that before us was an ancient Jewish settlement which should be redeemed and resettled. Andrews did all in his power to help us, but, soon after, he was murdered by a gang from Nazareth. How we mourned the death of our good friend!

Year after year, new tragedies befell us, yet Manya was never discouraged. She did not lose her faith that we would manage to redeem our land and it was she who motivated Hankin to acquire Tel-Shuk.

In order to advance the land redemption, Manya initiated the establishment of a joint association of Jews and Arabs—The Jewish-Arab League—one of whose purposes was to acquire unused land without dispossessing the Arabs. There was no support for this idea at the Jewish Agency in Jerusalem and so she decided to enlist supporters outside Eretz Israel while she was serving as a delegate of Plugot Hapoel—the sports division of the Histadrut which was to serve as a national reserve unit for security.

En route to London, she wrote to her friends in Kfar Giladi:

2.11.30
Shipboard

Greetings to my friends in Kfar Giladi!

Tomorrow I will be disembarking at Marseille. The trip has not been too great, because the waters have been rough and I—well you know, I don't love the sea.

Fourth class is not the most comfortable either.

The one good thing that has come out of the trip so far is that I have been able to write some of my memoirs about Hashomer and have sent them to Aaron Feldman.

Sometimes I think I am crazy for taking on the assignment that I have, one for which there is so little hope for success. Everyone seems these days to be totally concentrated on politics, unable to understand anything else.

I am not doing all this as a private person, I am not speaking for myself and there is no group that will support me.

Sometimes I think that I am forced to do what I do and that there is some unknown force pushing me, "nesib" (fate) like the Arabs say.

Peace to you, my friends.

Manya

In 1930, Manya arrived in London, but she had no resources and for quite a while had to sustain herself on one meal a day. And thus she wrote to Eliezer Krol on December 12, 1930:

"...I am healthy, but it is always cloudy here and I cannot seem to adjust to this strange climate. I have no money left—I had hoped to stay with a friend, but it didn't work out, so I am staying in a pension which is costing a great deal. At first, I tried to economize and eat only once a day, but I realized that this was affecting me adversely and weakening me. In this cold, one must eat like all the others..."

About her activities on behalf of Hapoel, she wrote to Kfar Giladi:

...There is here a sports organization "Habonim". A man named Aaron runs it. He was in Eretz Israel once and he has this idée-fixe about the sports movement in Eretz Israel. He created this group of Habonim and he organizes the youth in this direction. He promises to help us, he wants to come to Eretz Israel and work with us. He has good intentions...

I don't get into details with him, but rather request of him to organize Hapoel in the villages, since there are still more than eighty agricultural units where nothing is being done and only Hapoel is addressing this problem."

In London, Manya sought out Jews who would understand that it was of the utmost importance to reclaim the deserted and desolate government land, that only the Jews could bring it back to life.

In 1931, Manya travelled from London to the United States and there too she expended great effort to convince people of means to acquire land for the Jews without dispossessing their Arab neighbors.

23. Manya and the Arab Question

All of Manya's activities—in Hashomer, in the Haganah, in Aliyah Bet, in land redemption—were inextricably linked with the Arab question.

From its inception, Hashomer was formed to protect Jewish life, property and pride; yet, at the same time, it was considered essential to develop cordial relations with the Arab neighbors. It was therefore necessary to understand the Arab way of life as well as interactions among the various Arab tribes. Many outsiders did not appreciate this statesmanlike aspiration of Hashomer. The members of Hashomer strove to be accepted as an independent body of settlers in the midst of the surrounding Arabs, a nation returning to its homeland as its right and not as a favor.

Manya devoted much thought to the problem of relations with the Arabs and she received much pleasure when her friends told her stories of Arab folklore. In particular, she was enchanted by our recollection of the visit of Sheik Suleiman and an escort of several other sheiks from the Negev to the Hashomer unit in Rehovot. Tova and I were present at the time of that visit and Manya delighted in asking me to tell and retell the story.

In the early part of 1911, the senior members of Hashomer—Mendele Portugali, Zvi Nadav and Mordecai Yigal—were supervising the Watch in Rehovot. Consequently, they wandered about the area often in order to keep an eye on the many hired hands who guarded the vineyards of Rehovot. Sometimes they also went down to the Negev and visited the Bedouin camps. On one such occasion, they invited the noted sheiks to Rehovot.

The preparation for this visit was monumental. We removed the beds of the Watchmen from the room and Tova and I nosed around in our neighbors' houses borrowing a rug and straw matting, a round table and a copper tray on which we placed a kettle of coffee and pretty cups. On the walls of the room were hung different types of weapons which had been gathered from all the Watchmen: guns, rifles and swords. The Watchmen wore all their finery, plus ammunition belts from which were protruding shining revolvers.

The morning hours passed in an atmosphere of tension, particularly in the case of the three hosts. Tova and I wanted to be present in the room, but Yigal explained that such a thing was simply not done. At most, we could peek in through the crack in the door. The friends kept glancing nervously at their watches and listening to every outside sound. Finally we heard the sounds of hoofbeats and Yigal hurried outside. It had already been agreed that the boys from the Watch would tend to the horses. And behold, there were the Sheik Suleiman and another three Bedouins wearing magnificent abayas. The greetings and blessings began. Again and again they blessed their hosts until they finally sat down in armchairs while our friends stood by to serve them in the manner of our patriarch Abraham. Yigal, who knew how to brew Bedouin-style coffee, prepared it. The Sheik kept staring at his surroundings as well as at the three hosts who were tall and strong looking, doubtless making an impression on him. The Sheik appeared absorbed as though he were thinking about something, as though he were sunk in memories. Suddenly, he raised his head, gave the three a piercing gaze and asked, "Who are you?" Yigal, who spoke fluent Arabic replied, "We are Jews." The Sheik shook his head and argued that they didn't look like any Jews that he knew. He knew Jews in Jaffa and in Rehovot and in Jerusalem—all sorts of Jews—but these before him were not like them, therefore they were not Jews. The three retorted somewhat heatedly that they were indeed Jews, Jewish Watchmen. Silence hung in the air. The friends were amazed—did the Sheik think they were Circassians or Druzes? But the Sheik remained quiet and the silence began to grow oppressive. Then he looked up, stared fiercely at them and said, "I will tell you who you are: You are the children of the children of the ancient nation that lived in this land. Our fathers have told us about a powerful nation that was in this land, witness to which are their scattered grave sites. We were told that one day, a mighty army came from across the sea, which battled with the inhabitants of the land, who defended themselves valiantly. But the attackers were many and conquered the dwellers of the land, took them and scattered them over many lands. We have all heard from our fathers that one day they would return. And you are the sons of this returning nation."

"Indeed," answered the friends, "we are returning from the

faraway lands and we would be pleased to be friends and good neighbors to you." Yigal poured the coffee and presented the food to them.

The guests continued to talk about this and that, including politics, but we girls weren't listening anymore. We were touched very deeply by the words of the Sheik who had the wisdom to see in us the descendants of this ancient nation.

Manya loved to repeat this story to her American friends, Henrietta Szold, Dr. Magnes and others. Manya loved the Bedouin folklore that she heard from our shepherd friends, feeling sure that it was possible to establish strong relations between us and our Arab neighbors.

From the time of their arrival to their desolate post surrounded by Arabs, the members of Kfar Giladi worked hard to develop ties of friendship with their neighbors, often visiting their villages and the Bedouin tents. They did, in fact, gain the trust of many of their neighbors and Kfar Giladi was noted for its hospitality. Manya was very aware of this matter and often accompanied her Arabic speaking associates: the Illuwitz family, Tova Portugali and her brother Moshe, Nachum Horowitz, Meir Spector and others, who nurtured friendly relations with the Methualite Christians from Mettullah, the Druzes and the Moslems. An indication of their success was that on a number of occasions they were called to settle their Arab friends' family disputes.

Manya was very pleased by the ties of friendship that were woven with the family of Kamal Bak, the head of the Methualites. In particular, she was impressed by Tova, a native of Metullah, who had spoken fluent Arabic from childhood and who was therefore appointed by the kibbutz to be in charge of hosting a contingent of honored guests from Lebanon, which included many Christians. Tova was a frequent house guest at the Bak home, not only talking with the women, but also with Kamal Bak himself. His family often visited Kfar Giladi and Manya always made an effort to be present at these meetings.

Tova also had strong connections with the the family of Kamal Bak's nephew, Ahmed, who for a while was Chairman of the Lebanese parliament. When Ahmed's wife was about to give birth, she requested that her dear friend Tova be present with her. For this purpose Tova stayed in the Bak home in Beirut for several weeks, participating in all discussions, gatherings and festivities and feeling like a real member of the family. After this visit she was able to report to her friends about the feelings and attitudes of the Lebanese elite.

At one point, Ahmed Bak lost favor in the eyes of the French regime, which was about to arrest him. Together with his wife and children, he found refuge in Kfar Giladi where he stayed for several months. Tova was their gracious hostess and Manya often joined in their conversations. When the British came to incarcerate Ahmed Bak according to the French request, Nachum Horowitz told them that they would only take Ahmed over his own dead body and the British finally conceded. This was certainly a Manya-type response to a problem.

Manya would often say that neighborliness was a science which must be learned and explored in order to find new and better ways. She would emphasize the influence of the Jewish settlers on the development of the Arabs in Eretz Israel and the fact that in the eyes of many Arabs the Jews were considered friends—until they were convinced otherwise by the propaganda of the British authorities. She was full of faith that there was place in the land for Jews and Arabs alike.

At first the collective lifestyle seemed peculiar to the Arabs, who also could not understand the concept of independent work without utilizing outside help. But the more frequent the visits, the greater was the basic respect that developed. In particular, the Arabs were impressed by their friends' attitude toward work—all work—seeing in it a source of respect for the worker.

I remember how surprised Manya was when I recounted to her the story of the visit that Ben-Zvi and I made to Kafr Jish (known as Gush Chalav in Biblical times). On our way from Safed to Kfar Giladi, we wandered into an Arab courtyard inhabited only by a few beasts of burden, when we suddenly heard a man's voice speaking to us in Hebrew. When we looked up, we saw above the stable, a young man who asked us in Hebrew to climb up to him on the steps at the end of the yard. We did so. To our amazement, on his table, along with a copy of the New Testament, was the Old Testament together with several Hebrew books. The boy told us that his name was Atnas Akal and that his ancestors had dwelt in that village for countless generations. He knew that, in the past, there was a Hebrew settlement there called Gush Chalav, but that in Arabic the name had been changed to Jish. Perhaps, he was in fact a descendant of those early Jews who became Christianized long ago. In any event, he was a Maronite Christian.

This was a truly unusual encounter and Manya wanted to meet with this man. We invited the two of them to Jerusalem, where they spoke to each other at length. Atnas reinforced Manya's faith that we would live to see bonds of friendship established between us and our neighbors.

For many years Manya kept up her association with Atnas. During the days of terror of 1936, Ben-Zvi received a condolence letter in Hebrew from Atnas in which was the sentence, "The God of Israel will help his people in their homeland." Manya kept this letter in order to show it to her friends outside Eretz Israel.

During her entire life, Manya strove for ties of friendship with the Arabs. There were those who saw in this an inconsistency in Manya's personality, but she had no problem accepting herself as she was, contradictions and all. It was reasonable to her: her attitude toward her Arab neighbor came from her love of all people and from her belief that our development of our homeland was beneficial to the Arab community as well. Those who were displaced received compensation and those who sold portions of their land were able to improve their standard of living with the money received. One of Manya's guiding principles was that despite her goal of redeeming the land, the transfer of land to Jewish hands should not cause harm to those displaced.

Thanks to this forthright attitude, the Arabs felt respect for her— so much so, that even during the attacks in Haifa, they acted politely toward Manya. One day, in the Arab marketplace, Manya hurt her foot and was able to walk only with great difficulty. Suddenly one of the Arab dock workers who recognized her, left his group (which was right in the middle of planning an attack on a Jewish neighborhood) and extended his hand to Manya. Leaning on his arm, Manya limped out of the area until she stopped a passing Jewish car.

Despite her many efforts in the area of self-defense, Manya never stopped dreaming of peace and never ceased her efforts to find new ways of understanding between the two nations. On the one hand, she used every avenue to obtain weapons and armaments, and on the other, she kept contact with the people of "Brit Shalom"—Magnes, Benjamin and others—with the hope that, through their efforts, it might be possible to aspire to a life of coexistence without constant self-defense.

Way back in 1929, Manya had written this about the Arab question:

"Organization of the Watch in all agricultural settlements into a national union: the role of this group is simply to guard legally the rights to property and life, while at the same time establishing ties of friendship with all the surrounding Arab villages, for this to be the natural result of studying and knowing what transpires in the groups of Bedouins and fellahin...

...to establish ties of friendship with the Druzes who live in Eretz Israel. To help protect them from those who would do oppress them, and to extend medical help toward them through Hadassah, to establish a treaty with them, because they are trustworthy...".

One of the means to bring the Arabs closer was, in Manya's opinion, to raise the cultural level of the Arabs, and to this end she proposed a number of ideas. Thus she wrote:

"1. A weekly Arab newspaper (in 1925, Ben-Zvi established a newspaper called *Ittihad Al-Amal, Workers Union*)...
2. Establish joint agricultural teams...
3. Professional clubs for the Arab and Jewish city workers...
4. Help form a democratic, Arab national party...
5. Establish banking branches in the Arab centers...
6. Form one joint business venture...
7. Perform statistical work to find out more about the numbers of the various Arab sectors...".

When she was in the United States, Manya turned to Weizmann with these words:

New York, 3.3.1931

Greetings to Doctor Weizmann, our dear leader!

I have been in America for a week.

You remember the content of the letter that I received from America and of which I gave you a copy. Here I see that the situation is much worse and I bless the hour that you decided not to travel here at this time, but rather to go to Eretz Israel first. I hope that here I will be able to tell many influential people the truth.

Here there is the possibility to organize a group similar to the Sieff group in London in order to study the Arab problem. If this develops, it would be possible to also actively seek funding for a cooperative effort with the Arabs.

Pursuant to the advice of Henrietta Szold, we have decided not to go in this direction until you personally give your agreement and opinions and I ask you to respond as quickly as possible to my questions:

1. Is it necessary to organize a group for the purpose of studying the Arab question?

2. On what basis should it be formed?

3. Is it necessary at this time to raise money for coordination with the Arabs?

4. Do you agree with our self-initiated group for the question of the Arabs in Eretz Israel (Yisrael Shochat, Nachmani, Hankin, etc.)?

5. Have you come to some agreement as to the basis on which a joint Jewish-Arab group should be formed?

I hope that you will respond immediately, because the people here who are interested in this problem are awaiting your reply. Don't delay until your arrival here; please answer in writing. I hope that when you come to America you will find many devoted friends.

With devotion and respect,

Manya Shochat

During her stay in America, Manya sent Joseph Nachmani a suggestion for the establishment of the Jewish-Arab League:

FIRST STEPS FOR
THE LEAGUE FOR JEWISH-ARAB COEXISTENCE

Despite the mutual hatred that has developed in Eretz Israel during the terror between Jews and Arabs, there has lately been a willingness on both sides to improve relations.

On the part of the Arabs, this is a consequence of the economic ruin which has resulted from three and a half years of internal terror and from their complete disappointment in the Mufti's politics. As for the Jews, this is a consequence of the White Paper. The Jews have stopped believing that England will help them build a national home. The leaders of the League, who have always aspired toward cooperation between Jews and Arabs, see in this situation the propitious moment for a fundamental partnership in order to reach the Jewish-Arabic coexistence which is necessary for this land.

MEANS FOR COEXISTENCE

There have always been two approaches toward cooperation between Jews and Arabs. The first would be through the Arab leadership, to reach a political agreement with the official leaders, granting them political compromises as a price for reaching a peace with the entire nation. The extremists on this approach (who have yet to yield any positive results) are the members of Brit Shalom. The second approach would involve a direct contact with the masses, first creating neighborly and friendly relations between the Jews and the various strata of Arab society, leading to mutual understanding. Only after a protracted, systematic and continual effort is there hope for a healthy political agreement between the two nations. The League has chosen this path.

THE POLITICAL BASIS

Without going into details of the political agreement between ourselves and the Arabs, it would be an agreement which would, at long last, give a political direction to our future. The League bases its actions on the fundamental principle—not depending on the present Arab majority or the Jewish majority of the future—that there will be a mass immigration of Jews to Eretz Israel.

The first actions of the League will be in the cultural, economic and social fields.

CULTURAL ACTION

1. To bring Arab literature to the children and the youth which will educate them in a humanitarian spirit and will release them from the fascistic-chauvinistic poison which has thus far been fed to the Arab youth.

2. To organize seminars for the Arab teachers, to raise their cultural standard, to connect them with the cultural life of the Jews, and thus to weaken the reactionary influence to which they are accustomed.

3. To encourage Jews to learn the Arabic language and to publicize information about the Arabs and their customs.

ECONOMIC ACTION

1. To help the Arab fellahin to sell their crops in a cooperative manner through the appropriate departments in the Histadrut.

2. To encourage a union of the Arab and Jewish chambers of commerce, cooperation between the Arab and Jewish orchard growers, etc.

3. To help in the creation of joint labor unions in those fields in which there are no fundamental wage differences. In particular, government employees, transport workers, dock workers, postal employees, etc.

SOCIAL ACTION

1. To organize meetings between the Jewish and Arab leaders in all areas of the country in order to jointly consider the agricultural interests of the Jews and the Arabs.

2. To begin to include Arabs in the social institutions of the Jews, such as: hospitals, health care, etc.

3. To establish greater contact between Jews and Arabs in both public and private life.

These actions will lay a healthy foundation for the new political structure which will emerge in time and will guarantee cooperation between the two nations living in Eretz Israel.

Until her final days, Manya remained true to her dream for harmony with the Arabs through mutual respect. Two years before her death, she sent Ben-Gurion this note:

Jerusalem, President's home
24.3.59

To my dear and close friend Ben-Gurion,

...the time has come to stop the discrimination, to end the shame that rests upon us. There are in the defense department enough smart and capable people who could find the means to fight against a fifth column among the Arabs without resort to martial law.

With blessings and love,

Manya Shochat

And he answered her thus:

Jerusalem
3.6.59

Dear Manya,
I have kept letter of 24.3.59. I apologize for not answering right away—but what you wrote is very important to me. I will not argue with you about the military government. Both of us have doubtless heard all the arguments, pro and con, and we will not change each other's minds one bit; nevertheless, the spirit in which your opinion is expressed is not strange to me. I am a full partner with you in the aspiration for equality and justice, the difference is in our perception of the realities. But I was happy to hear from you, happy that you turned to me.
We are not so far apart as it sometimes appears and I wish you, from the bottom of my heart, health and strength for many long years.
With love,
D. Ben-Gurion

Today, with the distance of years, Manya is more comprehensible to us than she was in those days. She was often perceived as peculiar in her friends' eyes, who saw a contradiction between her nonstop efforts to obtain weapons and her contact with the people of Brit Shalom, who were so different from her. But, in retrospect, this was no contradiction but rather wisdom and perception which we understand today: hands outstretched toward peace, but at the same time preparation and readiness for war.

When Manya heard that Wingate, the Englishman who had been a friend to the Jews, was about to depart, she wrote to him:

22.5.1939

Greetings to our dear friend Mr. Wingate:

I heard that you must leave Eretz Israel. I send my blessings to you. We love you like a loyal brother and devoted friend. Our feelings of affection and devotion will accompany you wherever you are. You have won the hearts of all who knew you and listened to you. You have seen what is to come and you understand the meaning of justice. To our great sorrow, you are one of the few Englishmen in the country who have understood our problem. And I am certain that the day will come when the British nation will understand the sin that its government has committed. Our political direction will be:

1. Cooperation with the English nation and complete opposition to the fascist government which rules it today.

2. Cooperation with the Arab masses, and war against the fascist Arab segment headed by Haj Amin Al Hussein.

The day will come and we will win. We will succeed in establishing for the Jewish nation a working homeland which will be a shining example for the Arab nations in the east.

Our paths will cross again someday. And the day will come when you will see the fruits of your labor and you will have the satisfaction that you helped us in our difficult years.

With respect and devotion,

Manya Shochat

24. The Holocaust: Rescue Plans

By the year 1942, the reverberations of the Jewish annihilation in the Nazi camps had already reached us. In those days I did not see Manya very often, but in each of my meetings with her she gave me the eerie feeling that she herself had just come from those camps. She did not speak very much but her silence was a scream in the dark. Knowing about the efforts to send emissaries to the captives in the conquered countries, she volunteered to participate, but for obvious reasons, parachutists were preferred. Manya felt hopeless.

At the fifth convention of the Histadrut, which took place in 1942, her words seemed measured as though they were said with a tranquil heart, but I knew that Manya could not find a place for herself then in the land, she so yearned to get to the death camps, as though it were in her power to save the victims. At the convention, she spoke thus:

> I will talk only about one issue, about the central, primary task of Zionism today. How to open the gates of Eretz Israel to free immigration; how to realize the possibility of a mass aliyah after the actual completion of the war. To me it is clear, after two and a half years in England and America, that the diplomatic pipeline has been sealed. It will not do to take that path alone. There is another way we have overlooked in recent years, namely, explaining the facts to the masses. To my sorrow, many do not know of the great strides we have taken in Eretz Israel, do not know that after sixty years of experimental settlements at the cost of starvation, suffering, back-breaking labor, with stubbornness and great faith, we have finally managed to prepare our country for a mass immigration. Not only do millions of Gentiles not know. Jews and most of the Zionists do not believe, do not know. Even here, in Eretz Israel, most of our colleagues in the Histadrut do not know.
>
> ...We must strengthen Aliyah Bet. Just like the year 1923 when a million and a half Greeks were moved from Turkey to Greece by

134

decision of and with the financial support of the League of Nations. I do not know why we cannot take upon ourselves to prepare a minimum program like that. For me it is clear that the thing is possible if we just organize it.

...And I come to talk to you now about a small, but, in my opinion, important matter which we must start to do now. Since the many people who will have to come to Eretz Israel cannot receive training where they are and, since we will have to receive them as they are, we must here, in Eretz Israel prepare and train a youth movement which will serve as leaders, which will prepare to receive these immigrants. Concretely, I see that all the youth movements must accept this new idea: preparation of the youth for acceptance of the masses. The youth must prepare itself to train the newcomers in agriculture as well as in city labor. We must form workers groups who will be trained and ready to help the masses which will have to be organized. If we can accept and begin implementing this suggestion here, then a new spirit will suffuse us all.

...This is what I wanted to tell you in brief. I will bring this proposal—as is customary—to the standing committee and I will ask you to accept my idea in principle. Then we will be ready to act.

Manya's mind was working feverishly. Her reasoned proposal which she introduced at the convention was not practical enough even to her. I remember one night in the beginning of 1944, when Manya stayed with us in Jerusalem. All evening she listened to Ben-Zvi, who suggested that we demand from England and the United States the bombing of the death camps; that camps be built to transfer the escaping Jews to the shores of Eretz Israel where we would share with them our last crust of bread. But how? Demand from whom? From whom could we expect help?

A bizarre silence settled over the land, like an Arab ceasefire; we knew full well what awaited us at the end of the World War. And, true to form, at the termination of the war, the English established the Arab League. One of the Irish soldiers from Camp Allenby told me this news quietly, warning me that we had to watch out for the English....

Manya took an active part in the illegal immigration. Her physical stamina was already somewhat diminished, but her soul was aflame and gave her no rest. From Kfar Giladi, she roamed to the nearby kibbutzim and the seashores, meeting the new refugees.

25. The War of Independence

On the eve of the War of Independence, Manya responded to Yisrael's request to come to his apartment in Tel Aviv, despite the fact that he was not especially careful about concealing his women, even in her presence.

In the winter of 1947, during the days of siege, Manya transferred arms to the Haganah stations—on her own person.

One evening, Manya knocked on the door of Shoshana Persitz. Shoshana, who knew Manya from her early days abroad, was afraid to open the door and did so only after she was sure it was Manya's voice. In the threshold stood Manya, weak and pale, asking for a place to sleep. To Shoshana's question as to why she could not stay in her own home, she answered in a choked voice that for this night it was not possible; Yisrael was not alone.

Shoshana drew Manya in, locked the door, pulled down the window shade and helped Manya remove her clothes which were full of all kinds of ammunition. It was her custom to wear one dress on top of another; in each of the dresses were large wide pockets. Not only were all her pockets bulging with grenades and pistols—she was wearing a belt full of bullets on her hips. Shoshana covered the weapons with a blanket and went out with Manya to the next room. Manya was sad and tired. Shoshana had never seen her so broken-hearted. The next morning, before Shoshana awoke, Manya had already "packed" and had hurried to Haganah headquarters.

In the maddening days of the siege on Jerusalem in 1948, when shots were fired ceaselessly upon the city, Manya appeared in the Primus, the small airplane which served the arrivals to the capital. It is hard to imagine how she managed to be aboard, since only the most notable leaders were able to get a seat, and then only with difficulty.

After the people of Gush-Etzion were captured, Manya wanted

to go with them, believing that as a Legion** captive she could help them escape. Dressed in a white apron and clutching a first aid kit she marched over to the Legion forces, ignoring all the protests of her friends. We were still burying the dead and Manya was trying to talk with the Legion soldiers about peace. "Crazy woman," they laughed and called their commanding officer. After listening to her in amazement, he too figured she was insane and sent her away.

During the war days there was very little contact between us. I knew that she was involved in the war effort, racing between Kfar Giladi and Tel Aviv, between Haifa and the settlements, and appearing occasionally in Jerusalem. But when the siege on Jerusalem began, outside contact was impossible and we lost touch. After the so-called "Burma Road" was opened, she once again came to Jerusalem, looking very weak physically but spiritually elated, full of hope for the coming aliyah.

**Probably the Jordanian Legion.

26. In the Transit Camps

In the wake of the War of Independence, the backbreaking jobs of rebuilding and immigrant absorption began simultaneously. After the Holocaust survivors came, there began an influx of refugees from Yemen, Syria, Iraq and North Africa, when transit camps were erected for them. Near each city, adjacent to each settlement, these camps were erected, in the hope that a way would be found to absorb the new immigrants into Israeli life. But the road was long and the suffering was great, not only because of the large numbers but also because many had no job skills. Manya saw work as the means of salvation for the immigrants and she would reiterate time and again that a person could be redeemed only through labor.

It seemed that of all of us, Manya was the only one who was directly involved with the transit camp dwellers, giving them devotion and care, actually living with them in the camps, not caring if she had a place to lie down or a piece of bread to eat. She went from camp to camp, and hounded all the authorities, all the people she knew in public life. In those days, she had the appearance of a wounded lioness: a feeble body combined with a will of iron.

One day, Manya arrived and turned to Ben-Zvi who had in the past been head of the national council and was now part of the provisional government, and in a scream that came from deep within her, she demanded his help in saving the immigrants, in giving them work so that they would not turn into degenerates and in abolishing the accursed transit camps. She went to all the authorities, writing letters, offering solutions. Here is one:

Kfar Giladi, 25.4.1950

To the Honorable Golda Myerson**, Minister of Labor:

**later known as Golda Meir.

In accordance with our previous discussion, I am putting in writing my conclusions and suggestions based upon my having lived and worked in the camps for several months.

I am not proposing anything startling, since the condition in the camps is well known to everyone, but there is a need to pay particular attention to this matter, rather than getting used to the deplorable situation and delaying a solution which will require a great effort.

The life of idleness in the camps is destroying the souls of even the best individuals; they are becoming increasingly demoralized, and in a person who is naturally active and conscientious, his lot in the camps leads to even greater spiritual devastation. For several consecutive months I have seen how, in every corner, dependency and bitterness are growing, and even—to our shame—a hatred for the state itself.

Even though there are those who are working faithfully and devotedly to help the immigrants, the results are very grim because they cannot create the one essential ingredient for their salvation: work. Still, to our good fortune, there is one constant encouraging truth: the great majority, regardless of background or class, wants to work!

My proposal is not directed to those who have managed to leave the camps and are in the cities, work villages, etc. My proposal is geared principally toward the basic question: How can we put most of the people to work in agriculture? I know that the professional background of most of the immigrants is meager at best and only a small number have received any agricultural training. Some want to go only into business and only a small percentage would like to be farmers at this point. In my opinion, this is because they don't know what a life of agriculture entails, and I therefore have the following suggestions:

1. Establish a law that every immigrant who is unmarried be required to devote a year toward agricultural work.

2. These new immigrants should no longer be brought to the camps but should be directed to agricultural settlements immediately upon arrival. The kibbutzim must absorb them. They would receive training, living expenses and pocket money, and at the end of the year (if they choose to leave) would be given a sum of money.

Through this effort we will accomplish the following:

1. The Jewish Agency will save a great deal of money (estimates are that they are currently spending about 20 liras per month per immigrant).

2. The farms need working hands. Of course, we cannot ignore the fact that difficulties will be encountered in training people who are coming to the farms unwillingly, and only because of the law.

Still if we succeed in eliminating, for the new (unmarried) immigrants, the terrible period of idleness and degeneracy in the camps and immediately bring them into a life of work, and if this effort will be accompanied by compassion and personal attention, the probability is that most of them will succeed and will stay in agriculture.

3. The establishment of state farms or work cooperatives. State farms will serve those who are immigrating with families, who need to build themselves a stake. They would be hired to build these settlements, to build the homes, to pave the roads, to dig wells, etc. These farms would be a training ground for new immigrants. We have seen that the attempt to take workers with no previous training and expect them to succeed is only rarely successful.

It is important to bear in mind the simple truth: there is no possibility of implementing grand plans of immigrant absorption through agriculture if there is no program for training in place. It is also important to remember that a state farm could serve as a training ground for non-agricultural endeavors as well. This would enable the new immigrants to have a choice—those who were not suited to farming would be prepared for a successful life in the cities.

On state farms, the opportunity would be present to create a whole agricultural system, to serve as an experimental station which will help the surrounding settlements as well.

As you well know, millions of dunams of land are just waiting to be worked, built and developed. People in the know tell me that the state now owns large tractors, that there are able and willing agricultural trainers who could be enlisted in this effort.

We must begin to develop at least two state farms at once. I need not go into the technical details here. We have many able, experienced friends who can help in that area. With great respect and trust,

Manya Shochat

One of the people to whom Manya turned often on the issue of abolishing the transit camps was Abraham Herzfeld, who served as the head of the central agricultural committee. To one of her letters, Herzfeld responded:

"I feel positive about your suggestions. The truth is that several of them are underway, such as the issue of the unmarried immigrants who from now on will be taken immediately to an agricultural area and will learn either farming or forestry, as you suggested..."

Following is one of Manya's memos regarding a new neighborhood of 200 families from the Ramat Hasharon transit camp:

The settlement of these two hundred families is impossible in the conventional manner for the following three reasons:

1. They have no ready cash for investment.
2. They need a large living space (6-8 beds or more).
3. They cannot pay high rent.

In order to make it possible for them to achieve their stake in the land of Keren Kayemet Le-Yisrael and to receive loans from the government/Jewish Agency, it is necessary to:

1. Make it possible for these families to participate in the work of building.
2. Grant them, in addition to a loan, a fixed nonreturnable sum.
3. Leave completion of the building to the settlers themselves.
4. Engage the help of a local community group in order to lower building costs as much as possible and to save on administrative expenses.

Manya directed many new immigrants to labor camps in the Negev where they first worked as hired day workers and eventually planted roots and established, with their own hands, workers' settlements in the Lachish region.

In those days, Manya neglected all matters of Kfar Giladi and devoted herself wholly to the new olim, seeing in the method of absorption a test of Eretz Israel's future. The immigration bureau responded favorably to Manya's requests, by and large, allowing her to work as a volunteer in the transit camps and to live there. This was considered a mark of great respect, and not a door was closed to her—all were responsive to her even when her requests were somewhat extraordinary.

Manya was not one to follow normal channels. She never paid attention to formalities like regulations and restrictions and, when a matter needed attention, she broke through all obstacles until the issue was resolved. Workers in the immigration bureau could observe that when Manya passed in the corridor, she would look in the faces of the people who were standing in line, stop near anyone whose case appeared somewhat out of the ordinary and would bring him or her under her wing at which point he or she would be helped expeditiously.

A professor who was a Holocaust survivor requested from Manya that she find for him some physical work, since his state of mind would not allow him to spend time with his books. Since he saw that most of the immigrants in the camp were wearing torn shoes, he asked Manya to see if she could arrange for him to set up a small cobbler's shop to repair their shoes. She was able to fulfill his request and, when she visited him sometime later, she found him content and proud of his work.

Long months of unflagging effort left their toll on Manya and her strength started to fade. The doctor forbade her to live any longer in the camps and against her will she left the camp at Pardes-Chanah and went to Yisrael's apartment in Tel Aviv.

While she was forced to accept her fate and remain in Tel Aviv, her frail body did not prevent her from thinking and she remained alert to all settlement problems. On the fifth of November, 1955, she sent Ben-Gurion a letter of thanks on his speech in the Knesset. In it, she wrote the following:

> I feel an urgent need to thank you for the speech you gave at the opening session of the Knesset on 2.11.55. I listened carefully to your words, which I read the next day in the paper, sentence by sentence. I learned about the "security problem". You succeeded, Ben-Gurion, in stating what the great majority in the country wants to hear, exactly what I hoped you would say. Thus a great commander succeeds sometimes at a moment of danger, and my blessings go with you.

And thus Ben-Gurion replied:

> Your few and sincere words encouraged me greatly and reminded me of those early days in Sejera.

27. Eternalizing the Past

Every Shabbat, former members of *Hashomer* gathered in the Shochat home, dreamt the dreams that had not yet been fulfilled and shared each other's memories and deeds. Each member felt the need to put forward his own recollections and out of this need came the idea to publish a second volume of the book, *Hashomer.*

In 1957, we, the original core of Hashomer, had the opportunity to establish the Hashomer House, in whose charter Yisrael and Manya recorded the noblest of the thoughts and ideas of the Hashomer vision. Manya sent me the following letter on this matter:

4.8 57

Dear beloved Rachel,

As per your request, Yisrael is sending his proposal for the establishment of the Hashomer House, but since he just prepared it today, I am sending it to you quickly so that you have time to read the detailed proposal before Nachum visits with you.

The proposal is not fully developed because Yisrael was in a rush, and I pressed him to finish it.

All the best,

Manya

Soon thereafter, Nachum Horowitz was able to bring the proposal to fruition by establishing the Hashomer House in Kfar Giladi.

The second volume of the book was published, but both Manya and Yisrael cautioned again that the basic goal had not been achieved; that a thick, unappealing tome would not reach the hands of the young. After much deliberation, the proposal was made to distribute brief leaflets for youth. This was the detailed proposal sent to me by Yisrael and Manya:

Tel Aviv, 22 November 1960

To the Honorable Rachel Yanait Ben-Zvi
The President's Residence, Jerusalem

Dearest Rachel,

The matter at hand: stories from the lives of the Shomrim for young people from ages 10 to 15.

Manya has already written you about her idea of disseminating stories from the lives of the Shomrim about the Watch and about Aliyah Bet.

I have developed the idea and have transformed it from an abstract notion to a practical and feasible plan.

I will tell you in brief how I imagine the stages toward the completion of this plan:

1. Select a committee of three, two of whom will be you and Manya. You both pick the third.

2. Manya will gather the material.

3. Select an editor of children's books who will rework the material and ready it for publication.

4. Request all the members of Hashomer to write down episodes from their lives during the time of the Watch and Aliyah Bet. (I have already prepared a format).

I think that you and Manya should be among those who write, since surely events have happened to both of you which would appeal to children in this age group.

I propose that the title of the publication be *LaNoar (For the Youth)*.

The volumes should have only five or six stories apiece so as not to frighten prospective readers by the sight of a thick volume.

I have already made inquiries with the Dvir Publishing Company regarding their willingness to undertake this project; we can reasonably expect they will.

This is in brief my action plan.

Also, in the book *Hashomer* which has already been published there are many anecdotes which can be adapted to children's stories, if the language is appropriate. For example, the story of Dov who overturned the wagon of straw in order to hide the illegal immigrants who were being chased by the police, or the actual establishment of Kfar Giladi in the year 1916 during the war can be told as a heartwarming and interesting story for children.

All that I have written is at your disposal for comments and additional suggestions on your part. I look forward to the opportunity to speak with you in greater detail.

In any case, if we succeed in fulfilling even part of the plan, we will achieve two goals:

1. First of all, we will give strength and inspiration to Manya to continue living, because she does not want to become an intellectual invalid together with being a physical invalid.

2. We will impress the ideals of Hashomer in the minds and hearts of the youth. This is a holy mission which can yield much benefit in the future, something which we need for our developing nation, to conquer the wilderness and to absorb the refugees.

But do I have to spout Zionism to you?

I am sure that you understand me and I am awaiting your detailed reply.

With devotion and love

Yisrael

(Also regards to Ben-Zvi and best wishes to both of you from Manya)

And thus Manya wrote to the Hashomer members on the issue of pamphlets for the youth:

I was always concerned that our youth does not know or recognize the role of Hashomer in the past or in the days of the Biluim and this is a thing which would educate and inspire them positively.

Although we have published two volumes of *Hashomer,* the young people do not like and are not used to reading such big books, full of essays, and therefore we are still facing a worrisome situation that most young people have no idea about Hashomer. Therefore we have decided to publish pamphlets including 5-6 stories of the experiences of the early Hashomer members.

I am personally requesting each and every Hashomer colleague to write about the experiences which they had in the Hashomer period.

I would like to emphasize that it is our wish to receive the experiences of the members themselves and not stories that they heard from someone else or that happened to someone else.

The material that you send will be edited by experienced editors and will be put into a form that is suitable for young people between the ages of ten and fourteen.

In order to make things easier for our colleagues, we have decided not to worry about style or language. We are sure that you understand our purpose in this endeavor and will respond quickly.

From time to time, we received material from one or another of our friends, but the content was not riveting enough for young people. We did not give up on the idea, and spoke about it often, met often to reminisce, hoping that eventually we would able to act upon it.

28. Manya's "Social Work"

U nder doctor's orders, Manya was forbidden to exhaust herself running from camp to camp helping with social problems, but this is not to say that she refrained from continuing to help others. Now, her "social cases" came to her home, particularly the difficult ones, knowing that no one would understand their problems as well as Manya. Each case got attention and most of the time Manya managed to overcome the problem.

Even when she was in the hospital in Jerusalem after an eye operation, and was very weak, she did not cease taking care of others. She wrote the following note to one of her acquaintances:

Dear friend,

What is new with you? We have lost contact lately but our friendship remains in my heart.

I myself have been ill practically the whole year. Now I am in the hospital in Jerusalem after an eye operation and I will be half-blind for several weeks more.

I am asking you to extend your help to a very tragic case, which I cannot manage alone because it will be a while till I can get around.

Manya

Here is a typical "social work" letter which she wrote from the hospital:

Jerusalem, 15.1.59

Dear Mr. Hans Muhller, Ata Company.

Greetings! I am turning to you with a request to straighten out a tragic circumstance. I wanted to come to you and tell you the details, but I find myself in Hadassah Hospital in Jerusalem after an operation and will not be able to get to you very soon.

In the transit camp near Tel Aviv there lives a family: a woman, four small children and a husband who is a drunk, an excellent worker when he is not drunk. He never gives a cent toward family support—rather he supports his whoring mistress. The woman is about forty, not beautiful, but good to her children and good-hearted. She does day work in the houses to feed her children. She has never turned to an institution for help and does not wish to accept charity. Two years ago, when her youngest daughter was born, she decided to leave her husband in order to save her children from the murderous abuse that her husband doled out when drunk.

To put her plan to move to another place into action, she saved 300 liras for key money and acquaintances of hers promised her a room in the Montefiore neighborhood for 600 liras. I helped her get a bank loan and she had almost the whole amount.

In that same transit camp, there lived nearby an older man named Hyman. He was an unusual character in all respects, a native of Hungary, who came to Eretz Israel before the revolution, an intellectual; religious, honest, a writer in Hungarian and totally impractical.

He is about sixty, works when he needs to and in his free moments writes his memoirs. The woman hid her children at his home during her husband's drunken rages. He also helped keep her money in a bank account since she did not understand the mechanics of it. A few months ago, Hyman left the camp to be a part-time watchman in a warehouse in return for a small room. In this room was a small closet with his writings.

On the day before the tragedy, Hyman took the money out of the bank in order to give it the next day to the woman for the apartment, and he placed the money in his closet.

Early in the morning, a fire erupted—part of the warehouse was destroyed along with the man's room and his closet.

When Hyman saw that he was too late to save the money, he tried to hang himself. Workers found him inconscious and took him to the hospital. At Hadassah they found in his pocket a note addressed to me which said: "Since I did not know how to take care of Shrina's money I have no choice but to die."

Now I am asking you to give me 200 liras and I will have no trouble getting the rest.

Before I came into the hospital, I received a phone call from Hadassah that he refuses to eat or to receive medical care (he is burned on several parts of his body) because he wants to die.

After a protracted conversation with me when I promised that I will get the 600 liras, he agreed to accept medical care.

I hope you will help.

With great faith in you,

Manya Shochat

Hans Muhller's reply was not preserved, but that the matter was resolved is apparent from Manya's second letter to him:

My dear friend Hans Muhller,

I received your check for 200 liras.

I did not doubt for a moment that this would be your answer. I am sure that this will help me straighten out the family. I will never forget your generous attitude several years ago.

It is good to know that in our difficult times there are people like you who know how to help others in such a fine and gentlemanly way. This eases our life.

I have gotten out of the hospital, but it will be another month before I can see again and can get back to normal.

Manya Shochat

29. Last Days

While we were in the midst of preparing the youth pamphlets about Hashomer, Yisrael took ill and required a hospital stay. I travelled to Tel Aviv for a few days, but I saw Manya for only a few minutes a day. Yisrael was ill—while Manya blossomed anew. With a smile on her lips she said to me, "When Yisrael is sick, he wants only me by his side." Manya devoted herself as usual, without limit, day and night. It seemed to me that she forgot her own troubles when she catered to Yisrael.

She had had an eye operation. Her suffering was great, but she bore it in silence, knowing how to overcome pain with her inner strength. It was difficult to watch the strong Manya who battled every sign of weakness, disappearing before our very eyes.

After leaving the hospital, she stayed with me for several weeks at the President's residence; every day Tamar Wilbush, her brother Moshe's daughter, visited her. She talked a great deal to me about Manya. From childhood, she had been as attached to Manya as to her father. I remember in particular how she described Manya's character: "Manya is like an officer at the head of a brigade—when one of the soldiers falls on the way, Manya leaves the brigade and takes care of the man, instead of commanding one of the other soldiers to take care of him. And when she returns and doesn't find the brigade in place, she does not get discouraged, but uses all her powers and pulls them all together into a unit again."

Manya enjoyed Tamar's closeness and did not know that Tamar herself was ill with a debilitating illness. One day we were notified that Tamar was gone. All that day Manya was quiet, lying in bed in total silence. Not a word did she utter—not a tear, not a sigh. Thus she lived her sorrow.

Manya's children came for a few days: Anna,** who resembled Yisrael, and her son, Geda, the handsome pilot. This was a miracle: the boy's head was like Yisrael's, but his eyes were the magical eyes

**Note No. 23 of Documents added to this biography. (Interview with Anna)

of Manya. Later, he committed suicide, but by then Manya was no longer with us.

Manya's room in Tel Aviv looked like that of a student, full of books and notebooks, neat and organized like a young girl's. It was strange to see this room's inhabitant—old, weak and withered, but her spirit was still strong. Every word was measured, full of clarity and logic. She still had so much she wanted to do, if only her body would let her.

On the last Shavuot of her life, Manya wanted to be with her friends in Kfar Giladi. In a gathering of all the adults and the children, Manya raised herself up with tremendous effort and from her heart burst these words: "I love you, I love every one of your children, every tree that we planted, every clod of this earth." And they all stood up and said quietly: "And we love you".

In her last days, in her room in Tel Aviv, Manya seemed somehow stronger, as though signs of recuperation were appearing. The day before she died she sent me a short note, only a few words, but, as always, they jumped off the page with life:

> I am hurrying to write you my first letter since my illness which had closed my eyes. In the morning, when my eyes open again, I will write more.

The day before her eyes were shut forever, Manya did not know that the next sleep would be her final one.

Manya was buried near her friends in the Hashomer section of Kfar Giladi.

Afterword

Since Manya is gone, I continue to think about her. My soul is tied to her soul. In the days of Hashomer and in the days of Haganah, I absorbed within me her soaring spirit, her overflowing heart. So attached am I to Manya that I cannot get used to the thought that she is no longer with us. My ears continue to hear her deep and soulful voice, and my eyes still behold her magical eyes, full of warmth and wisdom.

When Manya would go to visit the gravesites of her friends in the cemetery at Kfar Giladi, she would talk to them as though they were still alive and would conclude by saying, "We will meet again, friends!" We felt the same way when Manya left us. It seems that she continues to live among us and we continue to hear her unique voice. Therefore, we will say to her, in her own words, "We will meet again, Manya!"

Readers' Guide to Names and Terms

(*starred in text)

Aliyah   To "go up" or immigrate to Eretz Israel. *First Aliyah* indicates immigration between 1880–1904, mostly from Russia after the pogroms. *Second Aliyah* refers to 1904–14.

baksheesh   From the Persian word for "present"; an Oriental term for gratuity; may connote a bribe.

Baratz, Yosef   (1890–1968) Immigrated to Eretz Israel from Russia in 1906 and became a labor leader. Helped found Degania, the first "official" kibbutz and settled there, writing its story in both Hebrew and English.

Bar Giora   Legendary leader of the rebellion against Rome, CE 66–70, Shimon Bar Giora, whose name was adopted by the Shomer as a secret society.

Biluim   An acronym (based on a passage in Isaiah 2:5) of Jewish pioneers who left Russia in 1882 as a response to pogroms. Though few in number they had a lasting and powerful impact on the nation's ideals.

"Black Hundreds"   Slavophile chauvinists, "Russia for the Russians" sponsored by the Czar, which gave the impetus to official anti-semitism. The first such pogrom was in Odessa in 1871. By 1882, there were over 50 such massacres in other locales.

Bundists   Member of the Bund, founded in 1897 in Russia, a first Jewish socialist mass organization, opposed to Zionism, for improving workers' lives. They influenced Jews in East Europe, England and the USA until W.W. 1; W.W. 2 ended their popularity.

Brandeis people   Supporters of Supreme Court Justice Louis D. Brandeis' proposal to form a group of businessmen devoted to the economic growth of Jewish settlement.

Brandeis, a Zionist, drew supporters like Rabbi Stephen S. Wise, Felix Frankfurter, Robert Szold and Julian W. Mack.

chalutzim   (sing. chalutz) Hebrew for "pioneer"—refers to early immigrants who built the land through physical labor, mostly in agriculture.

Chovevei Zion   "Lovers of Zion"; members of a popular movement of the late 19th century in Europe and the USA, whose purpose was to encourage a Jewish revival by settling in Eretz Israel.

Circassian   A native (or the language) of the North Caucasus in the south Soviet Union bordering on the Black Sea.

Decembrists   Those who were in conspiracy against Czar Nicholas when he ascended the Russian throne in December, 1825. A rebellion ensued and five army officers were hanged.

Dukhobors   A religious sect in Russia from 17th to 19th century, with Quaker-like beliefs opposing priesthood and military conscription. After persecutions, in 1887 they migrated to Canada: in 1908 spread over British Columbia and were known to practice nudism as a form of passive resistance.

dunam   A measure of land equal to 1000 square meters, equal to 0.247 of an acre.

effendi   A Turkish ruler or official; a title of respect.

mukhtar   An Arab village head.

fellahin (pl.)   Egyptian or Syrian farm laborers; a term used by the Turks to indicate Egyptians.

gymnasia   Post-high school and pre-college training course; derived from the German method of education.

Hapoel Hatzair   "Young Workers", A first indigineous workers' party of Jews in Eretz Israel, begun in 1905 at Petach Tikvah by Second Aliyah arrivals. Members of this group founded the first kibbutz (Degania, 1908) and the first moshav (agricultural cooperative) in 1921. In 1930, they merged with Ahdut Avodah to form the Mapai party.

Hashomer   "Shomer"   Self-defense organization of Jewish watchmen formed in 1909 in Eretz Israel to protect Jewish settlements in the lower Galilee—a first attempt to establish a Jewish armed force. A select group that never had more than 100 called "shomrim", in the 1920's it merged with the Haganah, the defense force. (This biography encompasses its development)

Haskalah   The Jewish "enlightenment" begun by Moses Mendelssohn in the 18th century, advocating reason and a knowledge of secular subjects to enable Jews to enter mainstream society. Hebrew was advanced and Yiddish neglected.

Hauran   Today this region is part of Syria, and is east of the Jordan River. In antiquity it was extremely fertile and densely populated.

Hussein   Aj Amin Al Hussein, an Arab leader, was Mufti of Jerusalem appointed by the British in 1921. As head of the Supreme Muslim Council, he soon used the combined power of his office to put down Jewish settlement and organized anti-Jewish riots in 1929 and 1936. Dismissed by the British in 1937, he fled. During W.W.2, he met with Hitler to propagandize against the Jews.

I.C.A.   Jewish Colonization Association begun by Baron Maurice de Hirsch in 1891 to help Jews emigrate from troubled countries. From 1904–14, I.C.A. formed hundreds of emigration groups with the approval of the Russian government. It resettled Jews in Brazil, Cyprus, Turkey, USA and Eretz Israel.

Katznelson   Berl Katznelson (1887–1944)
A leading figure of the labor movement in Eretz Israel; was editor of *Davar*, the first daily newspaper for workers begun in 1925.

Keren Kayemet L'Yisrael (Jewish National Fund) This group was formed to purchase land in Eretz Israel in 1905 at the request of the Zionist Congress. It continued such acquisition until 1948, when its functions were transferred to the government of Israel.

Kishinev pogrom   Anti-Jewish riots in the Russian city of Kishinev in April, 1903, with hundreds injured and 47 killed. This riot and those preceding it heightened Jewish self-defense and nationalism as well as emigration.

Lindheim   Irma Levy Lindheim (1886–1978) Later known as "Rima" Lindheim. Zionist leader in the USA and Israel, she was a leader of the Zionist Org. of America and national president of Hadassah 1926–28; a disciple of Henrietta Szold, settling on Kibbutz Mishmar Ha'emek. Her autobiography, *Parallel Quest*, was published in 1962.

lira   (pl. lirot) Israeli legal tender which replaced the Palestine pound on September 15, 1948. Unrelated to the Italian lira, and called the Israeli pound, it was currency until May 1980 when it was replaced by the shekel.

Dr. Magnes   Judah Magnes (1877–1948)
American Zionist rabbi who served as chancellor (1925–35) and president (1935–48) of the Hebrew University. He helped form *Brit Shalom* in 1929, seeking a bi-national state with Jews and Arabs, and in 1942 established *Ihud* for better Jewish-Arab understanding. In 1948 the Hebrew University officially dissociated itself from Magnes' views.

Maronite   Oriental Catholic of a church centered in Lebanon.

moujiks (or *muzhik*)   Russian peasants

Musselman (or Muselmann)   German for Muslim; also Nazi camp slang at Auschwitz; prisoners who were emaciated on the brink of death.

Nordau, Max   (1849–1923) Famous for being Herzl's aide in the early days of political Zionism. An essayist and philosopher born in Hungary; also a physician.

Narodnya Volya   "People's Will" or "People's Freedom", a Russian revolutionary group formed in 1879 advocating terrorist action as a means of forcing political reform and overthrow of Czarist rule. The group assassinated Alexander II in 1881.

Pale   Area of Czarist Russia to which Jews were confined; mainly the area of the former Polish kingdom and land annexed from Turkey on the Black Sea. Boundaries were in effect from 1791 to 1915, intended to restrict Jewish competition with Russian merchants and encourage settlement in southern Russia.

Poalei Zion   "Workers of Zion" movement in Russia in 1890's which tried to blend both Zionist and socialist aims. It expanded in Europe, USA, England and South America, and in Eretz Israel, where it became a political party, currently within the Israel Labor Party.

Ruppin   Arthur Ruppin (1876–1943)
Well known lawyer and Zionist leader who organized an agricultural settlement, and as an official of the World Zionist Organization in 1905, initiated the idea of Jews owning land in Judea and the Galilee. He also helped found the settlement which became Tel Aviv.

Rutenberg   Pinhas Rutenberg (1879–1942)
A Russian social revolutionary, he became an engineer and industrialist, began the first hydroelectric project in Eretz Israel and also developed the country's first irrigation system.

Sabbateans   Followers of Shabtai Tzevi, a false Messiah of 1676, who became various sects; one, the Donmeh, adopted Islam.

Subbotnik   Judaized Christians in Russia who practiced circumcision and other Jewish rites, appearing first under Catherine II.

Szold   Henrietta Szold (1860–1945)
Born in Baltimore, Md., she founded Hadassah in 1912. She was the first woman to study at the Jewish Theological Seminary, and became an important Zionist leader. After W.W.2, she helped rescue and resettle European children in Eretz Israel.

Terror of 1929   A rampage by Arabs in Hebron, which attempted to destroy the small Jewish community living there.

UPA   United Palestine Appeal, established 1925 by the Zionist Organization of America as a fundraising arm.

Vilna Gaon   Elijah ben Solomon Zalman (1720–1797)
A spiritual and intellectual leader and Talmudic scholar, versed in math, astronomy and grammar. He advocated mastery of secular subjects and opposed Hasidism as messianism.

Yevsekim   (Yevsektsiya) Jewish section of propaganda within the Russian Communist Party established by Lenin to bring about assimilation, thought then to be the best solution to the Jewish problem in the USSR.

Yishuv   "Settlement"—applied to the Jewish community which settled in Eretz Israel.

Zhids   A derogatory term used by some to refer to "Yids" or "Jews."

31. SELECTED BIBLIOGRAPHY*

Ben-Zvi, Rachel Yanait. *Coming Home,* Herzl Press, NY, 1964.

Izraeli, Dafna. "The Zionist Women's Movement in Palestine, 1911–27: A sociological analysis." *Signs:* A Journal of Women in Culture and Society, 1981, 7(1); 87–114.

Maimon, Ada. *Women Build a Land,* Herzl Press, NY, 1960.

Reinharz, Shulamit. "Toward a Model of Female Political Action: Manya Shohat, Founder of the First Kibbutz," *Women's Studies International Forum,* 1984, 7(4): 275–287.

(The most recent overview of Manya Shochat by a feminist sociologist; contains bibliography that includes Hebrew and Yiddish citations)

Samucha, Marlena. "Manya Shochat," *Pioneer Woman* (USA) Magazine** October–November, 1976, 11–12.

Shazar, Rachel Rubashov Katznelson. *The Plough Woman: Memoirs of the Pioneer Women of Palestine,* Herzl Press, NY, 1975, 2nd ed.

Syrkin, Marie. "Manya Shochat and Aziz," *Jewish Frontier,* May/June, 1987. (Reprint of an interview with Shochat first published in the same publication, January, 1941.)

---

*Does not cite works in Hebrew. Such readers may wish to know of a documentary film on the life of Manya Shochat shown on Israel Television in 1987.

**See also Document #25 from the same publication added to this English edition.

Documents

1. Handwritten draft of a contract between the Board of Sejera and Israel Shochat in the matter of the employment of two watchmen. (undated)

2. Handwritten draft of charter for the Board of Hashomer. (undated)

3. Manya's approach to Henrietta Szold on the matter of establishing a cooperative of itinerant farmers. (7 March 1909)

4. Arbitral verdict of 19 December between Hashomer and the Settlement Board of Mescha in the matter of a theft from one of the farmers.

5. Letter written by Yisrael Shochat to the Zionist Executive Council in Berlin the matter of monetary help for Hashomer (undated; probably end of 1913 or beginning of 1914)

6. Memorandum from Yisrael Shochat to the Zionist Executive Council in Berlin on the matter of funds for Hashomer. (20 June 1914)

7. Decisions regarding female membership in Hashomer, apparently from the Protocols of the Hashomer Council formed in Yavneel in 1915.

8. Contract between Hashomer and the Settlement Board of Kfar Tavor (Mescha). (1915)

9. Secret memorandum sent from Hashomer to the Provisional Zionist Committee in New York. [In English] (2 October 1916)

10. Demands of Atara Sturman (Krol), Devorah Darkler and Yehudit Horowitz in the matter of female equality in Hashomer. (25 September 1918)

11. Letter from Yisrael Shochat to Shmuel Hefter (8 August 1919)

12. Letter from Manya to Rachel Yanait in the matter of the Negev delegation and in the matter of obtaining the support of Henrietta Szold for Manya's efforts in the United States. (6 August 1921)

13. Letter from Manya to Rachel Yanait in the matter of the Negev, Poalei Zion in America and the controversy between Yisrael Shochat and Eliahu Golomb in land procurement matters. (21 September 1921)

14. Letter from Manya to Rachel Yanait in the matter of raising funds for the settling of soldiers in Tel Arad and in the matter of land procurement (undated)

15. Report on the activities of the First Delegation to the United States on behalf of the Histadrut in the matter of Bank Hapoalim; followed by letter sent to the Jewish Workers' Community. (3 February 1922)

16. Letter from Manya to Ben-Zvi in the matter of his participation in the convention of "Gedud Ha-Avodah". (7 March 1924)

17. Letter from Rima Lindheim to Manya in the matter of the negative attitude of Labor Israel toward Hadassah Organization. [English] (undated)

18. Letter to Manya written by Henrietta Szold after being elected to the National Committee. (3 October 1927)

19. Letter from Manya to Ben-Zvi in the matter of fundraising for activity within the Arab community. [English] (14 January 1930)

20. Manya on obligation to buy the Shekel. (in *Davar*, 12 April 1937)

21. Minutes of the first meeting of the Mishmeret Hagvul border guard. (1938)

22. Minutes of second meeting of Mishmeret Hagvul border guard. (1938)

23.* Manya Shochat through the eyes of her daughter, Anna. (*Haaretz* supplement, 17 October 1986)

24.* Manya Shochat Testimonials on her eightieth birthday (Excerpts) in *Al Hamishmar*, 23.10.59 p. 7–8.

25.* Our "Manya" by S. B. Russak, abridged, from March, 1932 *The Pioneer Woman*.

The following items are presented as written, except for minor orthographical corrections.
Key to symbols:
[ ] cannot be read
<>editorial addition

1. HANDWRITTEN DRAFT OF A CONTRACT BETWEEN THE BOARD OF SEJERA AND ISRAEL SHOCHAT IN THE MATTER OF THE EMPLOYMENT OF TWO WATCHMEN

CONTRACT

Between the board of Sejera and Mr. Yisrael Shochad <sic>, according to these conditions:
1) Mr. Y. Shochad <sic> proposes two Jewish Watchmen to guard the settlement of Sejera.
2) The Watchmen must be on duty from evening until morning.
3) The Board has the right to send one of the Watchmen to guard the fields, flocks, silo.
4) The Board is required to give the Watchman who is guarding the fields a horse, saddle and horsefeed.
5) If the Watch supervisor finds one of the Watchmen asleep at his post, he will be required to pay a quarter of a mejida* <*a Turkish coin, worth about five francs of that time> as a fine the first time, and a half of a mejida the second

---

*Three documents (Nos. 23, 24 and 25) have been added to this English edition. They do not appear in the original Hebrew edition.

time. The supervisor is required to bring one of the sleeping guard's possessions to prove that his accusation is true.

6) The Board will pay Y. Shochad <sic> or his representative eighty francs per month.

7) The Board is required to pay in full at the end of each month.

8) The Board is required to supply the Watchmen with two rifles and two ammunition housings. At the end of the year, these are to be returned to the Board.

9) The Board is required to give the Watchmen ammunition at its own expense.

10) The Board is required to give the Watchmen decent accommodations.

11) All gates must be closed at 9 P.M.

12) If the Watchmen find an open gate after 9 P.M., then the responsible farmer must pay a fine of a quarter of a mejida the first time, and half a mejida the second time.

13) If one of the Watchmen should become ill, then for one week, there will be only one Watchman. Or if the Board wishes, we can locate a substitute for him, on the condition that if the Board pay him without reducing it from the [—].

14) If one of the two parties moves to another [—] pay a franc to the other party. This contract is in force from today until the first day of Tishrei .

(Labor Archives, IV 112, file 8)

2. HANDWRITTEN DRAFT OF STANDARDIZATION FOR THE BOARD OF HASHOMER

MISSION OF THE BOARD

1) The Board of Hashomer has primary responsiblity in all matters and work of the organization such as Watch, defense, work, etc.

2) The Board is charged with the responsibility for ensuring that the principles of Hashomer are carried out.

3) The Board is trying to broaden the Watch and the work (accepting Watch in new locations, arrangement of work crews, both temporary and longer-term).

4) The Board is to try to arrange cultural events for its members (such as lectures, lessons, libraries, etc.)

5) The Board is to achieve the means to do intelligence work and investigation in the surrounding area.

6) The Board should try to bring leaders to the settlements, people in our spirit, and if possible, from within our ranks.

In order to bind the members to ethical and juridical organizational obligations:

1) The general responsibility of Hashomer is divided among all its members equally, and each and every member must submit a formal undertaking to this effect to the Board.

2) Those expenses which are incurred for non-Hashomer matters do not fall upon the Hashomer organization.

(Labor Archives, IV 112, file 2)

3. MANYA'S APPROACH TO HENRIETTA SZOLD ON THE MATTER OF ESTABLISHING A COOPERATIVE OF ITINERANT FARMERS

Tiberias, March 7, 1909

Most honored Miss Szold:

You are probably surprised that after a year and a half of silence I am suddenly sending you this long letter. I was quiet because we were not involved in a joint effort, although, without a doubt, we have common goals. It is out of character for me to write love letters, but you are nevertheless very dear to me and I value and love you dearly.

Now I would like to propose to you a joint effort; I do not know why I feel this way, but I do believe that you will answer yes to my suggestion.

Listen closely to what I have to say.

Many things have changed in Palestine in the last two years, to transmit to you in writing all that has transpired is impossible. Once must live in the land or at least stay here for awhile to feel the progress of Eretz Israel. I will speak with you about the problem of obtaining land.

We have managed to overcome the pessimism that was prevalent in the administration of the I.C.A. in Eretz Israel matters. I.C.A. has now entered a period of fruitful activity to some extent. Hankin, whom I have told you much about, and about whom you have doubtless heard from Dr. Magnes as well, is in charge of this effort. He bought new land, about 20,000 dunams which was almost lost to us; he succeeded after much effort to retrieve it from the Arabs. The settlement has begun anew. In the past year, 30 young people have settled there with the help of the I.C.A. This year they have decided to settle an additional 60 farmers. If the new element obtains positive results from their agricultural, moral and nationalist endeavor, I.C.A. will broaden their activities greatly. But if the results are negative, then nothing will help and I.C.A. will completely abandon the colonization effort. This is my intuitive understanding of the situation. How we can reach the new element of settlers with an appreciation of its tremendous role in our future is a question to which we will doubtless return, but not in this letter.

Now I want to address the other side of the coin. When land is purchased in Palestine, for the most part it cannot be settled immediately. From the time of purchase until the construction time, a year or usually even more passes. And this is due to the legal complexities involved with land title transfer. I have already told you once that in Palestine, it is forbidden for land to remain fallow; when an Arab sees that a piece of land is not being worked, he moves in. And once he has eaten a piece of bread grown on that land, he will never leave. And then he must be extricated by force. Then the justice system takes over, and the sheiks are put in jail. As a result, the feeling of hatred between Arab and Jew is growing and festering and the atmosphere grows increasingly dangerous. Since it is impossible to leave the land fallow, it must be rented out and it returns again to the Arabs, and the cycle repeats itself, perhaps with minor deviations. At the end of the year, the Arabs refuse to leave the land they have worked and the results: agricultural uprisings, court cases, prison, hatred of the Jews, and even pogroms on the Jews in the Galilee, where we hope to continue living after all this is over.

After the Turkish constitution was established, the situation deteriorated a great deal. The Arabs who achieved "Huria", freedom, understood this achievement as no less than a social revolution. They state: "The land that the Effendis* once took from us by treachery and which they are now selling to the Jews, this land will once again belong to us."

I mentioned earlier that Hankin succeeded in retrieving from the Arabs 20,000 dunams of land which had been all but lost to us. Do you know why this land was about to be taken away from us, despite the fact that we paid the full price for it? The land was bought about ten or twelve years ago. We had no opportunity to house the settlers there right away, so we rented it to the Arabs. In the end, they did not want to leave. Injunctions did not help, they stayed and continued to work the land. Only after several years had passed did the Jews manage to evict them. But the Jews still did not settle there, but rented it to other Arabs. And the matter started afresh. Again the Arabs considered themselves landholders, and again there were uprisings, court battles, fighting, etc. And only now have we retrieved the land once again.

Do you have any idea how these ten years of battle over land title have poisoned the atmosphere?

All this is preventable if we do not, right from the outset, allow the Arabs to work land which is owned by the Jews. In other words: We need Jews who will come to replace the Arabs, and under the same conditions rent the land and work it. And they must continue working it until normalized settlement is possible.

This can only be accomplished by a group which would be called the Cooperative of Itinerant Farmers. This group must have the following attributes:

1. People who are strong and healthy and accustomed to the climate of the land.

2. Ready and willing to live in Arab huts or tents, and to move on as the need arises.

3. They must be experienced and capable farmers so as not to fail, particularly in the first, crucial year.

4. They must be brave and stout-hearted, or else they will suffer greatly from the immediate Arab assaults.

5. The group must be continually replenished by new blood, since this itinerant life is not tenable for long periods of time, but if they can be relieved periodically, this will not be so difficult.

6. The group requires its own inventory: horses, oxen, work implements and stipulated sums of money to buy seed and food for the people and the animals during the course of the year.

We have in the Galilee, a group of young people, who have the characteristics mentioned. This group has committed itself to forming a transient farmers' organization as described above. They have all the required qualities and they will accomplish what is needed in an excellent manner.

What they are lacking is the sixth ingredient, namely, the funds required to begin their work. They would like to begin a small pilot program: A collective of twenty people. For this purpose, they will need 40,000 francs or 800 dollars. I must emphasize that each of these individuals has the opportunity to obtain, on his own, from the I.C.A., easier and better conditions for settlement. They have received such offers several times, and have turned them down thus far, because they would like to accomplish their original purpose.

Here, it is impossible to obtain the needed funds, and certainly not from the administration of the I.C.A.—but if our first experiment succeeds, they will be more supportive of this effort. They are still very cynical, and say they want to see evidence that the Zionists can effectively deal with the colonization problem in Palestine.

And I ask you, Miss Szold: Do you want to help us solve this burning problem? You should know that the more property we acquire, the larger the problem becomes. There is an urgent necessity to begin our collective of itinerant farmers this year, or else we look forward to very sad times.

This year, land will be acquired by the I.C.A. as well as by private individuals. And once again following precedent, the Arabs will be invited to be "pioneers" and work the land; and we can look forward to agrarian unrest next year, unrest which can explode all that we have built thus far with so much work and pain.

My dear lady, all that I have told you now cannot be repeated to the individuals who are buying the land; we also must not communicate this to the I.C.A. offices in Paris, because then they will all conclude that if it is so difficult to hold on to the land, there is no point in buying it in the first place.

Also, the Jews do not have a burning desire to work the land in Eretz Israel, and we must be very cautious in telling them the truth. Yet, despite all this, it is very easy for you to help, if you wish to.

I believe that the following method is best: Begin a foundation, called the "Inventory Fund." When the 40,000 francs have been raised, let this amount be loaned to the cooperative group in Palestine. (The term of the loan and such will be decided here.) This fund must have an undersigner in Israel, such as Dr. Ruppin or Mr. Hankin, who will deal with the administrative details of the loan.

This money must reach us two months before Shavuot. Otherwise, the group cannot begin, because the critical factor in their success is that they must start working the land three months before the rains.

I have spoken about this with both Messrs. Lubarsky and Rozovsky <of the I.C.A.>and they agreed to help. The three of you can get together to set up this inventory fund.

I hope to hear from you in the affirmative. Please respond either way. I admire and respect you greatly.

Manya Wilbushevitz

PLAN FOR THE COLLECTIVE AND FINANCIAL ASSESSMENT

Twenty people leasing 5500 dunams:

Inventory:	Oxen, Horses and Farm Implements	20,000 f.
Seed:	To plant 5500 dunams	5,500 f.
Maintenance:	For animals/one year	6,500 f.
Food:	For 20 people/one year	8,000 f.
		Total 40,000 f

At the end of one work year:

In the worst case, the land will yield 6.5 francs per dunam less 20 percent of the income as rent paid to the I.C.A. administrators. The collective will remain with the inventory (20,000 francs less 10 percent depreciation) or 18,000 francs.

Income:	35,750 francs
Rent:	(7,150) francs
Net Income:	28,600 francs
Inventory:	18,000 francs
Net Worth:	46,000 francs

Thus: in the worst case, the collective will have a 16 percent profit on its investment.

(Archives of Hashomer, Kfar Giladi)

4. ARBITRAL VERDICT FROM 19 DECEMBER 1912 BETWEEN HASHOMER AND THE SETTLEMENT BOARD OF MESCHA IN THE MATTER OF A THEFT FROM ONE OF THE FARMERS

The decision of the arbitration panel composed of Mr. Shimon Levin from the Hashomer side and Mr. David Cohen from the settlement board and a third member selected by both, Mr. Yosef Krol reached on Thursday, 9 Tevet, 5673.

After examining and deliberating all the claims, we have come to the following conclusions:

1. The Watchmen must pay the settlement board for the theft which took place from Mr. Ashbal, as the damages will be estimated, since by terms of their contract of the second day of Cheshvan, 5673 in paragraph 1 without room for further discussion, since according to paragraph 5 of the above contract, they are responsible for all thefts which occur within closed doors, and although they warned the board on the ninth of Cheshvan that the doors were broken, and that they would no longer be responsible if repairs were not made, this was not stipulated explicitly in the legal agreement, and they therefore retain complete responsibility.

2. As for the demands of the Hashomer for the board to pay them a fine of 500 francs because of the material damage that they caused through not performing the needed repairs and thus being instrumental in causing the theft, we find that since the Watchmen had the same problem the previous year, and since the board did not do the necessary repairs then either, and furthermore, since the Watchmen were apparently able to continue their guard duty in the previous year despite the broken doors, therefore we find that they are entitled to only half the sum they demand, and we award them 250 francs.

Signed: S. Levin, Y. Krol and D. Cohen, Haifa, Thursday, 9 Tevet 5673.

(Archives of the Editorial Board of the Book of Hashomer, at the Ben-Zvi Memorial Foundation)

5. LETTER WRITTEN BY YISRAEL SHOCHAT TO THE ZIONIST EXECUTIVE COUNCIL IN BERLIN IN THE MATTER OF MONETARY HELP FOR HASHOMER (UNDATED; PROBABLY THE END OF 1913 OR BEGINNING OF 1914)

Honorable Councilmen:

I would like to speak at length about the matter of Hashomer and the Watchmen. Everyone who is the least bit interested in resettling Eretz Israel is well aware of the value of the Jewish Watch and its place in settling the land. I will address only the matters of the foundation and organization of the Watch and in particular the issue of broadening its scope.

Organizing and broadening the Watch requires, a great deal of money, (the Watchmen are divided into infantry and cavalry; uniforms and ammunition for the infantry cost approximately 150 fr. and for the cavalry about 600 fr.) but we are not asking for administrative funds, only for guaranteed loans which we will repay in time or as a perpetual fund, that is, inventory, from which we may draw for Hashomer. We require an annual credit line as well as long term loans. As we take on each Watchman, we must give each one about sixty or seventy francs to buy warm clothing for guard duty. This is in the form of a loan which the Shomer repays over the course of the year. Thus, if we have on average a standing group of 150 Watchmen, we require credit of approximately 10,000 francs. We would therefore like a revolving credit line for this amount in the bank. The long-term loan is for another purpose. This credit is necessary for us to build the stock of Hashomer, such as horses and ammunition. Every foot Watchman receives arms and ammunition valued at 150 francs and each cavalryman receives 600 francs worth. To increase the number of Watchmen by sixty, we require 15,000 francs We would repay this loan over five years, three thousand per year. Perhaps our credit is not so well-known at the bank, but anyone who is familiar with our work knows that we always repay our loans on time, and not a cent will be lost.

Aside from these two lines of credit, we need one additional fund, a reserve fund This fund must be non-returnable, since we need it to add additional functions to our work. You must realize that Hashomer is not satisfied to do only the Watch, that we wish to make new beginnings which the individual worker is not able to accomplish. One of these jobs will be shepherding flocks. For this work we need study and training. We need money to support our colleagues who are sent to do this work. Shepherding has, to date, been inaccessible to Jews. Another purpose for the reserves: More than money, Hashomer needs a supply of people who will help to expand our ranks. We must bring these people from other countries, from Russia (such as the Caucasus). We cannot correspond with and recruit these people by letter, since it is impossible to explain the intricacies of the work and its value in writing. And therefore we must send a special emissary who will select appropriate recruits for our work. This entails an expense of 8,000-10,000 francs. As explained above, this money is not for repayment. The individual Watchman who receives a tiny stipend will not be able to afford to participate in this fund. We believe that this money must come from the Zionist Organization or from private individuals who believe in our cause.

Finally, I wish to address the matter of a legal fund. We feel the need for it, and cannot pass over it quietly. You know that in times of disputes between the settlements and the Arab villages, the first to suffer are the Watchmen. I only need to remind you of Yavniel, Merchavia and others. And, in general, the nature of the work leads to conflicts with the Arabs. In those events, we are always left without help and without the means to obtain justice. We have already had two members sentenced to three years of hard labor despite their innocence, something which has never before happened to Jews in Eretz Israel.

We suggest the establishment of a general legal fund and the Watchmen will also contribute to the extent that they are able. We have discussed this for some time, and nothing has been accomplished thus far. We believe that such a special fund must be established immediately for the Watchmen, since they are the first to suffer each time trouble comes. When a general fund is started, we will pool our funds into this one as well. It is untenable for us to send people out on such responsible and important work without being prepared to support them in times of trouble.

I will summarize our requests:

1. Revolving Credit Line: 10,000 francs
2. 5-year credit line: 15,000 francs
3. Reserve fund: 8,000 francs
4. Legal defense fund: ....

I must tell you that without these credit lines, it is impossible for us to continue our work. Do not think we are asking too much. Everyone who knows us and our work knows that we ask only the minimum. Give us the ability to work and to accomplish that which we have begun at the cost of tremendous labor and personal sacrifice.

I am confident that you will help us, but I must repeat that our fate is in your hands.

With the blessings of Zion,
On behalf of the board of Hashomer,

Yisrael Shochat

(Central Zionist Archives, Z 3/1629)

6. MEMORANDUM FROM YISRAEL SHOCHAT TO THE ZIONIST EXECUTIVE COUNCIL IN BERLIN ON THE MATTER OF FUNDS FOR HASHOMER

Tiberias, June, 1914

When I attended the last Congress we spoke about assistance for Hashomer. We decided that Hashomer would receive a loan of 33,000 francs apportioned thus: 15,000 francs to be paid over five years, 10,000 francs to be paid over one year and 18,000 francs subsidy by the Council. Guarantor letters have been written by several people. Of this amount, we immediately received notes of 16,200 and the rest was to be sent us shortly. I returned to Eretz Israel and we organized our work according to these expectations. We were sure that we would soon receive the rest of the letters of credit, but regretfully, *we have received no response to our repeated requests* for same. The summer is arriving, the Watch must expand to the fields and vineyards, and all this requires money. Had we known from the outset that these were empty promises, we would have worked out something else.

My dear colleagues, your assistance is so minimal that I think you could have fulfilled your promises already. This is the first time that we have turned to you for help, and I will tell you the truth, we expected a better response from you, particularly when we heard of your positive attitude toward us from the podium at the Congress. The truth is that *if by the end of one more month we do not receive credit for the amount of 16,800 francs,* I am not sure we can continue the Watch. I am requesting that you attend to the matter immediately and send us notes for 16,800 in the following manner: 6,800 francs subsidy and 10,000 francs to be repaid over the course of a year. Thus you will allow us to continue our work.— This entire matter has been made very clear to Dr. Shemaryahu Levin. I repeat that I am not exaggerating the seriousness of the matter.

I have told you the complete truth, and you will be responsible if we cannot succeed in our work. I request your response as quickly as possible.

With blessings of Zion in the name of the Board of Hashomer,

Yisrael Shochat

(Central Zionist Archives, Z 3/1629)

7. DECISIONS REGARDING FEMALE MEMBERSHIP IN HASHOMER, 1915

1. Since Hashomer has purposes which are broader than guard duty, there is room in the organization for active female members as well as active male members, both from the wives of the Watchmen and from the outside.

2. In order to absorb the wives of the Watchmen into the organization, we will allow for passive membership.

3. The female members as well as the male are elected by the general assembly.

4. To include into the organization all the wives of the members, they may have the right of discussion without voting rights until such time as the general assembly finds them worthy of becoming active members.

5. The wives of the Watchmen may be present at meetings, without the right to make motions or voting rights.

(Labor Archives, IV 112, file 2)

8. AGREEMENT BETWEEN HASHOMER AND THE SETTLEMENT BOARD OF KFAR-TAVOR (MESCHA), 1916

Between the Board of Kfar-Tavor on the one side and the representative of the Watchmen on the other as set forth in the following conditions:

1. Hashomer takes upon itself responsibility for guarding the fields, the plantings of Mescha and Umm-al-Jibel from the first day of Tishrei, 5676 to the first day of Tishrei, 5677 . The guard duty includes all crops without exception.

2. Hashomer will pay damages for each theft or burning of crops.

3. Damages will be determined by a joint evaluation by representatives from both sides appointed by their respective leaders for each tour of duty.

5. The Watchmen will not be responsible for damages incurred because of a farmer delaying his harvest five days more than his neighbor, similar delays in cleanups or transports or damages incurred by extraordinary events which were out of their control.

<The remainder of the document describes in greater detail the stipulations agreed to between the settlement board and the Hashomer delegation.>

Signed,
Y. Nachmani, Y. Giladi

(Archives of the Editorial Board of the *Book of Hashomer* at the Ben-Zvi Memorial Foundation)

9. SECRET MEMORANDUM SENT FROM HASHOMER TO THE PROVISIONAL ZIONIST COMMITTEE IN NEW YORK.

The social security of a person and his property was always, in comparison with other European countries, slightly protected in Turkey, particularly in the district provinces. Palestine was no exception in this respect. True, in the central localities, as for instance, in Jerusalem or Jaffa, a man is almost as safe and secure as in New York. This, however, cannot be said of the roads between the colonies and villages, and also in the colonies themselves.

The Turkish Government left considerable place for private initiative, as far as self-defence and maintenance of order is concerned, to every village, every town and every separate community. The work of the watchmen in the colonies consists of watching, during the night, the streets, courts and boundaries of the colony; to see in advance every suspicious sign, to stop, betimes, suspicious persons; and at certain seasons watch the growing crop on the field, the produce in the gardens, etc. During the seasons, the watch is increased and strengthened. The watchmen must always be ready to protect and defend, with weapons in hand, their colonies, when the robbers are so daring as to raid and openly attack and steal the cattle and stock, or produce on the fields. In this way the work of the watchmen in the colonies is of greater importance than superficially appears. The work of watching involves also the task of local militia.

Naturally, the watch often requires a large expenditure of money which is a burden to the colonies and villages. This, however, cannot be prevented, and it can easily be understood that if a well-paid watch is not maintained, the damage would be far larger than the expense connected with the watch.

As we said before, the Turkish Government does not interfere in the inner organization of the watch in the villages and Jewish colonies. The Government also granted the colonies the right to appoint watchmen, in order to defend their property against marauders and robbers. Nevertheless, in spite of this autonomy in their own affairs, the Jewish colonies never thought that this function, which is full of danger and responsibility, should be performed by themselves, or, at least, by hired Jewish watchmen. It is superfluous to say that the robberies were exclusively perpetrated by the Arabs working in the colony or in its neighborhood. The Jewish colonists were in the habit of appointing wild Bedouins, Cherkesses or Algerian Arabs, famous for their robberies, and these were the responsible watchmen of Jewish property and honor in Palestine!

The intention was to be protected against outside attacks. It turned out, however, that the watchmen of this sort were themselves often mixed up in various pilfering, and even when one's "own" watchman was caught redhanded, the latter, instead of paying a fine, took flight on his horse. He could be sure that nobody would pursue him.

Naturally, the alien watch did large material and still more moral damage to the colony and to the whole Jewish settlement. The watchmen-robbers felt as true masters in the Jewish colonies, and, on more than one occasion, they used to show their contempt for the Jews, who were unable to defend themselves, and had to employ hired men for that purpose; and the colonists themselves, by their passive attitude, confirmed, as it were, the opinion that Jews, even in Palestine, were unable to defend themselves; and did nothing to change the situation. The Jews were nick-named "Wlad-el-Muth"—children of death—and, like the brand of Cain, it burned and tortured our Jewish national conscience.

What the colonies neglected was taken up by Jewish workmen.

Some eight years ago a few Jewish workingmen organized a group to contest against this shameful and harmful position of national demoralization, and to raise the honor of the Jewish name in the eyes of the Jews themselves and in the eyes of their neighbors, the Arabs. They at first applied to the colonists themselves and appealed to them, in the name of their own interests and in the interests of the Jewish colonies. This, however, was not sufficient, for the colonists did not believe that Jewish young men were capable of undertaking such responsible work. Where would they get weapons? But after some accidents with the Arabian Cherkessian watchmen, one of two colonies (first the ICA farm "Sedgera", and afterwards "Masche") decided to invite a group of Jewish watchmen and to entrust it with the defence of their property. Their work was carried out earnestly and successfully. The group, by its heroism, acquired respect even with the Arabs, and the year following, many of the colonies applied to the group to supply them with watchmen. This encouraged the watchmen, and the watch attracted the best of Jewish workmen in the country. The organization grew year by year and spread its activities over the colonies of Judaea and Gallilee, and influenced the organization of the Jewish watch in Jaffa, Jerusalem and Tel-Aviv. In conflicts with robbers and thieves many Jewish watchmen shed their blood upon Jewish soil. Many suffered in Turkish prisons, but they had won their point: the "Jewish Watch" became the pride of the Jewish colonies. Jewish power is recognized, and the shame of passiveness and fear was washed off from our conscience.

The Organization "Hashomer" likewise formed groups to settle upon the land which was newly acquired, and upon which attacks were expected from the neighboring Arabian villages. Thanks to this group, it was possible to maintain and consolidate such important centers as "Merchavia", "Charkur" and "Tel-Adash". The name of the Hashomer grew so popular that German and even Arabian villages demanded Jewish watchmen.

But, at the same time, when the present moment increased tenfold the importance and task of the Hashomer, its existence became more difficult. The Jewish colonists, as it is well known, are suffering from a shortage of money, and this is reflected, above all, upon the condition of the Jewish workmen and watchmen. True, the watch is offered to the Hashomer, but on condition that only small portions of their wages be paid, and the rest after the moratorium. The money is naturally safe and guaranteed by the committee of the colony; but where can the Hashomer get now the necessary cash? And so it was hard for it to accept the watch in Segera only because it was short of $200, on the guarantee of the "Plantation Society". In the same way it was also unable to accept the watch from Richon-le-Zion and Beer-Jacob only because it could get nowhere another 30% of its necessary cash budget.

It must be taken into consideration that the present crisis in Palestine brought with it a heavy advance in prices of food articles and other necessaries, while clothing and shoes are almost unobtainable. The Winter period of showers and piercing cold finds the watchmen bare-footed, without warm garments, and hungry; and as a result—many illnesses and deaths. Watchmen have to care not only for their families, but also for their weapons and horses, without which their work is impossible. Many weapons have to be hidden until the war is over, and other weapons must now be bought. Weapons are hard to obtain, and, if obtained, are expensive. Ammunition is necessary. Food for the horses is also dear, and horses were taken by the Government for military purposes and many died of starvation, and a certain number of additional horses must be acquired.

The Hashomer has also comrades whose health has been ruined by their work, and by conflicts with Arabs. It has to maintain widows of comrades fallen while performing their duty, and to support the few who suffered for the sake of their organization, having been sent forever to distant parts of Turkey.

In ordinary times the expenses and deficits of the Hashomer were covered, in a certain measure, by the loans from the Odessa Palestine Committee, the Workingmen's Bureau of the Poale Zion in Palestine, and by the Zionist Organization. Now this support is reduced to a minimum, while the expenses are constantly increasing. Irrespective of the hard condition of the work at the present time, none of the watchmen allowed himself to be carried away by the panic-stream of refugees. They all remained on their post of honor. It is possible that now a great part of them will be compelled to join the army. *Their position is critical in the fullest sense of the word.* If it is impossible to obtain the means whereby their exemption from military service could be procured, it is still necessary that an immediate loan of a minimum of $10,000 to secure the existence of the watchmen, their weapons, their horses, their clothing, and the upkeep of their sick sentenced comrades be secured.

Surely, we cannot remain indifferent and see the destruction of the organization which has sanctified, with blood, our national regenerative work in Palestine. We cannot leave weaponless those whose sole task in life is to defend, with their weapons, our work in our Homeland. We cannot tear in tatters the flag of our struggle for independence and activity in the Land of Israel.

It is the serious obligation of the Zionist Organization to supply the Hashomer with this loan, and by it to consolidate and secure the basis of Jewish self-protection in Palestine, at a moment which is full of surprises.

The Hashomer only accepts, in its lines, such watchmen as have already acquired experience. Every new comrade must first watch at least one year under the supervision of the Hashomer, in order to be accepted into the organization. The Hashomer figures as a large cooperative comradeship which undertakes work by contract. All members have an equal voice in all matters concerning the organization. Every year a report is submitted. An Executive is elected, which bears the responsibility for all the members. Every member is obligated to comply with all the requirements of the organization, and is subjected to the discipline which rendered possible the success of the Hashomer. The organization has several working funds; an Insurance Fund for members and horses; a Weapon Fund; a Sick Fund; a Loan Fund; an Inventory Fund; a Guarantee Fund to ensure the colonies against possible burglaries; a Legal Aid Fund, and others. All these funds were provided, up to now, by the payments of members; and, in the year before the last, the Hashomer had a budget of 100,000 Francs, counting not less than 100 members. The present budget can naturally be reduced.

BUDGET OF THE HASHOMER

15 riders, family men, 150 Fr. ($25.00) each per month............	Fr. 2,250
11 riders, single men, 100 Fr. ($17.00) per month.................	1,100
24 pedestrians, 60 Fr. each ($10.00) per month...................	1,440

TOTAL 50 Watchmen	Monthly . . . Fr. 4,790
	approximately $800.00

For the year, approximately Fr. 60.000—$10,000
The minimum support as a loan necessary for the Hashomer is 50% of this

sum, i.e., $5,000 a year for watchmen's wages. The colonists pay now not more than 30% of their usual pay; naturally, not in cash.
The loan will go for the following:

Wages for watchmen this year, 50%	$ 5,000
Fund for horses	1,200
Weapons and ammunition	2,000
For sick and arrested comrades	1,800
	$10,000

CS
2/10/16

10. DEMANDS OF ATARA STURMAN (KROL), DEVORA DARKLER AND YEHUDIT HOROWITZ IN THE MATTER OF FEMALE EQUALITY IN HASHOMER

To the membership of Hashomer!

We the young women who have worked together with you for several years and who have always been at your side under the most difficult conditions, do not feel it is possible for us to continue our work in the manner which we have done thus far. We do not wish to call your attention to facts and events of which you are well aware. We have come to the decision that joint work and joint responsibility is possible only when there are equal conditions in all areas. Only then will we be able to strive our utmost for our common goals. And if we are equal members in our daily work, let us be equal members in all aspects. No meetings which exclude us, no secrets from us, and if the membership does not trust us enough for this, then you must openly declare this. At least then we will know where we stand and we will find other means to achieve our common goals. We await your answer.

Tel-Adash, 25.9.1918   Atara, Devora, Yehudit.

(Labor Archives, IV 112, file 9)

11. LETTER FROM YISRAEL SHOCHAT TO SHMUEL HEFTER

12 Av 5679
<August 8, 1919>

Dear Shmulik,

It is possible that I will shortly be travelling abroad, definitely to Paris, and since one of the matters I will take care of is the settlement, I must prepare a detailed agenda, etc. I think that the settlement board should work out all the details, but don't procrastinate since I think most of the Council members are present in Tel-Adash and Merhaviah. What's doing with Tel-Adash for next year? Have you succeeded? Have you recruited new members? I spoke with Haim <Sturman>, he is very depressed—not seemly for a Hashomer member....

Please let me know if you have recruited new members, and who the candidates are. In general, try to write at least once a week to let us know what is doing with you.

We hear talk about concessions of land being made in London, top secret, how true we do not know.

In any case, before I leave we will have another Hashomer board meeting to iron out all the details.
Good-bye for now.
Yours,

Yisrael

(Labor Archives, IV 112, file 26)

12. LETTER FROM MANYA TO RACHEL YANAIT IN THE MATTER OF THE NEGEV DELEGATION AND IN THE MATTER OF OBTAINING THE SUPPORT OF HENRIETTA SZOLD FOR MANYA'S EFFORTS IN THE UNITED STATES

Mania Shohat
c/o Shelupsky
1490 Croton Park East
Bronx, N.Y.

6.8.1921

Dear Rachel,

What's new? Why haven't you written? You promised to let me know the results of the Negev delegation. I cannot begin until I hear from you. One cannot speak in mere generalities—America is even richer in generalities than Israel. I wrote to you several times while en route. I asked you to visit Szold to find out her final decision. Without her name it is impossible to do anything serious here. The time is passing. Why don't you understand this simple thing, haven't I explained it enough to you, and didn't I ask you to respond immediately?
I do not know how to extricate myself now from this situation. Another two months will pass until I hear from you.
Listen, go to her, tell her in my name that I am asking that she let us use her name. Her name is well-trusted here. Explain to her how serious the situation is, there are moments which require that we demand. The day will come that she will demand and I will do. Have her send a telegram in Magnes's name if she agrees or not.

I love you.

Manya

(Archives of the Ben-Zvi Foundation, file no. 2/6/1/32)

13. LETTER FROM MANYA TO RACHEL YANAIT IN THE MATTER OF THE NEGEV, POALEI ZION IN AMERICA AND THE CONTROVERSY BETWEEN YISRAEL SHOCHAT AND ELIAHU GOLOMB IN LAND PROCUREMENT MATTERS

21.9<1921>
My dear, dear friend,

Today I received your letter of September 3. I am very happy since this is the first time that I got such good news. I think that I will be able to send you the $1000 needed for the Aqaba expedition. How I believe in your intuitive ability! I think that without this strength we would never build anything. Here this is a great possibility to fund the Negev project. We are awaiting your report. I laid the groundwork, in case there is the slightest possibility that Samuel will provide the land. Then we will make a revolution in labor conditions. And we will succeed, dear friend.

Here the party does not work well. Everything is superficial. In all of America, there are maybe 2000 members, a real joke! In New York, there are no more than 180 members, and there is no peace among them, "Left", "Right", "Left", "Right", discussions and discussions, and speeches and noise and finally, finally a tempest in a teacup. The entire movement here is worthless. These members are waiting for some new, big, momentous event and then they will work and devote their efforts. They are fed up with the way they have worked thus far, and Di Tzayt, their newspaper, is folding. It is amazing how much money this paper has eaten up and it has not survived. It ate up all the energy of the members, all their money and in the end there is no possibility of continuing it. I am afraid that bankruptcy will arrive together with Berl and then we will have to get out of here. And all this is not because in fact there is no place for a newspaper such as this, on the contrary it is needed and very important. It is because the administration of the newspaper is totally ineffective. Is it true that we workers have no administrative ability? I do not understand it. Don't tell anyone about this—I do not want them to know that I am telling their secrets. Maybe they will get stronger, or maybe by the time you get this, the newspaper will have been put to sleep.

What will be in the matter of Yisrael and Eliahu, is it possible to make peace? This will destroy everything. What to do? I said that the committee consists of Yisrael and Ben-Zvi. The people here who give money, give it on the condition that the matter will be in the hands of people who are known to them. Rosenblatt is travelling to Eretz Israel, if he will know that there is no peace there between us, he will insist that the money should fall into the hands of the steering committee. Can't you make peace, or at least explain to them that they must absolutely not behave this way? I am very saddened by this and I do not know what will happen in the end.

Regards to all.

Manya

(Archives of Ben-Zvi Foundation, file no. 2/6/1/32)

14. LETTER FROM MANYA TO RACHEL YANAIT IN THE MATTER OF RAISING FUNDS FOR THE SETTLING OF SOLDIERS IN TEL-ARAD AND IN THE MATTER OF LAND PROCUREMENT

Dear beloved Rachel,

I do not understand why Feller <of the settlement committee for soldiers> did not send the report of the delegation. We are waiting for it here. I am sure that we will be able to do much about the Negev, but I need data <.> How is it that you, people of experience, do not understand this? We have decided here that the money which we will collect in the workers groups will be sent to the attention of Ben-Zvi. The money that the Zionists of Keren Hayesod are giving is in the name of Novomaisky <creator of the Dead Sea Works (this is what they want) and the Brandeis followers will give it on behalf of Henrietta. They could have collected a lot, until Aaronson came in and disturbed matters. I will have to

fight him, but this is a difficult matter and so far there is no success. Magnes does not want to help in this.

From Berl there is no news. This man is very strange. He completely disregards his friends. I spoke to <Brandeis's representative> Dehaz in regard to the Negev. They want it a great deal. I do not know if it is good for us to get tied in with them, if Berl would agree perhaps I would too. I am afraid. The hatred toward them is so great that it is hard to imagine, it is hard to explain this to an outsider, and I do not want to fall in the midst of all the politics.

What's with Yisrael? I think that he has to travel to Vienna for land purchase, for several reasons he must do this. This separation is unavoidable. He will interfere with all the work. We have already bought one motor boat, we just have to fix it up, it is not new. When we buy another one we will send them together. The fund in America is quite depleted, bills must be paid, and they will be able to send maybe $10,000 to Israel if they succeed in collecting $20,000. Here there is no faith in Poalei Zion. The community does not want to support them. For something real, we could raise money from the American Jews, but to a general fund, they will not give.

Send the report quickly. You are helping me very poorly. I love you.

Manya

(Archives of the Ben-Zvi Foundation, file no. 2/6/1/32)

15. REPORT ON THE ACTIVITIES OF THE FIRST DELEGATION TO THE UNITED STATES ON BEHALF OF THE HISTADRUT IN THE MATTER OF BANK HAPOALIM

The first activity which our delegation members attempted after receptions and publicity was the preparation of the bank committee. The goal was to draw toward bank activity groups from the broadest elements of the worker community. The personal meetings and special assemblies seem to promise success. Union leaders, spokesmen and well-known people from all over the labor spectrum seem eager to join.

One of the first to work for the bank was Dr. J. L. Magnes. He also tried to break the stone wall at the <Jewish Daily> Forward for the bank, in an open letter to the editor written in honesty and in an appreciation of the value of the matter at hand. The response of the editor was ambiguous. The matter still required "further investigation." However, this open letter led to commentaries from other directions. Dr. Zhitlovsky wrote two essays in the columns of the "Tzeit", pulling out all his weapons and attacking Dr. Magnes with the eternal Yiddish question. And then all the Zion-haters came out of their corners and added their arguments to the fray.

A lot of people who were ready to participate in our effort began to retract. The delegation members saw a need to set things straight. In a series of essays, which they published themselves, our comrade B. Katznelson demolished the false idols and the lies and poured light on the dark sea of ignorance, but explaining the truth of the matters in Eretz Israel.

Our broadside was finally published. In it was recounted the story of the delegation that came to America, the purpose of its coming, about the party formed for the Bank Hapoalim. Also in it was a plea for all the cities and towns to form chapters for this committee.

This letter was sent to the Jewish workers community:

Comrades:

We are not coming in the name of any party, and we are not addressing one particular group. The united workers of Israel have sent us to the Jewish workers of America...ties must be established between us.

We have come to you after years of trials and efforts. We began alone. Empty-handed and inexperienced...We fought conditions of cheap labor, unstable markets, low technology. We have created a collective life, we have brought strength to the settlements. We create work not only for ourselves, but also for all those who follow us and join us.

The worker in Eretz Israel does not need help. He lives by his work...From his earnings, he sent help to the victims of the pogroms in Europe, and he sends his coworkers abroad for the sake of the Aliyah, and even the new pioneer scrapes off part of his meager earnings to fund his family and friends to come to Eretz Israel.

Thus, it is not to help us that we came to you but to help the work that we do. There is an aliya to Israel, but it is not enough. But thousands are coming. Ships are bringing young workers. The worker of Eretz Israel must welcome them, help them find work and then join forces and work together.

And it is for this purpose, for the immigration absorption that we need your attention, your awareness. We wish to explain everything openly, about our lives and our work. We want to tell you about our economic activities, explain about our cooperatives and kibbutzim, describe our work in agriculture and industry. We want to reveal to you the light and the shadows, the trials and the victories, the motivations and the obstacles which we meet on our path. We also want to share with you the strength and the conviction that we carry within us; the strength that draws even upon the depths of destruction; the burning conviction that grows as our work grows and which is validated by all the pioneers who stream to us from all over the world.

Our camp has grown. And our work has grown. We have established tens of workers' cooperatives in the villages and cities. Tens of cooperative kitchens, a large supply institution, "Hamashbir". The development of the worker community is what brought us to create the central monetary institution for our economic activities: Bank Hapoalim.

Bank Hapoalim was created on a healthy foundation. And we are confident that it will be a motive force in strengthening aliyah and in building the workers settlements. We believe that our efforts deserve to be understood and participated in by the Jewish working class all over the world.

And now we turn to you, American Jewish workers. We give ourselves permission to come to you with our words, with our requests. You are, after all, the only ones who were saved from the great destruction. And you do not have the right to sit peacefully by with folded hands when this matter comes before you. The Jewish exiles now have a refuge. The Jewish worker is building roots in the earth, building factories, accomplishing his dreams and aspirations. You who have been saved from the sea of tribulation of the Jews, you can do something worthwhile. You can lend your hand, your strong worker's hand, to the creators of modern Jewish history to aid in pioneering and social creativity.

In you, and only in you, are the means for opening the gates for the wandering Jew who is requesting no handouts, only work and you can help the worker in his battle. You can put the stamp of labor on the realia of life.

You have the power to act. Your obligation is to do so, and we sincerely hope that you will.

Workers' Representatives in Eretz Israel
Yosef Baratz, B. Katznelson, Manya Shochat
(Kuntres [Notebook], Vol. 106, No. 5, 5 Shevat 5682 = 3 February 1922, pp. 13-15)

16. LETTER FROM MANYA TO BEN-ZVI IN THE MATTER OF HIS PARTICIPATION IN THE CONVENTION OF "GEDUD HA-AVODAH" <WORKERS BRIGADE>

Jerusalem
7.3.1924

Greetings to you Ben-Zvi,

In my name and in the name of Yisrael and in the name of the people of the brigade's executive committee, each of us individually requests you to arrange matters so as to be able to join the convention on Monday.
Yisrael will pick you up by car and arrange everything so that you can return easily.
I know you are very busy, but sometimes there are situations which require one to put aside some important matters and deal with others.
I myself do not have the time to speak with you in person. But you will understand that it is necessary for you to make a genuine peace with the brigade members. They love you and believe in you and if you go the atmosphere will be cordial and warm.
Please do this, I will try to see you tomorrow. But if by chance I can't, I am writing this to explain to you that you must make every effort to give us your time for 2-3 days.
Send me your answer with Tuvia. He will come to you tomorrow, get your answer and bring it to me.
With great affection and respect,

Manya

(Personal Archives of Ben-Zvi, file no. A 116/14)

17. LETTER FROM RIMA LINDHEIM* TO MANYA IN THE MATTER OF THE NEGATIVE ATTITUDE OF LABOR ISRAEL TOWARD HADASSAH

(English text)
(Archives of the Ben-Zvi Foundation, file no. 2/6/1/49)

Mrs. Manya Shochet,
Box 98
Jerusalem, Palestine.

Dearest Manya,

I cannot even apologize for not having written to you for all of this time. There is no excuse, and I am not going to offer one.
Your recent letters have left me with a feeling of deepest depression, they have been the one live contact that I have had with Palestine and therefore of the

*In the USA she was known as Irma Lindheim. The text says that the children of Kfar Giladi renamed her "Rima."

greatest value. I hardly know where to begin. There are so many things that are crowding into my mind which I feel I must discuss with you. First of all, the situation at Kfar Yeladim. I spoke to Mr. Spector,* whom I saw for the first time yesterday, and he seemed to feel that there was some hope of a settlement between the Gedud and the Histadruth. I hope and pray that this may be true. It is terrible for me to think of the Labor group being torn apart by strife such as you pictured in your letter. I am deeply concerned to know more details about the reasons for this upheaval, and am looking forward with eagerness to the letter in which you promised to give me more information. I have spoken to various people here, but have failed as yet to arrive at the fundamental causes. Is the cause a political one? This question almost answers itself. As I see it, the differences of political views are always the rocks upon which causes go to smash. The thing that makes me so fearful about this whole complication now is that I feel that there is growing up in America a bitter antagonism to the labor ideals of Palestine. This, I believe, comes from two causes: one, that America is suffering from a wave of reactionism, and second and by far the most important causes are the actions of the Labor group itself. I find myself at every meeting and at every conference in the position of defending the Labor group. Why do they make it necessary? I need not convince you of my belief in the ideals which the labor group represents in Palestine, but I cannot be too strong in my condemnation of many of their methods. In relation to Hadassah; as I see it, Hadassah represents in Palestine a great humanitarian movement which expresses in its ideals and through its activities the highest social principles, principles which parallel and support the ideals of the workers. Hadassah today is in a position which may make it necessary for it to cease operation,—and why? Because of the workers. Instead of assuming that Hadassah has ideals which are compatible with their own, they are making these ideals impossible, because Hadassah happens to be represented by people of a different nationality from their own. I saw when I was in Palestine how deep the antagonism was to Americans. It is true of almost every country in the world today, and yet for us as Jews to adopt a biased attitude because the whole world is doing it, is unworthy of consideration. That, I believe, is at the very base of the situation between the Hadassah and the Histadruth. I know that immediately the protest would come that it is not that,—that the Hadassah is an outside organization, that it gives larger salaries than are compatible with the other salaries given in Palestine, that it tries to introduce methods which are foreign to the country, etc., etc.,—but if all of these things were being done by an organization which was being run by Eastern Jews I am certain that the attitude would be vastly different. The manner in which Dr. Bluestone has been treated since his arrival in Palestine has made it impossible, should he return to America, to find another man to assume his responsibilities. Without a fine administrator, how could the Hadassah work and grow in effectiveness? Without this growth, how can the population of Palestine be served? In other words, because Dr. Bluestone has not been allowed to attend to his administrative work and has met with a spirit of non-cooperation on the part of the workers, the effectiveness of the work for Palestine must suffer and be seriously menaced as far as its future is concerned in America. At every meeting now, you will hear: "The workers? Look at the way they have treated Hadassah! They are arbitrary,—nobody can cooperate with them." This is typical of the remarks made at the Zionist

*Meir Spector, a member of Hashomer.

meeting. Outside of Zionist circles, or even in Zionist circles which are not of the inner group, it already has become common talk that, if Hadassah is so hampered in its humanitarian work of healing that it cannot operate effectively, then how can anything else be successfully done in Palestine? I am not exaggerating. Manya dear, it is a question of really serious import, and a problem which must be faced by the labor group in Palestine. The collections this year are being seriously enough menaced by the work of the Joint Distribution Committee, by the crisis in Palestine and by the emigration, but, when the attitude of the workers is such that it may make impossible the future participation of the women Zionists of America in medical work in Palestine, this as an obstacle to the collection of money overshadows all of the previous difficulties.

My heart is heavy when I realize the sufferings that all of you are undergoing. No country has ever been built up on a finer spirit of sacrifice and love than Palestine. I know the magnificence of the group of workers; I know that without their ideals Palestine had better never be built up at all. But I want other people to know these things too. I do not want them to feel that this group of workers is oppressive in its methods and imperialistic in its ways. I am beginning to be known as a Bolshevik here, at every meeting I take up your cudgels, but it is unjust to make my task so heavy,—unjust from the point of view of Palestine and from the point of view of the workers' ideals.

For the last three weeks I have been involved in my new tasks; I love them more each day. The responsibility is a heavy one, and I feel weak and humble in the face of it. I consider it one of the great privileges of my life to be in constant and close association with Henrietta Szold; she is the greatest educational force I have ever met, and I hope that with her example before me I will learn to follow in her footsteps. It breaks my heart, though, to see how she has been broken up by the conditions of which I spoke before. She, with all her beautiful social vision, with her ability to make them concrete and put them into life, has been made to feel impotent because of the retardation of the achievements of these ideals by the methods of your protagonists. I find her deeply unhappy and pessimistic, and though she is firm as ever in her assertion of her beliefs in the ideals of labor, her condemnation of their methods is unequivocal, and are bound to influence unfavorably those who hear them.

I feel that if we could work out some method by which Hadassah and the workers could come to an effective understanding, that a really creative piece of work for Palestine would then be done. Work in this direction is being started, and I hope that some means will be found to work a way out of these difficulties. It must be found. I really feel that the future of Palestine depends upon it. You need our work as much as we need you, and Palestine must not cut itself off from the possibility of getting whole-hearted American support. I really hate to write a letter like this to you, when I know how many troubles you have and how patiently you face them, but all of this is part of the same thing, Manya dear, and only with the solution of these problems can our future be made secure.

Your letters, even those with bad news, always are a source of great happiness to me. I love you as much as ever, and I am looking forward more than I can say, to my return next summer. I expect to leave here immediately after our Convention, and to come direct to Palestine. I wish it could be before, but I am needed here now and cannot leave.

Give my fondest love to Anna, and tell her that I think her drawings are really lovely, and I am looking forward to getting some more. To you, dear Manya, as always, my love and my deepest admiration. I only hope that you may be able to give to others in Palestine some of the great wisdom which is yours.

Yours,

18. LETTER TO MANYA WRITTEN BY HENRIETTA SZOLD AFTER BEING ELECTED TO THE NATIONAL COMMITTEE

(English text)

(Archives of Beit Hashomer, Manya file 15/6)

October 3, 1927

Dearest Mania,

What you wanted has come to pass. If only your confidence in me was not misplaced! Yes, my intentions are good, free from self-interest—so much I can say. But what of my knowledge, my experience with affairs, my strength, my wisdom? What, indeed, can the wisest and the strongest among us do when we are faced by deficits, a curtailed budget, a problem of eight thousand unemployed? What can a movement do which in its hour of trial has to resort to a woman of sixty-seven, a tired woman, who wanted rest and needed rest?—a movement which apparently has developed no personnel—no men, no sacrificial spirits.

I wish I could feel about myself as you feel about me. I confess to you that I have not had a moment of serenity since the Congress. I have just come from the organizing meeting of the new Executive in London. The whole panorama of problems was unrolled before us—the inadequacy of our prospective means was made cruelly clear. And I have acute personal difficulties—certain duties towards my family, and, worst of all, a commitment to outsiders to which I am pledged, and which I can meet only in New York.

Well, the dice is cast, I am going to America for three weeks. Not only did I have to go to arrange my personal affairs, but the Executive wanted me to go for certain reasons connected with the collection of funds. The understanding is that I am to be in Palestine as soon after the middle of November as possible.

I must return to the question of confidence in me. The election did not show that others share it. The Right voted against the combination, the Left abstained from voting. The only members of the Left who had a word of encouragement for me were Rachel Yanait and Dr. Rieger,* and even that was faint, and was prompted by a recollection of past, friendly personal relations.

It had been my firm intention, when I left Palestine last April, after my conversation with you and Israel in the presence of Mr. Lindheim, to write to you on reaching America about the possibilities for getting the leaders to accept your attitude. I had hardly set foot on American soil than I knew the utter impossibility of it. The situation which I found in our American organization was as deplorable as the situation I had seen in Palestine. And between Palestine and America lay the Actions Committee! There was no use writing to you, even if there had been time. Instead we all had to plunge into the sea of our own troubles and difficulties—a deficit of $136,000, no money coming in for the United Palestine Appeal, opposition to the existing management without hav-

*Dr. Eliezer Rieger, a physician and educator, a member of the National Council.

ing other forces to put into power—a repetition of Palestine and London, a forecast of the Congress. All we can do is to make ourselves whole and sound. In America at least that is the only method of restoring confidence. I know what that method means to Halutziut. But in certain cases all a physician can do is to treat each symptom of a disease as it appears. That must be our method now.

I have read and re-read the letters you wrote us last winter. I have them with me now, and I am reading them again. In coming to certain conclusions as to what is needed, I have been guided by them. You will have to give me the benefit of your guidance in Palestine, too.

A Happy New Year for us all—for Palestine.

My love and good wishes to Miss Lasker.**

Affectionately,

Henrietta Szold

19. LETTER FROM MANYA TO BEN-ZVI IN THE MATTER OF FUNDRAISING FOR ACTIVITY WITHIN THE ARAB COMMUNITY

Tel Aviv, 14.1.30 Let Rachel read this letter.
Ben Zvi, I am sending you a copy of my suggestions to the Executive Committee.

To the Executive Committee of the Workers' Federation, Tel Aviv:

Friends,

I recommend that you send me to America to obtain funds needed for wide-range activity within the Arab community:

1) Arab newspaper, 2) Organization of the Watch, 3)Information and constant communication with the Fellahin, 4) Statistical study of the workers, Fellahin, Arab sharecroppers, 5) Joint clubs for Jewish and Arab workers in the cities, etc., etc.

2. I can raise the required funds with Lindheim's help from private people from pacifist groups who do not belong directly to the Zionist Organization, but are interested from humanitarian reasons in coordination between the Jewish nation and the Arab nation. Also, it is possible to organize a group of individuals, who will support us with regular annual contributions.

3. This fundraising will be unofficial, unpublicized and will not interfere with the Fund of Eretz Israel Workers nor with the United Jewish Appeal.

4. I will get a loan of 70-80 Eretz Israel lira for the trip and expenses for the first few months in America and from the sums that you receive, you can pay off my loan.

5. My trip must be kept very quiet, no newspaper publicity either here or there.

6. I can also do some work for Haganah in America if I am given an assignment. I can help the Women's Workers' Council to obtain a fund for the creation of a network of day nurseries for the children of urban and rural working women.

7. I must leave immediately. Every delay will deter from the possibility of

---

**Manya's close friend from London who moved to Eretz Israel and was killed in an explosion in the buildings of the national authorities in 1948, together with Leib Yaffe.

success. I, myself, am confident in my success, because this Arab question has become an *idée fixe* to me.

Respectfully,
Manya Shochat

20. ZIONIST TAX (SHEKEL) OBLIGATION—APRIL 12, 1937

Many of my acquaintances have come to me lately with the question: "Is it true that you refuse to buy the shekel and are opposed to participation in the Zionist Congress?" I decided to answer in writing.

I don't know who is interested in spreading this rumor, which is a lie to its core. I decided to squelch this rumor in writing, not because I think that the Jew who buys the shekel is a good Zionist and the one who doesn't is a bad Zionist.

I know many Jews who continually buy shekels and at the same time destroy the settlements, and hundreds of other young men and women who do not buy the shekel, whether out of principle or laziness, and the latter are building the land. Nevertheless we are now in a period in which all the revolutionary forces in the work force must participate in the Zionist Congress.

The Congress is in effect the parliament of the Jewish nation, and the institutions of the Zionist Organization influence all our actions in the land in daily life. Also, in addition to the established reasons which require working people to participate in the Zionist Congress, there is an additional factor: The necessity to save the soul of the labor movement, because the movement has, in recent years, shown a dangerous tendency to erode much of its socialist character within the general framework of the Histadrut.

Therefore, it is incumbent upon the movers and shakers within labor, for whom the socialist ideal is not simply a metaphor, that celebrate it so vociferously the first of May, for whom it is the direction that life must take in the building of a working homeland, not to stand on the sides now, muttering and mumbling criticisms, but to participate fully in the Zionist Congress in the most active way, and to create an internal power base which will preserve the founding principles of the labor movement and will not allow its image to be tarnished.

Manya Shochat

(*Davar*, 12 April 1937)

21. MINUTES OF THE FIRST MISHMERET HAGVUL MEETING, JANUARY 9, 1938

(Internal Document 3110/A7)

Weekly Review.

On 29.1.38, the council met. Participating: Yisrael, Manya, Yosef, Nachum, and Charit.*

1.a. Discussed recruitment for new members. Suggested that former Hashomer members not be subject to further initiation procedures.

b. Those who are particularly important in the group of "Mishmeret Hagvul" (border guards) should be encouraged to join.

Resolved: Have to meet with: Ben-Zvi, Kaplanski, Paz, Shaul, Wolf, and Yigal**

2. On the issue of bringing in the youth, the responsibility was given to Manya, and also to gather information as required for the council's evaluation.

3. *Relationship with institutions.* As a first step, should seek to co-opt members of those institutions and, as possible, to expand this activity.

4. The subject of the Watch was tabled for now, despite the fact that its importance and inherent difficulties were expressed.

5. Information gathering to take place in Tel Aviv.

6. Appointed secretary—Charit. Liaison—Manya.

7. The council to meet in another two weeks.

On 4.2.38, the secretariat met. Present: Yisrael, Charit. After a discussion of how to organize the material, it was decided to hire a secretary for half days.

It is necessary to pay particular attention to the ecoomic value and topographic quality of the land, villages and boundaries where settlement is investigated and to their demography.

Yisrael will procure detailed maps of the country's boundaries. Once the maps are received, border inspection duty is to be split up among the members.

To set up a standing membership file.

Try to get Zvi Nadav to work in aviation on a regular basis.

On the question of money, it was agreed to suggest that the council impose upon the members an annual tax of 10 percent of their monthly wages. (For example—a member earning 20 liras a month would pay 2 liras a year).

(Labor Archives, IV 112, file 29)

22. MINUTES OF THE SECOND MISHMERET HAGVUL MEETING
FEBRUARY 8, 1938

Internal

Weekly Review:

On 8.2.38, the secretariat met. Participating were Yisrael, Manya and Charit. Manya reported on her activities. She met with Kaplanski. He promises to help and expressed a desire to learn what's going on. Manya promised that when Yosef or Nachum would be in Haifa, they would go see him to explain the matters that are their area of activity. Manya also met with the youth of Kfar Giladi. They expressed the opinion that maybe it would be easier if this organization had a clear political direction. In order to reach the youth, their leaders must be contacted. There are about five groups getting ready to settle. They should be approached and encouraged to join.

Decided:

1. To prepare two programs.

2. Programs for filling in our membership rolls.

3. Establish two schools. One in Hulah and the second in Kfar Giladi. In them, the members will learn about their surroundings and about security and agriculture.

4. As to the youth, we must begin recruitment efforts, to organize them in groups for specific places. To arrange lectures for them.

*Yisrael and Manya Shochat, Yosef Nachmani, Nachum Horowitz and Yosef Charit.
**Shlomo Kaplanski, Saadia Paz, Shavl Karbel, Zvi Wolf and Mordechai Yigal.

(Labor Archives, iv 112, file 29)

5. Independent preparation required as well. One must study the Arab question pragmatically by direct meetings.

The opinion was expressed that other institutions should not be approached until something concrete has been accomplished. The council will meet on 15.2.38 in the evening.

(Labor Archives, IV 112, file 29)

*23. MANYA SHOCHAT THROUGH THE EYES OF HER DAUGHTER, ANNA. (HAARETZ SUPPLEMENT, 17 OCTOBER 1986)

Caption under photo:

What is it like to be the daughter of legendary figures? How does one grow up in a home where the parents are engrossed in building the land? Anna Shochat, 70-years-old, daughter of the Hashomer personalities Manya and Yisrael, about her parents and their other loves, about the special relationship between them, about the rate of suicide in the family, about the old values and the remnant that still haunt her today. "I am an orphan," she told Ben-Gurion when she was still a young girl...

Question:What is your most early memory of your parents?
Answer: My first memory, and I am not sure if this is an actual memory or a piece of a story that my mother told me at age fifteen. It is that I got lost at the age of a year and a half in Turkey, and my father was ready to leave me there in order to speed his trip to the Congress in Stockholm.
This was in Turkey. I was told that I was born in prison, but the truth is that I was born in exile in Brusa, where my parents had been sent after my mother's trial in Damascus for concealing weapons. They were each seized individually, but at the end their sentence was reduced to exile. They lived with Joshua and Olga Hankin, and had no means of support. Father tied his feet in burlap sacks, because they did not even have shoes, and he would take me walking in some rickety carriage, and when I would cry, he would stick sugary candies in my mouth.
In that period, he later told me, he tried to escape twice. He shaved his head and tried to disguise himself, but he was caught. When I was about a year and a half, they succeeded in getting out because my father was appointed as a delegate to the Congress in Stockholm.
They were with the Benjamini family, friends of my parents. The Benjaminis had a daughter slightly older than me, about two and a half, this was already in Constantinople. They packed their belongings. We, the two little girls, went down, and holding hands we crossed the road. We crossed the street, two tiny girls. And some policman took us to the edge of the city. Suddenly our parents realized we were missing and started looking for us. Like finding a needle in a haystack. They searched in all the places that they could think of.
Mother ran a fever of 40 degrees (104F.), and felt as though her daughter was lost forever. The girls were gone, and there was no way to find them. Father told her, as she recounted to me when I was fifteen, "Let us leave the children and go, we will leave people here who will continue to search for them." I remember my emotions when I heard this story. My knees grew weak, and I had the feeling of abandonment, because if I had not been found I would have been a

*Excerpt permission from *Ha'aretz*, by Rut Baki.

poor little girl, a little Turkish whore, all because he felt this desperate need to return to Israel. This is the way I pictured it to myself, that he figured that we would somehow be found, but maybe not. We were found entirely by accident. We were sitting all dirty from grape juice and mud at the edge of Constantinople. One of my mother's friends happened to see us. Mother felt that she would not have been ready to leave us like that. This was the story, and it still haunts me today. I still have the feeling of being disoriented, of being lost, but at the end I always find my way. In every situation, my first reaction is that of being lost, the feeling of a small girl crying because she has been abandoned.

Question: How was it to grow up feeling less important than the state of Israel?

Answer: I absolutely felt that Israel was more important. I felt the priorities. In fact, I accepted those priorities uncritically. I never dared to ask myself—why am I less? Is it because I am not good enough, not successful enough, or is it because values such as country and homeland have more pepetual meaning than an individual? I didn't consciously think about it, but the deep sense of loss that Father could ignore me was a feeling that accompanied me for many years.

Question: Did your mother ever cry? You say that she was fearless. Did you ever see any external signs of emotion in her?

I saw my mother cry once. No, actually twice. Other than that, never. The first time was when I was ill with typhus. I was eleven years old. The fever kept going up. At first they thought I had malaria. I had six attacks. During the last attack they took me to Hadassah. I remember lying there, they came in to take my temperature, the thermometer was on my hand, not even under my arm and the temperature was 42 degrees. I was delirious and they put ice on my body, and the ice kept melting. I remember my mother sitting there with tears running down her face. I felt myself passing away, as though my soul was being lifted out, yet I somehow mustered up some strength and survived. They diagnosed that I had typhus, took me to Wallach and I recovered.

The second time was when she came to Kfar-Giladi to visit. We talked and I told her that the teachers were beating us violently. They really hit us, Eliezer, Shmueli and the others. She stood up, grabbed me by the shoulders and screamed: "Liar!" I remember that when I told her this I was choking with tears. I felt as though a huge canyon had formed between us, a black cloud. I got up, turned around and went. I walked between the bushes until I reached the children's house, lay down in bed and cried bitterly. Mother made the rounds among the children, asked others, and found out I was telling the truth. And then she came to the children's house, sat down beside my bed, and when I woke up I saw that she was sitting and crying, really crying, crying from the depths of her heart. She felt that her mistrust in me had been unwarranted. But more than that, maybe these tears expressed something of the price that she had paid in her children. Until that point she had trusted the teachers completely. There was complete specialization at that time, each worked only in his own area. The parents figured that if the teachers were beating the children, they probably deserved it, and did not concern themselves with what was really happening. When she found out that I had not lied, she came to find me.

I was angry. I pretended to be asleep and let her cry. I thought that she deserved to cry. I never saw her cry again, not in any situation, and there were difficult times when people died, and also hardships with Father. She was a strong person. She also did not cry when she told me about her own hard life. When I became fifteen, she started telling me more about her experience, her feelings. She spoke passionately, but the passion was an intellectual one, not accompanied by heartbreak, she never fell apart except for that moment in the children's house. I could never forgive her, not for all those years. There was a split between us. I did not tell her I was angry, but I never let her kiss me. When she would come over to embrace me, I would push her away, we had no physical contact. Nothing, nothing. All those years I had no mother, I grew up without a mother, without the feeling of a mother. We had an intellectual bond and she helped me politically. We identified in our thoughts and in all sorts of things, she respected me, valued me, loved my daughter very much, and expressed feelings, but I could not forgive. It was as though a curtain had fallen. Only in her final years, did the feelings come back. But for my whole childhood, I had no father and no mother even though I saw my mother more.

This was a period of great poverty. When we consider the rations of the refugee camps today, we should remember that we had much less. But there was no one to compare ourselves with then. We walked barefoot in rain and snow, found food with great difficulty, but we were not extraordinary, because we were all in the same boat. After being in Tel-Adash for a time, we went to Tel-Aviv for a while. Perhaps this was a transitional period, perhaps this was one of the frequent times that Father was ill and Mother took care of him, and this is the period that I also remember Geda, my brother, and the relationship between us. My brother was a street child. He was really abandoned. They were imprisoned, and he spent some time with an Arab family. Before that he was in Kinneret, and there it seems he sniffed out the arms cache and began to demand sweets so as not to inform on them, so they were forced to get rid of him and put him in some Arab home where he contracted an eye disease, and he told me how he would wake up in the morning with his eyes glued shut and the Arab would wash his eyes with the filthy waters of the Kinneret.

Geda was a boy who exploited and scrounged, a real street child. When we came to Tel-Aviv, he stole money from Father, bought shoelaces from a shoemaker, and tried to sell them on the street corner like all the other ragamuffins. Friends of Father told him, "Look, your boy is selling shoestrings on the corner." He got the belt for that. In general, Father did not beat him, but this was a matter of pride. Geda was an inveterate liar, he would deny everything. I recall mother screaming at him, "Don't lie."! She would drag him by the hair. They never touched me, not at all, and my brother was my protector. I remember I once broke a glass, it fell out of my hand and broke, and Mother asked who broke it, and I said, "I did." At the same moment, Geda said, "I did." He always protected me as though he was the only one who could do wrong. This was the period in Tel-Aviv.

Later, our parents sent us to Kfar Giladi. Mother was the treasurer, and was constantly taking out loans from one bank and transferring the money to previous creditors. The money got moved around, but she managed to keep up Ramat Rachel, Kfar-Giladi, Tel-Yosef, and maybe even Tel Hai.

In Kfar Giladi our parents did not even have a room. When Mother came to visit, she slept at the Krols. There was a bed there under their beds. We, the children of the kibbutz, grew up in two houses, six-seven in a room. There weren't enough beds, and we would sleep four in a bed. I still remember sleeping four in a bed head to toe, and we would remove the thorns from each other's feet, because we were always barefoot. Later, it became better and we only had two to a bed.

Many have asked me what I did after four o'clock when all the children went to their parents. I had nowhere to go. Geda and I had no home at all. I felt that I had nothing, that I was all alone. I pitied myself, but never really gave it serious thought. This was a feeling of great, inconsolable pain. Mixed up with my feelings of not being good enough was the concept of "homeland". I felt alone, but I knew it was for the homeland. They always spoke to us about how we must do great things for the sake of the homeland. And my parents carried the burden of the homeland relentlessly on their backs. Once, during one of our festivals, Ben-Gurion asked me something about my parents, and I told him that I was an orphan. I don't know how those words escaped, but he got very angry and said that I should not dare speak like that again, that thanks to my parents the settlement exists.

Question: What were the values that the Hashomer children grew up with—the children of Giladi, Hankin, Boker, Portugali, you and Geda?

One of the central things was work and hard labor. To stand on your own, to work, to earn a living, to help others and to be a working, laboring group. We worked hard, as children we practically did not learn, just worked, beginning from the age of five, from six in the morning. I do not remember vacation at all, only work. We, the children, were responsible for the sheep. We would milk the goats at ten and four and in between took them to graze. We could never go far, because we had to get back for milking. We also did seasonal work, cleaning and threshing and shepherding—and always barefoot.

Another important tenet was loyalty. Not to inform and not to tell on friends. There were weapons, and we heard many stories that if they catch you and beat you, you must stand firm in the tortures and not tell. This was a complete culture. I remember thinking what would I do if they would catch me and how I would stand the torture. And I also remember how we spent entire nights in the storehouse, cleaning the bullets and shining them, removing the rust and making piles and piles. We were simply little children and big children discussing all sorts of problems, and especially what to do if they caught you. We learned to handle weapons at the age of eleven, to dismantle and assemble rifles. Then there were exercises with guns, like taking them apart in the dark with our eyes closed. We practised in the hayloft, but there was another special place, a secret place that we did not even dare to say its name out loud. Secrecy and loyalty were holy values. And this loyalty, this unwillingness to ever inform on a friend extended itself into also being always ready to help others.

The secrecy was a founding principle from the days of Hashomer. This was the only way to guard our land and to change the image of the Jews. Yet, despite the secrecy, which was to my parents the loftiest value, they were accused of hiding arms and exiled. Absalom Feinberg was the one who gave my mother over to the Turks at the beginning of the World War. (Years later he said: "I informed on the person I loved most, because I thought that from an ideological standpoint, it was necessary in order to save the rest of us").

24. MANYA SHOCHAT, TESTIMONIALS ON HER EIGHTIETH BIRTHDAY (EXCERPTS) IN AL HAMISHMAR BY L. TERNOPOLER, 23.10.59

"One of the most riveting characters in the annals of the labor movement in Russia and Israel."

"Unique traits—burning idealism, unbridled enthusiasm, deep social consciousness and a constructive approach to solving national and societal problems."

"In 1941, Manya participated in the establishment of the League to Assist the Soviet Union. She found ways to obtain medical supplies to assist the Soviet army. In those days, with Israel still under Mandate, there was no official diplomatic relationship with Russia, but the League nevertheless welcomed dozens of Soviet representatives, who visited Israel from time to time. Manya was especially popular because of her wide knowledge and her fluency in Russian."

"For more than fifty years, Manya put her personal stamp on the evolution of the Zionist creation, the settlement of Eretz Israel, and the Labor movement."

*25. OUR "MANYA" BY S. B. RUSSAK**

Such a soft tremor of the soul was heard at the farewell gathering for Chavera Manya Shochat who returned to Palestine after a ten months' visit in this country.

Few people knew that Manya was here, few knew the purpose of her mission and still fewer knew of her departure. A handful gathered in a corner of a hotel to bid Manya Bon Voyage. It was attempted in the "proper" manner, with a chairman, representatives of organizations and speakers, but things would not move in an orderly fashion. No one knew where to begin nor what to say and one felt that soon someone might place his two fingers in his mouth and sound a loud shrill whistle, as the speechless expression of our mood.

Chaver Ehrenreich as chairman designated her as one of the Lamed Vov and—how truer than true that is. At times I see Manya washing clothes in Kfar Gileadi, in that distant village on the Syria-Palestinian border; at other times Manya is in Tel Aviv on "some" mission . . . and again you find her rushing through the roads of the land as a "nurse" to heal and comfort.

"Don't worry Samuel!" she used to speak to me in that forsaken village, "If you will not fit into the Kvutzah, it will be no loss for you. There are many ways in which one can build the land. In my own eyes the essential thing is the collective, but the prime need is to build."

Chavera Lindheim on bidding Manya farewell told a story. There was once a painter who made wondrous pictures. Artists from all the world came to him to discover the secret of his colors, but in vain! Only when he died they found a hole in his heart; there he dipped his brush. With the blood of his heart he had mixed his paints, "That is Manya Schochat."

It seemed we would never close the evening for no one had said anything and no one knew what to say . . . until they asked her to speak, and there arose the beaming face of Manya Schochat. Her voice quivered. She, the hardened revolutionary, could hardly control her emotions.

"I came to you that you should help us build the Palestinian Youth, which is the spiritual and physical guardian of the land. I will also tell you that you must yourself come and help in the upbuilding, for 180 thousand cannot revive a country—that must be done by a nation. We, there, are only the vanguard!"

And Manya, too, told a story.

"It was three or four years ago. We had gathered up the earthly remains of the Shomrim who had fallen throughout the land and we buried them in Tel Chai, on that mound where Trumpeldor and his comrades rest. We did not cry, for— we have already become accustomed not to cry. But a web of memories was woven into the surrounding atmosphere, and apparently this atmosphere was transferred to the children of the village. The next day my child, Anah—at that time ten years old—came to me and told me—

"Mother, I had a dream and I saw: it is dark and I am alone on the cemetery, all alone, but I am not afraid. Suddenly I see the graves opening up and before me arise our fallen comrades. I spoke to them—'Chaverim, the grown up people, have told us that dead ones can never rise.' "

"True, child, true! The dead can never rise, but we, we must rise. During the day everyone works and at night they sleep, so we must awaken and guard the Gallil."

"Is it difficult to rise from the grave? Will you always have to do it?" I asked them.

"It is very difficult, the earth is so heavy . . . but we will have to do it so long until the Gallil will be settled with hundreds and thousands of new comrades" . . .

For a moment a silence descended upon our gathering. It seemed we could see the mound in Tel Chai, that we heard the voice of our fallen comrades— 'Come . . . and give us our peace.' " . . .

. . . "I have come," continued Manya, "to awaken in you your latent powers. You can and you must become the leaders of American Jewry in the present hour. You need only the belief that you are capable of it. We in Palestine have a song—hineni muchan umezuman—I am ready and prepared for work, ready for joy and for sorrow, ready to die if need be. We in Palestine have rejected all Jewish and Gentile Messiahs. We believe only in our own powers! And we in Palestine believe, we are certain, that you will come; from all corners of the earth you will come. You will help the living to build and give the dead their rest. . . ."

***

Thus spoke Manya. I don't know whether she is of the Lamed Vov, or like that wonderful artist; possibly she is like Joan d'Arc or like Deborah, the prophetess. No, she is all of them in one.

**Abridged, from March, 1932, *The Pioneer Woman* Magazine, with permission, Pioneer Women—Na'Amat, the Women's Labor Zionist Organization of America.

INDEX

❦

Note: Items with asterisk (*) are listed in Reader's Guide to Names and Terms. Documents section is not indexed here.

191